AF323912

THE THEOCRATIC IDEOLOGY
OF THE CHRONICLER

BIBLICAL
INTERPRETATION
SERIES

Editors

R. ALAN CULPEPPER
ROLF RENDTORFF

Assistant Editor

DAVID E. ORTON

Editorial Advisory Board

JANICE CAPEL ANDERSON · MIEKE BAL
PHYLLIS A. BIRD · ERHARD BLUM · ROBERT P. CARROLL
WERNER H. KELBER · EKKEHARD STEGEMANN
ANTHONY C. THISELTON · VINCENT L. WIMBUSH · JEAN ZUMSTEIN

VOLUME 33

THE THEOCRATIC IDEOLOGY OF THE CHRONICLER

BY

JONATHAN E. DYCK

BRILL

LEIDEN · BOSTON · KÖLN

1998

This book is printed on acid-free paper.

Library of Congress Cataloging-in-Publication Data

Dyck, Jonathan E.
    The theocratic ideology of the Chronicler / by Jonathan E. Dyck.
        p.   cm. — (Biblical interpretation series, ISSN 0928-0731 ;
    v. 33)
    Based on the author's thesis (doctoral—University of Sheffield,
1994) presented under title: The purpose of the Chronicles and
the critique of ideology.
    Includes bibliographical references and indexes.
    ISBN 9004111468 (hardcover : alk. paper)
    1. Bible. O.T. Chronicles—Theology. 2. Theocracy—Biblical
teaching. I. Title. II. Series
BS1345.6.T43D93   1998
222' .606—dc21   98–16756
                                                            CIP

Die Deutsche Bibliothek – CIP-Einheitsaufnahme

Dyck, Jonathan E.:
The theocratic ideology of the chronicler / by Jonathan E. Dyck. -
Leiden ; Boston ; Köln : Brill, 1998
    (Biblical interpretation series ; Vol. 33)
    ISBN 90-04-11146-8

ISSN   0928-0731
ISBN   90 04 11146 8

PRINTED IN THE NETHERLANDS

לנעמי
יאר יהוה פניו אליך

CONTENTS

PREFACE

This book is an extensively revised version of a PhD thesis submitted
to the University of Sheffield in 1994 under the title "The Purpose
of Chronicles and the Critique of Ideology." A number of important studies on Chronicles have appeared since 1994 and I have
tried to take account of this in my revisions. But more significant
than this perhaps is the ability that time affords one to see what
one has written in a new and critical way. As a result I have reorganized and rewritten almost all of the original thesis adding a new
chapter in the process. I trust that the final result is a clearer, more
convincing (and interesting), argument.

I owe a great deal to my supervisor Prof. John Rogerson who
knows how to blend encouragement and critical comment in the
right proportions and I hope that some of his capacity to ask new
and significant questions of the biblical text with clarity has rubbed
off and is reflected in this work. I am also endebted to my two ex-
aminers Professors Philip Davies and Robert Carroll for their comments and for encouraging me to seek a publisher for this work.
Since then the genuine interest and collegiality shown to me by my
colleagues in Trinity College, especially my fellow biblicists Professors
Seán Freyne and Andrew Mayes, has given me that additional energy
and purpose to see this project through. I thank Prof. Rolf Rendtorff
for accepting this work in the Biblical Interpretation Series and am
grateful for the efforts of Dr. David Orton and the staff at E. J. Brill
in preparing the manuscript for the press. I also want to acknowledge the generous financial assistance of the Arts and Social Sciences
Benefactions Fund of Trinity College.

The generosity, steadfast love and prayers of my parents Rev.
John and Joyce Dyck and my parents-in-law Dr. Erwin and Anna
Penner will never be forgotten. I thank Annaliese, Heidi, Hans, and
Susanna for putting up with a father with too much on his mind.
Finally, I thank my wife, Naomi, who invested more of herself in
this effort than I did. I dedicate this book to her with love.

Jonathan Dyck
Trinity College, Dublin
Hilary 1998

INTRODUCTION

This book is about the religion and politics of the Chronicler. The Chronicler's thinking on these two subjects is labelled here "theocratic" because what we see as two spheres—the religious and the political— he sees as one; in Chronicles, Israel is "the kingdom of Yahweh". What I want to explore in the following study is the relationship between the Chronicler's theocratic ideas and the socio-historical context within which he worked; hence, the term ideology. I use the term ideology, not as a synonym for ideas, thought or theology but rather for ideas or language with a particular social force. Applying this to Chronicles, what I will argue is that the theocratic ideas of the Chronicler had a particular social force in the context of the Jewish community centred on Jerusalem in the late Persian period.

The Jewish community of which the Chronicler was a part can be described as theocratic in constitution. The word "theocracy"— literally "rule by God"—was invented by Josephus to describe the blending of religion and politics which characterized the Jewish nation in the Second Temple period and set it apart from other forms of government:

> There is endless variety in the details of the customs and laws which prevail in the world at large. To give but a summary enumeration: some peoples have entrusted the supreme political power to monarchies, others to oligarchies, yet others to the masses. Our lawgiver, however, was attracted by none of these forms of polity, but gave to his constitution the form of what—if a forced expression be permitted—may be termed a "theocracy", placing all sovereignty and authority in the hands of God. To Him he persuaded all to look, as the author of all blessings, both those which are common to all mankind, and those which they had won for themselves by prayer in the crises of their history. He convinced him that no single action, no secret thought, could be hid from Him. He represented Him as One, uncreated and immutable to all eternity; in beauty surpassing all mortal thought, made known to us by His power, although the nature of His real being passes knowledge (*Against Apion*, 2.164–7).

Insofar as "rule by God" meant in effect "rule by priests" Judah was a theocracy for most of the Second Temple period. Indeed for much of this period Judah was ruled by the high priest, either in a dyarchy

with governors appointed by the Persians or as sole ruler and representative of the people as was the case under the Ptolemies. The
Hasmonean kingdom was a theocratic kingdom as well in that the
Hasmoneans were both kings *and* high priests. When Josephus wrote
the above description of Judaism, the "theocratic period" had already
passed, having fallen victim to Rome's iron will. Under the Romans
and prior to 70 CE the high priest had much less power than in
earlier times, but the temple was still the centre of life for the Jews
both in Palestine and the Diaspora.[1]

Josephus's nostalgia for the theocratic period comes through in
the story he relates of Alexander's visit to Jerusalem. On hearing
that Alexander was on his way up to Jerusalem from Gaza, Jaddua
the high priest was, according to Josephus, justifiably concerned about
the fate of Jerusalem. He had earlier refused to submit to Alexander
on account of his prior commitment to Darius and therefore expected
the worst. However, Jaddua is assured by God in a dream that no
harm would come to Jerusalem and is further instructed on how he
should meet Alexander. Thus,

> When he learned that Alexander was not far from the city, he went
> out with the priests and the body of citizens, and, making the recep-
> tion sacred in character and different from that of other nations, met
> him at a certain place called Saphein. . . . [And] when Alexander while
> still far off saw the multitude in white garments, the priests at their
> head clothed with linen, and the high priest in a robe of hyacinth-
> blue and gold, wearing on his head the mitre with the golden plate
> on it on which was inscribed the name of God, he approached alone
> and prostrated himself before the Name and first greeted the high
> priest (*Antiquities*, 11.5.329–31).

This story is a legend but the image is not that far off the mark.
For much of the Second Temple period Jerusalem could indeed be
described as a theocratic city-state "sacred in character" made up
of priests and citizens with a high priest at it head. Hecataeus of
Abdera, the earliest Greek author to refer to the Jews, describes the
Jewish nation in similar terms:

> The colony [in Judea] was led by a man called Moses, who was out-
> standing both in wisdom and bravery. On taking possession of the

---

[1] See L. L. Grabbe's discussion in *Judaism From Cyrus to Hadrian* (Minneapolis: Fortress, 1992), pp. 73–5 and 607–16.

country [having been expelled from Egypt] he founded many cities including the one which is most conspicuous, which is called Jerusalem. He also founded the Temple which they hold in greatest honour, introduced the honours and ritual paid to (their) god, established laws and organized the form of their state. . . . He picked out the men of greatest accomplishment who would be most able to lead the entire nation and appointed them priests, and prescribed how they should occupy themselves with the Temple and the honours and sacrifices (paid) to God. He also appointed them to be judges in the most important cases, and entrusted to them the guardianship of the laws and customs (of the nation). That is why the Jews have never had a king, but the leadership of the mass of the people is always vested in the priest who appears to excel in wisdom and virtue. They call him the High-Priest, and believe him to be the mediator of God's commands to them. According to (Hecataeus), it is he who in their assemblies and their other meetings proclaims what is ordained, and the Jews are so obedient in such matters that they immediately fall to the ground and do obeisance to the High-Priest who expounds (these commands) to them. The statement is even added at the end of their (code of) laws that "Moses heard from God these words which he declares to the Jews".[2]

In the case of Chronicles I use the word theocracy, not in the specific sense of rule by priests, but in the broader sense of a temple-centred polity or (as Weinberg puts it) a citizen-temple community. Chronicles was probably written in the second half of the fourth century BC; perhaps just before Alexander's conquest of the Persian empire. If Josephus's story were true one could well imagine the Chronicler taking part in the procession that greeted Alexander. As it turns out, though, we know very little about Judah in the fourth century other than the fact that the temple was all important.[3] The fourth century has not entered into the narrative history of the Jews, biblical or otherwise,[4] and this reinforces the idea that Judah lived in relative isolation from the world in the first half of the Second Temple period. Chronicles thus represents a rare window onto the

---

[2] As cited in M. M. Austin, *The Hellenistic World from Alexander to the Roman Conquest: A Selection of Ancient Sources in Translation* (Cambridge: Cambridge University Press, 1981), pp. 274–5.

[3] F. M. Cross has attempted to reconstruct the high priestly succession for this period combining data from Josephus and the Samaritan papyri, but even this bare skeleton of history is speculative ["A Reconstruction of the Judean Restoration," *JBL* 94 (1975), 4–18; cf. G. Widengren, "The Persian Period," in J. Hayes and J. M. Miller (eds.), *Israelite and Judean History* (Philadelphia: Fortress, 1977), pp. 506–9].

[4] Not including Josephus's legendary anecdotes about the high priests of this period in *Antiquities*.

thinking (if not the historic-chronological data) of the theocratic community in Judah from this time period.[5]

Just as the temple was all important in Second Temple Judaism so too is the temple the central theme of Chronicles and it is for this reason that I speak of *theocratic* ideology. The theocratic ideology of the Chronicler could mean two things: on the one hand, it could refer to the Chronicler's own particular thoughts about the temple as opposed to another writer's theocratic ideology. On the other hand, it could refer to the ideology of the theocratic community as expressed by the Chronicler. In light of the significance of the temple in Judah, what Chronicles tells us about the latter is the more interesting of the two from a socio-historical perspective and it is in this area that I want to concentrate. In my reading of Chronicles I treat it as cross-section of the discourse which enveloped the Second Temple at a particular point in time. It is this discourse, and the practices associated with it, that made the temple what it was in the minds of the priests, patrons and peasants who organized their lives around it.

By speaking of theocracy and ideology I also intend to foreground the socio-political implications of what the Chronicler says. Josephus treats the status of the temple as an accomplished fact or at least as a feat accomplished by Moses in the very distant past. The Chronicler, on the other hand, makes David the founder of the theocratic kingdom of Yahweh. What I aim to demonstrate in the following is that the theocratic constitution of Judah in the Second Temple period was not so much a "reality" to be taken for granted as an ideological achievement in which the Chronicler played no small part.[6]

Interpreting Chronicles in light of its historical context is not new; what is new is that I do so with reference to the concept of ideology as understood in the social sciences. The first two chapters are devoted to explaining this new approach: the first, retrospectively, with reference to the debate about the Chronicler's purpose; the sec-

---

[5] By "window" I am not suggesting that Chronicles is "a 'source of information', but as information in itself; not as an opening on a reality laying beyond, but as an element which makes up that reality" [M. Liverani, "Memorandum on the Approach to Historiographic Texts," *Orientalia* 42 (1973), p. 179].

[6] Assuming for the time being that if a text survives from the Persian period it must be representative of a relatively significant group within Judaism.

ond, prospectively, with reference to the social theoretical issues involved in the concept of ideology.

In chapter one, I examine the notion of purpose and the relationship between purpose and ideology in the interpretation of Chronicles. The differentiation between aspects of purpose—intention, motive, and contextual function—and ideology and the interpretative interests that go with them is a central feature of the argument. The survey of research which follows the analysis of these concepts is a critical assessment of modern Chronicles scholarship with a view to highlighting the ways in which the relationship between text and context is conceptualized. The problem as I see it is that the notion of purpose, as it is used in the interpretation of Chronicles, is too cumbersome and undifferentiated. The implication of this view in substantive terms is that the current juxtapositioning of "exclusivist" versus "inclusivist", "theocrat" versus "royalist" interpretations needs to be re-examined.

The concept of ideology raises a number of important theoretical issues which are addressed in chapter two. Of particular importance is the role of the concept of ideology in interpretation. Ideology is most often associated with critique—Marxist critique in particular—which raises serious questions about the typical hermeneutical stance of the interpreter. There is a tendency to place hermeneutics on one side and critique on the other: interpreters try to *understand* while critics try to *explain* in terms of causal forces and *expose* the false-consciousness involved. The attitude of the former is empathy; the attitude of the latter suspicion. In opposition to this juxtaposition I will argue that interpretation and critique are complementary moves within a broader hermeneutical perspective. At the core of this argument is Ricoeur's three-stage analysis of ideology as it relates to distortion, legitimation and integration/identity. Ricoeur argues that aspects of the social phenomena called ideology are intertwined and demand a number of attitutes, approaches and conceptual models ranging from suspicion and critique to interpretative empathy.

The three readings which follow in chapters three, four and six deal in turn with each of the three dimensions of ideology identified by Ricoeur (though in reverse order).

In chapter three I examine the Chronicler's ideology of identity using the notion of exile as my point of reference and comparing his ideology with that put forward in Ezra-Nehemiah. My aim in this chapter is to uncover the nature of the difference between the

Chronicler's more inclusive ideology of identity and the so-called exclusivism of the writer of Ezra-Nehemiah.

In chapter four I look at the way the Chronicler identifies "Israel" though now from the point of view of legitimation. The relationship between identity and legitimacy is explored from the theoretical side by Ricoeur and Geertz and I draw on their analyses in order to demonstrate the way in which the "broader" definition of Israel is inextricably tied to the question of the legitimacy of the "kingdom of Yahweh in the hands of the sons of David" (2 Chron. 13:8). My aim is to show that the Chronicler's ideology of identity is at the same time an ideology which legitimates Jerusalem's role as the sole legitimate centre of Israel for all Israel and in the Chronicler's day.

Prior to my third reading of Chronicles, I explore the internal social situation in Persian Judah (chapter five). The objective is to uncover the hierarchical structures within Judean society and the exploitation which they enabled. I argue that there was a system of hierarchies within the post-exilic community with the Second Temple at the centre and reaching all the way down to the בתי אבות or "houses of the fathers", the primary social unit in Judah.

Finally, in chapter six I explore the possible consequences of believing the claims put forward by the Chronicler on behalf of the Second Temple. It is my view that such belief was taken up in the interests of power and did contribute to the maintenance of the power and prestige of the temple. These ideological critical deliberations presuppose the distinction between intent and consequence; between what the Chronicler consciously intended to say and do and the consequences of what he said and did. From the point of view of the contextual functions of the Chronicler's ideology, his work should be characterized as ideological in the sense of supporting the dominant position of the Second Temple within the post-exilic community. Furthermore, the degree to which the Second Temple was an oppressive presence in the community is the degree to which the Chronicler's ideology—insofar as it supports this presence—is distorted. This is not a judgement about something intrinsic to Chronicles but a judgment about the functional properties of Chronicles in the context of the Jewish theocracy of the early Second Temple period.

CHAPTER ONE

PURPOSE AND IDEOLOGY
IN THE INTERPRETATION OF CHRONICLES

It has been said that ideological criticism involves asking "who is saying what to whom and for what purpose."[1] There are a number of substantial theoretical issues wrapped up in this definition as in the identities of the who and the whom but for the moment I will look at just one of them, namely, the notion of purpose. The issue I want to explore is the relationship between the notion of purpose as used in historical criticism and ideological criticism. The above definition of the latter leaves one with the impression that ideological critics have something in common with historical critics as regards asking about the purpose of a text in its context. Upon closer inspection, this impression turns out to be false insofar as the way in which this question is asked and answered by ideological critics is substantially different. The point is, however, that ideological criticism can be situated vis-à-vis established lines of inquiry in biblical studies with reference to "purpose" which means that I can situate what I am doing with Chronicles within established lines of inquiry as well.

"Purpose" as it relates to authors, texts and contexts is an imprecise concept and needs to be defined more closely before being used, if at all. Thus, in the first part of this chapter I look more closely at this concept, differentiating between different aspects of purpose, intention and meaning and, corresponding to this, different interpretative interests. I then locate the concept of ideology within the spectrum of interpretative interests using a map of ideology based on Raymond Geuss's analysis of the concept.

In the second part of this chapter I survey Chronicles research and critically evaluate both the ways in which the relationship between Chronicles, the Chronicler and his context has been conceptualized as well as the substance of competing proposals. I will use this discussion of previous interpretations of the "purpose" of Chronicles as

---

[1] T. Eagleton, *Ideology: An Introduction* (London: Verso, 1991), p. 9.

a launching pad for a new look at this problem, as informed by theories of ideology and critique, and indeed a new substantive proposal as to the Chronicler's purpose.

Part One: Purpose and Ideology

Purpose, Motives, and Intentions

The purpose of a work is commonly associated with the author's intended meaning in its historical context. By and large, the purpose of an author in writing a text is determined with reference to what he/she intended to say in the context in which it was said. To determine, for example, the purpose of Chronicles one begins by looking at what he said, correlating this with what we know of the author's context. This is essentially the procedure of those who have had occasion to comment of the purpose of Chronicles. However, as I will now argue, this is an inadequate way of proceeding because it conflates a whole range of separate issues and interpretative procedures. A more nuanced account of what is going on with regard to purpose has to take into account issues such as the relationship between prior intentions in the mind of the author and the meaning of the text, our ability to retrieve these intentions via the text, and the question of whether our notion of what the text means and what its purpose is should be determined in this way.

I begin with the related problem of the author's intended meaning, building on Skinner's and Brett's analyses of the problem.[2] The author's intended meaning is an undifferentiated term combining an authorial element and a textual element and thus the first step in developing more precise categories is to disentangle these two elements.

Skinner distinguishes between three senses of "meaning". In the first sense, *meaning 1*, meaning is the literal level of the text; what the text says in itself without reference to the motives or intentions of the author. As is well known, Wimsatt and Beardsley argued that

---

[2] Q. Skinner, "Motives, Intentions and the Interpretation of Texts," *New Literary History* 3 (1972), pp. 393–408. M. G. Brett, "Motive and Intention in Genesis 1," *JTS* 42 (1991), pp. 1–16. See also M. G. Brett, "Four or Five Things to do with Texts," in D. Clines, S. Fowl, and S. Porter (eds.), *The Bible in Three Dimensions: Essays in Celebration of Forty Years of Biblical Studies in the University of Sheffield* (JSOTS 87; Sheffield: JSOT Press, 1990), pp. 357–77; and A. D. H. Mayes, "On Describing the Purpose of Deuteronomy," *JSOT* 58 (1983), pp. 13–33.

the meaning of the text is independent of the author's intentions and the historical context of its production and should not, therefore, be a criterion in determining the meaning of a text.[3] Skinner's overall point is to challenge the view that there is but one legitimate sense of meaning, thus, *meaning 2*. This refers to the what the text means to me. Accordingly, interpretation which focuses on this level of meaning must, therefore, take into account the actions involved in responding to the text.[4] To inquire about the third sense of meaning, *meaning 3*, one would ask: What does the author *mean by* what he or she says? An example of meaning at this level of meaning would be the allusions an author may be making in the text. Why did the author use this or that particular phrase? One can summarize these three senses of meaning in terms of three different questions:

(1) What does the text say?[5]
(2) What does the text mean to me?
(3) What does the author *mean by* saying what he/she said?

The third sense of meaning is by far the most common sense in the interpretation of Chronicles. As a synoptic work both the presence and the absence of Vorlage, as well as the "purely Chronistic" material, are seen to be pregnant with meanings of this kind. What did the Chronicler *mean by* including this or leaving out that or adding the other? And it is in relation to this sort of meaning that the concept of purpose is applied. But what does purpose mean in this context? Does meaning 3 require consideration of motives and intentions?

The answer to the last question depends, of course, on what one means by motives and intentions. In agreement with Wimsatt and Beardsley, Skinner argues that it is not necessary for us to know about the author's motives in order to inquire about meaning 3. But contrary to Wimsatt and Beardsley, Skinner argues that one does have to take intention into account. The difference between motive and intention, as he sees it, is that motives are prior causes which lie outside the text and have no direct bearing on our understanding

---

[3] W. K. Wimsatt and M. C. Beardsley, "The Intentionality Fallacy," in D. Lodge (ed.), *20th Century Literary Criticism* (London: Longman, 1972), pp. 334–45.

[4] Thinking in particular of W. Iser, *The Act of Reading: A Theory of Aesthetic Response* (Baltimore: Johns Hopkins University Press, 1978).

[5] Brett calls "what the author is trying to say" the communicative intentions of the author, which are to be distinguished from the author's motives. I feel that it is helpful to distinguish more clearly between verbal meanings and intentions.

of what was said. The author's motives for writing are to be distinguished from the author's intentions in writing.

Skinner clarifies his definition of "intentions" via Austin. Intentions have to do with illocutions whereas motives have to do with perlocutions. According to Austin, an illocution is the "performance of an act *in* saying something as opposed to the performance of an act *of* saying something [a locutionary act]."[6] Promising, urging, advising or ordering are all examples of illocutionary acts or of statements which have an intended illocutionary force. To "take up" the intended illocutionary force of a text is equivalent to understanding what the author *meant by* writing in a certain way. On this account of meaning and intention the text itself embodies a certain intention just as the utterance "I do" before the priest at the altar embodies a certain intention. Both of these aspects are relevant, according to Skinner, to understanding what was said. Paying attention to this level of meaning is not, of course, the whole of the interpreter's task just as studying the original context is not "a final criteria of correctness" in interpreting the meaning of a text, but nonetheless it is part of the interpreter's task.[7] There are, of course, very real practical problems in "taking up" the intended illocutionary force of a text as old and as large as Chronicles. It is one thing to determine the direct communicative intentions of an utterance the size of "I do" and quite another to feel confident about such a determination when it involves an "utterance" sixty five chapters long. When so much is said and not said the reality of the matter is that such an assessment will, for the most part, be an assessment of *indirect* communicative intentions, inferences, allusion and the like, not *direct* communicative intentions.

A *perlocution*, on the other hand, is a speech act which has "consequential effects upon the feelings, thoughts, or actions of the audience, or of the speaker, or of other persons."[8] Perlocutionary motives have to do with the desire to achieve a particular effect. To say that the "purpose" of the Chronicler was *to urge* his audience to support the Second Temple as the leading institution of his day is to say that he had a particular illocutionary intention, whereas to say that

---

[6] J. L. Austin, *How to Do Things with Words* (Oxford: Clarendon, 2nd edn., 1975), pp. 99–100.

[7] Skinner, "Motives," pp. 404–5.

[8] Austin, *How to Do Things*, p. 101.

the "purpose" of the Chronicler was *to persuade* his readers to support the Temple is to impute a perlocutionary motive to the Chronicler. The important point is that the desire to perform a perlocutionary act is fulfilled only if the desired effect is achieved and both desire and effect lie outside the text. There is no necessary connection between a perlocutionary act and what the Chronicler said or how he said it. To ask about perlocutionary motive is simply to address why he wrote. It just so happens that the "normal" way of assessing why the Chronicler wrote what he did begins with (and is largely confined to) asking what he said, which obscures this important analytical distinction.

One can summarize the above distinctions as follows:

- Locution = what the Chronicler *said*
- Illocution = what the Chronicler *meant by* what he said, which has to do with *intentions*
- Perlocution = what the Chronicler *did by* saying, which has to do with *motives*

Generally speaking these three aspects of a speech act will cohere but the point being made here is that one should not assume that they always do so.

If we come at this problem from the point of view of the purpose of a work rather than the meaning of the work the same sort of distinctions apply. If we define purpose in terms of author's motives then to know what the text says (meaning 1), or even to know what the author meant by saying what he or she did (meaning 3) may not in fact be relevant. But to inquire about the purpose of the author in terms of intentions will necessarily involve attending to the what was said and what was *meant by* what was said.

Those who (unwittingly perhaps) limit their understanding of purpose to those purposes which can be correlated directly with what the text says (meaning 1) unnecessarily restrict the scope of what might be considered relevant to the understanding of a text. An equally unnecessary and restrictive move would be to identify meaning 1 with meaning 3. From this point of view the author could not have *intended* to say anything which he does not say directly. Allusions, for example, are not strictly speaking "inside" the text. Whilst no one in the following survey of Chronicles research does this, it seems to be an underlying criteria for some by means of which one judges assessments of purpose.

In light of these considerations, Brett calls for the recognition of a plurality of interpretative interests in biblical interpretation. These interpretative interests can be plotted in relation to the intersection of two domains: text and author.

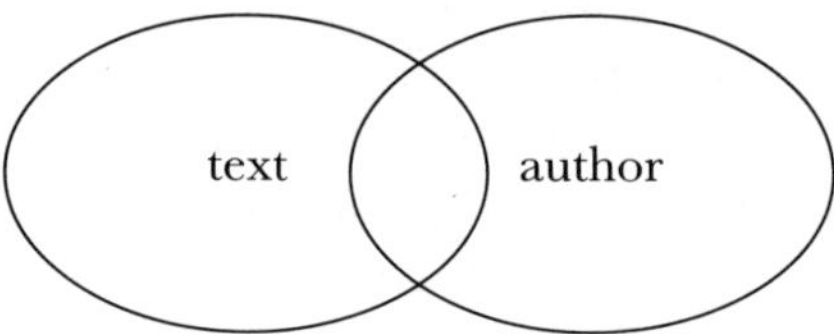

Let us say that the centre of the author's circle is the author's motives and that the centre of the text's circle is the verbal meaning of the text.[9] The areas of non-intersection indicate the analytical distinction or gap between what the text says and the author's motives. The area of intersection, on the other hand, has to do with the illocutionary force of what is said.

If we conceive of this as a continuum we could further differentiate between direct communicative intentions and indirect intentions. Indirect intentions can be defined, according to Brett, with reference to the area of linguistics which is concerned with indirect communication or implicature (as in the synoptic interpretation of Chronicles).[10]

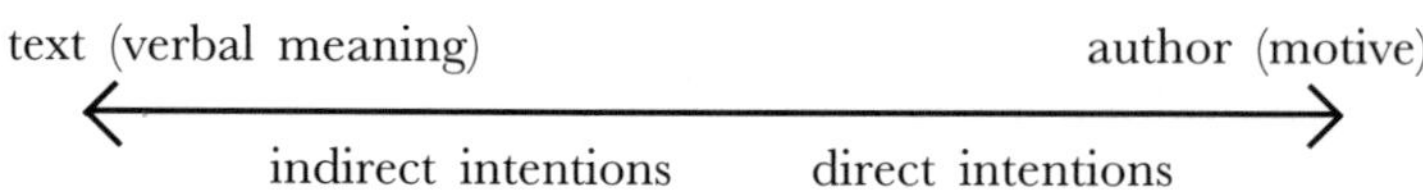

On the basis of this diagram we can identify three interpretative interests:

(1) an interest in the text as such
(2) an interest in the motives "behind" the text
(3) an interest in illocutionary intentions

We have not yet considered a third dimension of text interpretation, namely, context and it is with reference to context that the question of ideology becomes significant.

---

[9] And let us not agonize at this point about the stability of the subject and the text even though the metaphor of the circle with a centre is asking to be de-centred.
[10] Brett, "Motive," [p. 10].

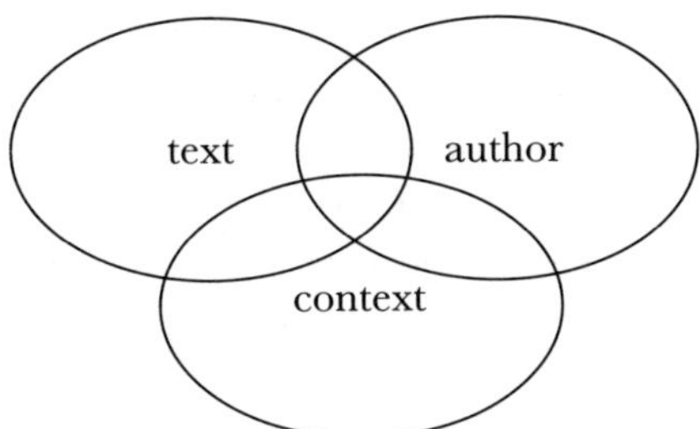

The new area of intersection indicates that the context of production (linguistic, literary, cultural, historical, and social) is relevant to the above interpretative interests in a number of ways. An interest in what the text says (meaning 1) does presuppose a knowledge of the linguistic and literary conventions of the day (the linguistic and literary context). An interest in the motives and intentions of the author involves making some sort of inference from knowledge of the wider context of production. These inferences are usually restricted to those aspects of the context of which (in our estimation) the author was conscious. An author cannot have a conscious motive or intention in relation to a social reality of which he or she is unaware, or so the argument goes. If, however, we were to restrict our account of the relationship between author, text and context to the realm of consciousness a good deal of the "territory" mapped out in this diagram would be left unaccounted for. As in the area of verbal meaning, one needs to recognize the conventional, here applied to intentions and motives. Skinner speaks in this regard of the conventional intentions which speech acts embody. In this view speech acts are also social acts governed to a greater or lesser degree by socio-cultural conventions. The degree to which an author is aware of the "intentions" embodied in the conventions he or she adopts will vary. The author may be following conventions in an unselfconscious way, may be incompetent at stating them, may not fully understand them, or may be self-deceived about them. Thus, characterizing an author's "intentions" need not depend on the author's own statements about his intentions. To put this in terms of the three aspects of meaning, one could say that conventional intentions refer to what is meant by what is said, as opposed to what he or she meant by what he or she said (using the passive verb to play up the social nature of convention and play down the role of the author's consciousness).

All this is to use the word intention rather loosely and so I propose that we use the term *contextual functions* to cover not only these conventional illocutionary acts but also conventional perlocutionary acts: what is meant by *and* what is being done by what is said. An interest in the *contextual functions* of Chronicles concerns what was *meant by* and what was *being done in* the writing of this text, considered from the point of view of the social context of the speech act. This is our fourth and final interpretative interest.

To summarize, I have argued that in discussing the purpose of a text a greater precision in what we mean by that term is desirable; specifically, that one observes the following distinctions where possible:

A. Between three aspects of meaning
   (1) What does the text say?
   (2) What does the text mean to me?
   (3) What does the author *mean by* saying what he/she said?
B. Between verbal meaning, motives and intentions in terms of speech act theory
   Locution = what the Chronicler *said*
   Illocution = what the Chronicler *meant by* what he said, which has to do with intentions
   Perlocution = what the Chronicler *did by* saying, which has to do with motives
C. Between four interpretative interests
   (1) an interest in the text as such
   (2) an interest in the motives "behind" the text
   (3) an interest in illocutionary intentions
   (4) an interest in the contextual functions

Ideology: A Map for Biblical Interpreters

How does the concept of ideology fit into all this? The crucial distinction in dealing with relationship between text and context from the point of view of the theory of ideology is the distinction between conscious intentions and motives and "unconscious" contextually-determined functions. The study of ideology asks about meanings embodied in the text of which the author was not necessarily aware. The study of ideology as it relates to texts is thus (among other things) an example of the fourth interpretative interest. It is an interest in the context of the text's production which takes into consideration those aspects of the context of which the author need not have been aware, but which, nevertheless, influenced what was said.

Before exploring this issue further it is necessary to differentiate between the various senses of the term ideology. The broadest definition of ideology refers to "a set of ideas, beliefs, attitudes held by a person". This definition makes no reference to the social status of these ideas, is not part of a particular social research agenda, and is thus not located on the "map" below. To ask about the ideology of the Chronicler in this sense (as, for example, Sara Japhet does)[11] is to ask what the Chronicler said about various topics; a sort of systematic biblical ideology concerned primarily with the verbal meaning of the text. The "ideology" of the Book of Chronicles is simply the set of ideas characteristic of the Chronicler. Perhaps she wanted to use a more secular term than "theology" or maybe she simply needed a synonym for "thought" since "The *Thought* of the Book of Chronicles in the History of Biblical *Thought*" would not do. To the extent that the Chronicler's ideas are compared and contrasted with other biblical texts is the extent to which Japhet can also say something about what the Chronicler *meant by* what he said. In other words, she infers intention on the basis of the allusions the Chronicler makes and on the basis of what he does and does not take over from Samuel-Kings. What did the Chronicler *mean by* leaving out the history of the northern kingdom? His intention was to show that "the northern kingdom was established in sin, its existence constitutes a rebellion against YHWH, and its history is an unbroken chain of transgression leading up to destruction."[12] From this we can draw the implications about his attitude to the North. And what is the Chronicler's attitude to, his ideology concerning, the North? In contrast to Samuel-Kings, it is clear that the North "is a part of Israel, and without the members of the northern tribes, the people of Israel cannot be complete."[13] Japhet is characteristically silent on the contextual significance of these attitudes and therefore restricts her account of the Chronicler's ideology to his conscious motives and intentions.

The definitions of ideology that are of interest in this study are those which can be located within a social theoretical framework. Geuss's analysis of the concept of ideology tries to make sense of

---

[11] S. Japhet, *The Ideology of the Book of Chronicles and its Place in Biblical Thought* (trans. A. Barber; BEATAJ 9; Frankfurt: 1989).

[12] Japhet, *Ideology*, p. 324.

[13] Japhet, *Ideology*, p. 324.

the different meanings of ideology in terms of the different social research contexts in which the concept is used.[14] His distinctions are summarized in the following chart, or map of ideology.

Research Context: Anthropology	Research Context: Social Criticism
Definition I Ideology as one part of the socio-cultural system	Definition II Ideology as false consciousness
discursive and non-discursive elements	Definition IIa Ideology as *epistemologically* false
Subsets of Definition I e.g. religious ideology vs. political ideology Differentiated according to . . . manifest content or functional properties	Definition IIb Ideology as *functionally* false 1. Functionally false in virtue of its role in supporting or legitimizing domination 2. Functionally false in that it hinders the development of the forces of production 3. Functionally false in that it serves to mask social contradictions
Definition Ia Ideology is a worldview	Definition IIc Ideology as *genetically* false
Definition Ib Ideology in the programmatic sense	

Ideology in the Context of Anthropology
Taking the broadest definition of ideology as referred to above, one only has to change "held by a person" to "held by a group" in order to "enter" the map at the top left side. In definition I (ideology as one part of the socio-cultural system) ideology is used in a broadly descriptive sense in that it does not require judging whether it is a good or a bad thing. The research context is anthropology,

---

[14] R. Geuss, *The Idea of a Critical Theory: Habermas and the Frankfurt School* (Cambridge: Cambridge University Press, 1981), pp. 4–22. These distinctions should not be taken to imply that no mixing occurs or should occur. Interesting instances and theories of ideology will typically combine a number of definitions or aspects of ideology.

the initial goal of which is to *describe* socio-cultural systems. Beyond that, comparative description tends toward the formation of generalized hypotheses and quasi-scientific explanations all of which are also potentially relevant to studying the ideology of a group.

Although the approach taken to the study of ideology in the broadly descriptive sense is non-evaluative and non-judgmental, how one divides the socio-cultural system into its constituent parts and how one conceptualizes the relationship between the "ideological part" and the "other part" is crucial *and* controversial. Should one use the categories of the participants themselves or should one adopt extrinsic categories? At what point does description cross over into explanation? Looking at this problem from the point of view of interpretative interests, the issue is this: How does one reconstruct (a) the relationship between text-author-context; (b) the contextual functions of the text; and (c) the role of the author within this reconstruction.

I have already noted two broad options to these problems, namely, sociological description and sociological explanation. One can *describe* the author's social context reconstructing the author's ideology (as in system of ideas) and context "from the inside" attempting to understand what it is like to live in the situation being described and how his or her motives and intentions relate to this context. One can also *explain* how the text relates to the context of its production using sociological models without referring to the author's or participant's point of view.[15] The emic-etic distinction corresponds to the description-explanation distinction and refers specifically to the perspective adopted in describing or explaining something. "Emic approaches to anthropology centre on what people think about themselves, whereas etic approaches seek to frame quasi-scientific theories about culture which are open to general discussion and falsification."[16] For the purpose of mapping ideology one can conclude

---

[15] W. G. Runciman, *A Treatise on Social Theory*: Vol. 1, *The Methodology of Social Theory* (Cambridge: Cambridge University Press, 1983). For the application of these distinctions to biblical interpretation see J. W. Rogerson, "The Use of Sociology in Old Testament Studies," in J. A. Emerton (ed.), *Congress Volume Salamanca, 1983* (VTS 36; Leiden: Brill, 1985), pp. 245–56; idem, "Anthropology and the Old Testament," in R. E. Clements (ed.), *The World of Ancient Israel: Sociological, Anthropological and Political Perspectives* (Cambridge: Cambridge University Press, 1989), pp. 17–37.

[16] Rogerson, "Anthropology," p. 31. Prime examples of emic analyses are Evans-Pritchard's studies of the Nuer and the Azande. They are "an account of Zande and Nuer beliefs in relation to the social mechanisms that regulate their lives" [Rogerson, "Anthropology," p. 32]. The *emic approach* has much in common with

that ideology according to definition I can be studied from an emic and etic point of view. Or alternatively to look at it from the point of view of interpretative interests, one way of asking about the contextual functions of a text is to ask about the relationship between the ideological part of the socio-cultural system as embodied in the text and the "other" part. Again, this may be done emically or etically.

A further distinction relevant to definition I is the distinction between *discursive elements* and *non-discursive elements*.[17] The discursive element—the content of our discourse, our ideas and beliefs—is more commonly associated with ideology than the non-discursive element—our attitudes, rituals, gestures and artistic activities. But taking the example of religion one could say that it contains discursive *and* non-discursive elements within one symbolic system. There will most likely be a close connection between belief and ritual but it is unlikely that a ritual such as Christian baptism, for example, will be associated with the same ideas and beliefs over the two millennia in which it has been practised. A theory of ideology at this general level will take into account both aspects of this symbol system, allowing of course for the blurring of boundaries between the discursive and the non-discursive and indeed between the non-discursive ideological "activity" and other "activities" in other parts of the socio-cultural system. As Geertz puts it, "thought [or ideology in terms of its discursive aspect] consists of the construction and manipulation of symbol systems, which are employed as models of other systems, physical, organic, social, psychological, and so forth, in such a way that the structure of these other systems . . . is, as we say, 'understood'."[18]

---

humanistic scholarship as practiced in biblical studies. The traditional orientation of biblical scholarship since the Enlightenment has been to understand the meaning of the text in its own terms and in light of the author's conscious intentions. The aim was to get at the ideas or the mind of the mostly ancient author as expressed in the ancient languages (hence the interest in grammars and lexicons) and as illuminated by knowledge of the "historical background" (hence the notion of historical-grammatical exegesis). Thus, the sociological de-centring of the authorial subject need not be construed as a radical departure from the humanistic agenda. The emic tradition within sociology is quite compatible with "understanding the text in its own terms" for it proposes understanding society (the author's social context) in its own terms [see Brett, "Four or Five Things," pp. 359–60].

[17] What Geuss means by discourse—that about which one talks—is to be distinguished from the more technical sense of discourse as referring to the social force of language to be discussed in chapter two.

[18] C. Geertz, *Interpretation of Cultures: Selected Essays* (London: Hutchinson, 1975), p. 214.

This last point leads us to the most important distinction to be made within definition I. Our example of religious ideology presupposed that the ideology of a group can be divided into various subsets, ideologies in the narrower sense such as religious ideology, political ideology, economic ideology, aesthetic ideology, etc. There may be a significant overlap between the various subsets of a group's ideology and indeed a point of interest would be exactly the intersection between subsets. These ideological subsets can be identified on the basis of their *manifest content* or on the basis of their *functional properties*. Again, the more common approach is to identify the ideologies of a group on the basis of the content of their beliefs. Religious ideologies are commonly identified on the basis of the beliefs the group holds about religion, and so forth.

Of greater interest, however, is the relationship between manifest content and functional properties. To identify ideologies on the basis of functional properties is to classify beliefs in terms of the kind of behaviour they give rise to or influence.[19] A religious ideology in this sense would be a set of beliefs which influences religious behaviour whether or not the content of ideology has anything to do with religion. As a rule one might expect the content of an ideology and its functional properties to mesh, as in our example of Christian baptism, but a religious ideology (in terms of manifest content) may also serve to influence political behaviour or a political ideology may serve to influence economic behaviour. There will be differences too between the way in which the participants classify the manifest contents and functional properties of their ideologies and the way outsiders might classify them. But in keeping with the overall descriptive aim of definition I, "[i]t will in general be an important fact about a given society how the various kinds of acts and institutions are individuated, how large a class of acts are considered to be 'purely economic transactions' or what acts to which religious beliefs are directly relevant. . . ."[20] Clashes between content and function would be of particular interest to ideological theorists, though to identify such a clash need not entail that one is making a pejorative judgement about them.

A problem with this analytic distinction has to do with the view

---

[19] Neither of these terms should be understood to imply the causal priority of beliefs over function.

[20] Geuss, *Critical Theory*, p. 9.

that language is itself an activity (speech-act theory) or practice (discourse theory): "what is said" (manifest content) merges with what is meant by what is said" (illocutionary force), merges with "what is done by what is said" (perlocutionary force), merges with the non-discursive social conventions in which this "saying" is embedded (contextual function).

Geuss identifies two further definitions of ideology within definition I, namely *ideology as a worldview* (definition Ia) and *ideology in the programmatic sense* (definition Ib). As opposed to the ideology of a group in general which includes everything the group believes, a worldview can be defined as a set of ideas which are widely shared, systematically interconnected, and central to the groups conceptual scheme. Worldviews strongly influence individual and group behaviour and typically deal with central issues of life. In my study of the "theocratic ideology" of the Chronicler, I will be putting forward the view that the Chronicler's ideology expresses the ideological worldview of the theocratic community of Jerusalem and consequently that the beliefs held by the Chronicler were central to the community's conceptual scheme and significantly influenced the activities of the community.

Ideology in the programmatic sense refers to a program or plan of action based on a particular theory of how society works. A political ideology is perhaps the clearest example of a program of action, although in common usage one tends not to describe one's own political position as an ideology: "I have a political philosophy, you have a political position, and she has a political ideology".

Ideology and Social Criticism
The last definition on the "anthropological side" of our map brings us to the threshold of social criticism for ideology in the context of social criticism also presupposes a theory of how society works. The only difference is that within the context of anthropology one is describing and explaining in a non-evaluative way how someone else's ideology works, whereas in social criticism one is evaluating another ideology in light of one's own social theory (or ideology, though again the social critic tends not to label his or her social theory an ideology). Critical evaluation tends to be a negative evaluation—ideology in the pejorative sense—but it needn't be.[21] To

---

[21] See D. J. A. Clines's discussion in *Interested Parties: The Ideology of Writers and*

use an analogy from medicine: anthropology is to social criticism what anatomy is to pathology. In the former, ideology is a "normal" part of social life whilst in the latter it is a "distortion" within social life. The trouble with these ideological distortions (and indeed with this analogy) is that they don't have the objectivity of an ailment for they involve distortions within complex linguistic symbolic systems. This along with the absence of an unambiguous "cure" means that the diagnosis itself will always remain in dispute. Attempts at circumventing this problem via recourse to the science of "material causes—ideological effect" have in my view (and anticipating the conclusion to chapter two) failed.

Ideology within the context of social criticism no longer refers to an aspect of the socio-cultural system which one describes or explains in an non-evaluative way but to a type of thinking or consciousness which one evaluates, finding it to be false or distorted in some way when considered from the point of view of a particular theory of how society does or should work.[22] Marx's historical materialism is the most well known theory of society upon which critique is based (and indeed the concept of false consciousness is Marx's) but critique need not imply some unequivocally correct way of viewing society. It need not first seek to ground itself in a "scientific" theory of society but can and does operate in an intuitive way.[23] Nor is critique necessarily anchored in a comprehensive theory of society (as in historical materialism); it may be more ad hoc or eclectic than that. An example of the latter is Clines's definition of ideological criticism: "It is a measure of our commitment to our own standards and values that we register disappointment, dismay or disgust when we encounter in the texts of ancient Israel ideologies that we judge to be inferior to ours."[24] In the following I simply want to point to the kind of things that are labelled "ideological" and why they are so labelled. No distinction is made at this point between the producers and consumers of ideological distortions. At issue is the existence of

---

Readers of the Hebrew Bible (JSOTS 205; Sheffield: Sheffield Academic Press, 1995), pp. 16–21.

[22] Critique of this sort tends to be transcendental versus immanent, etic versus emic, but some of the following examples of false consciousness could be thought of as involving immanent critique, though it is likely that the critic is in sympathy with the values that the person or community is thought to espouse and to which they are now being held accountable.

[23] Eagleton, *Ideology*, pp. 11–13.

[24] Clines, *Interested Parties*, p. 19.

socially-significant forms of thinking which, when looked at from a particular point of view, appear distorted.

Geuss identifies forms of false consciousness:

1. *Epistemologically false consciousness* (definition IIa) is a type of thinking which contains an element of faulty logic with a particular social force. These errors are not to be construed as simple logical errors on the part of any individual but are errors that are built into the discourse of the community itself.[25]

2. More important for our purposes is ideology as *functionally false consciousness* (definition IIb). Functionally false forms of consciousness are false "because my retaining it depends in some way on my being in ignorance of or having false beliefs about its functional properties."[26] This definition of ideology builds on the distinction between manifest content and functional properties. An ideology may be true in what it says but false in what it doesn't say; true as a piece of language but false as a piece of discourse; true in its empirical content but deceptive in its force. This definition is particularly pertinent to the interpretative interest in the contextual functions of a text.

(a) Geuss's first example is an ideology which may be criticized as *functionally* false in virtue of its role in supporting domination.[27]

---

[25] Geuss cites four epistemological errors, none of which presuppose a systematic social theory: (a) The first error is thinking which is dependent on mistaking the epistemological status of its beliefs. An example of this would be when statements of belief are mistaken for statements of fact. To positivists, for example, theological disputes about the nature and activity of God (a dispute which has had significant social consequences from time to time) are ideological in the sense that they do not have a valid (i.e. empirically verifiable) cognitive content.

(b) A second error is thinking which contains an objectification mistake in that social phenomena are treated as if they are natural phenomena. The classic example of this is Marx's analysis of the fetishism of commodities whereby the social character of exchange value is mistaken for the objective value of a thing.

(c) A third error is thinking in which the particular interest of a sub-group is mistaken for the general interests of the group as a whole. A good example of this would be a sexism which assumes that "man's" interests are representative of humanity's interests.

(d) A fourth error is thinking which doesn't recognize the "self-fulfilling/self-validating character of its beliefs. For example, "[i]f we think that the members of a subgroup G are lazy, unreliable, and unintelligent, and hence act toward them in ways which make them become lazy, unreliable and unintelligent, the belief that the members of G are lazy etc. is self-fulfilling" [Geuss, *Critical Theory*, p. 14]. This example also contains an objectification mistake.

[26] Geuss's way of defining functionally false consciousness is stated in individualistic terms and implies that one can cure it.

[27] An ideology of legitimation may contain epistemological errors as well. An ide-

To say that a form of consciousness is false in this sense presupposes either that no forms of domination are legitimate or that there are legitimate and illegitimate forms of domination. Take, for example, the belief that the dominant group is so powerful that to rebel against it is futile. This sort of thinking on the part of the dominated may lead to passivity over against the dominant group and hence help to stabilize its power. The beliefs as such may in fact be true (in terms of their manifest content) and the group holding such beliefs need not intend to support this system of domination, but the functional properties of holding such a belief—the consequences of such a belief—actually contribute to the problem. If the dominated group comes to realize this functional error in their thinking they may choose to resist the ruling class consciously and/or actively. Because the issue of power and legitimation are central for this study, I will return to this subject in the next chapter.

Geuss identifies two other definitions of ideology which address functional properties, both of which presuppose a Marxist framework. (1) The first is an ideology that is functionally false because it hinders the development of the forces of production which assumes that the development of productive forces is an inherent goal. (2) The second is an ideology that is functionally false because it serves to mask social contradictions. It need not contain false ideas, simply diversionary ones. Again, because Marx's work is seminal, I will discuss his definitions of ideology at greater length in the next chapter.

3. The final definition of ideology (definition IIc)—ideology as *genetically false in virtue of its origin*—is also the most problematic given that it seems to involve the genetic fallacy. Geuss attempts to reconstruct the logic of this definition of ideology by defining ideology of this sort as "systems of beliefs and attitudes accepted by the agents

---

ology may legitimate the power of a dominant social group by putting forward epistemologically false ideas such as the idea that the role of the dominant group in society is ordained by God or "natural" as opposed to being socially-constructed and hence contigent. The degree to which this ideology is accepted by the ruled and is successful in stabilizing or supporting domination, is the degree to which one could say that this is also an example of functionally false thinking. Those who believe these claims are in ignorance of the true origin of power which is in fact their belief in the dominant ideology. If they knew that their belief functioned in this way they may no longer hold such beliefs. In this example the manifest content of this ideology also contains an epistemological mistake and hence obscures the significant distinction between manifest content and functional properties as applied to the question of legitimation.

for reasons which they could not acknowledge," though he wonders whether or not there have ever been cases like this.[28]

Conclusion

I introduced Geuss's map of ideology as a way into a complex and controversial theoretical· terrain. Instead of telling us what different people think ideology is, Geuss outlines two research agendas in which the concept is used, reconstructing in the process the range and intelligibility of its use. This approach is particularly useful in the context of discussing the notion of purpose and the interpretative issues that go with it. In both cases my interest has been to differentiate between different research agendas.

The concept of ideology, as outlined here, fits within the fourth interpretative interest—an interest in the contextual functions of the text. It should also be clear that ideology does not fit within the interpretative interest in texts as such. To put it bluntly, ideology is not an inherent property of the text but an aspect of its use.[29] Ideology has to do with socially-significant modes of thought; thus, what is at issue in studying the ideology of the Chronicler is not so much what the texts says as the social force of what is said. This study is not an exegetical exercise focusing on the verbal meaning of the book but an examination of the contextual functions of this text and the relationship between these contextual functions and the motives and intentions of the author.

Part Two: Interpreting the Chronicler's Purpose: A Critical Survey

The aim of Part II is two-fold: (1) on the substantive level, this critical survey of Chronicles research will focus on the interpretations of the Chronicler's "purpose" as it relates to the question of the relationship between text and context. I am interested in both the way

---

[28] Geuss, *Critical Theory*, pp. 19–22. A possible example of this might be implied in Engels's description of bourgeois conscious when he states that "the real motive forces impelling him remain unknown to him" which seems to suggest that were these "real motive forces" known to the bourgeoisie there would no longer be a bourgeoisie. The use of "motive" implies consciousness but the use of "forces" points to the origin of this consciousness in external processes, an origin that must of necessity remain unrecognized by the participants.

[29] S. Fowl, "Texts don't have ideologies," *Biblical Interpretation* 3 (1995), pp. 15–34.

"purpose" is constructed and in the substance of these proposals; in other words, the conclusions I reach set the stage for this study on both fronts. I am not examining those studies which are concerned with the generic definition of Chronicles[30] nor with those which are aimed largely at an ever closer reading of the verbal meaning of Chronicles and the communicative intentions of the Chronicler. The contextual implications of these studies is generally of a more limited nature. (2) On the theoretical level, I will seek to demonstrate that the debate about "the purpose of Chronicles" is confused since the concept of purpose is undifferentiated in terms of motive, intention, and verbal meaning. Proposals range all over these interpretative interests giving rise to debates over false alternatives.

There are four main proposals regarding the purpose of the Chronicler consisting of two contrasting pairs and one minor proposal: (1) the Chronicler as exclusivist versus the Chronicler as inclusivist; (2) the Chronicler as theocrat versus the Chronicler as royalist; and (3) the Chronicler as apologist for the Levites.

Exclusivist?

The "exclusivist" interpretations of Chronicles range quite widely both in substance and in terms of how purpose is conceived. The most influential viewpoint up until recent decades has been Noth's hypothesis about an anti-Samaritan purpose, but before examining this hypothesis more closely I will review its pre-history.

W. M. L. de Wette's first volume of *Beiträge zur Einleitung in das Alte Testament*[31] marks the beginning of the historical critical study of

---

[30] Such as T. Willi, *Chronik als Auslegung: Untersuchungen zur literarischen Gestaltung der historischen Überlieferung Israels* (FRLANT 106; Göttingen: Vandenhoeck & Ruprecht, 1972); or, more recently, M. P. Graham, K. G. Hoglund and S. L. McKenzie (eds.), *The Chronicler as Historian* (JSOTS 238; Sheffield: Sheffield Academic Press, 1997).

[31] W. M. L. de Wette, *Beiträge zur Einleitung in das Alte Testament*: Vol. 1: *Kritischer Versuch über die Glaubwürdigkeit der Bücher der Chronik mit Hinsicht auf die Geschichte der Mosaischen Bücher und Gesetzgebung* (Darmstadt: Ohms Verlag, reprint ed., 1971). The overall purpose of the *Beiträge* was to lay the groundwork for a history of Israelite religion by examining the sources for such a history and setting out the historical method required. In volume one, de Wette examines the historicity of Chronicles in comparison to Samuel-Kings, and the consequences of this for the study of the Pentateuch. In volume two, he defines criteria for historical research that are then applied to the Pentateuch. See further J. W. Rogerson, *Old Testament Criticism in the Nineteenth Century: England and Germany* (London: SPCK, 1984), pp. 28–49. For the history of Chronicles research prior to de Wette see T. Willi's discussion in *Chronik*, pp. 12–26.

the books of Chronicles and whilst he had very little to say about
the context of Chronicles his reading of the Chronicler's *Tendenzen*
(as he calls them) is the starting point of the "exclusivist" interpretations of Chronicles. De Wette's study of Chronicles is based on a
comparison of Chronicles and Samuel-Kings. When comparing the
two histories he notes examples of alterations, embellishments, trans-
positions, omissions, the lack of precision, and the addition of supernatural elements.[32] Some of these differences were, in his view, of
no great consequence other than establishing that Samuel-Kings is
a more reliable source. A large majority of these differences could,
however, be attributed to "a peculiar manner of thinking, a certain
predilection and partiality, even a certain design. . . ."[33] He analyses
this "peculiar manner of thinking" in terms of three *Tendenzen* or
biases: Leviticism, vindication of the Judean cultus, and preference
for Judah and hatred of Israel.[34]

The textual evidence he cites in support of the last tendency—the
Chronicler's preference for Judah and hatred of Israel—is limited
but this evidence has remained central to the exclusivist argument.

(1) The most important observation has to do with what the text
doesn't say, specifically the absence of a history of the northern kingdom after the division of the kingdom in Rehoboam's reign (2 Chronicles 10–36). This contrasts sharply with the book of Kings which
devotes as much of its history to events in the North and consistently correlates the chronologies of both kingdoms. This sort of
argument whereby what the Chronicler is saying is determined on
the basis of synoptic comparison with Samuel-Kings is characteristic
of de Wette's treatment of Chronicles in general and indeed is characteristic of Chronicles research since his time. It represents an interest in the intentions of the Chronicler, not in the verbal meaning
as such. What the Chronicler *meant by* what he did and did not say.
Assuming that Samuel-Kings is the *Vorlage*, the presence or absence
of Samuel-Kings as well as the "purely Chronistic" material is seen
to be pregnant with intentional meanings.[35] What he *meant by* what

---

[32] De Wette, *Beiträge*, pp. 42–79.

[33] W. L. M. de Wette, *A Critical and Historical Introduction to the Canonical Scripture
of the Old Testament* (trans. T. Parker; Boston: Little and Brown, 1843), p. 274. The
substance of *Beiträge*, vol. 1 was repeated in his introduction.

[34] De Wette, *Beiträge*, pp. 80–32.

[35] A. G. Auld, *Kings without Privilege: David and Moses in the Story of the Bible's Kings*

he did *not* say relates, in my view, to the indirect intentions or implications of the text and not to direct communicative intentions of the Chronicler.

(2) The plausibility of this reading is, of course, strengthened by explicit statements found only in Chronicles castigating the North in some way or another. De Wette cites what is perhaps the most important statement in support of his hypothesis as found in Abijah's speech in 2 Chronicles 13. In his speech to Jeroboam and the rebellious northern kingdom, Abijah claims that the Israelites cannot defeat "the kingdom of the LORD in the hand of the sons of David" (v. 8) for to fight against a descendant of David is to "fight against the LORD the God of your fathers" (v. 12). He also cites a couple of references to Jehoshaphat's dealings with "wicked" (רשׁא) Israel in 2 Chronicles 19:3 and 20:35–37.

De Wette's *Tendenzkritik* does not fit neatly into the interpretative interest schema. A *Tendenz* or bias lies somewhere in the region of intention in that it is a statement about what is meant by what is said (or not said). But to describe these direct and indirect intentions as *Tendenzen* suggests a social form of consciousness or conventional bias which is to be explained more with reference to the context of production than to the individual conscious motivations of the author.

A more positive statement of the intention of the Chronicler is found in his *Introduction* written some ten years later.

> The design of the author was obviously this—to give an account of the theocratic kingdom of David, which was obviously, but slightly, connected with the earlier history of the people of Israel,—an account of that kingdom, which at first embraced all the twelve tribes, and afterwards only the tribe of Judah, and the tribes belonging to it,—the kingdom which observed the Mosaic law, and the Mosaic worship,—and to show how, in this, the true worship of God was preserved in all its perfection under pious kings, or restored by them, and how apostasy from this brought on distress and ruin. This he does in such a manner that the light far surpasses the dark side. Everything is tried by the priestly standard.[36]

(Edinburgh: T & T Clark, 1994), has recently challenged the idea that Samuel-Kings is the Vorlage of Chronicles. In his view they are both dependent on a common source.

[36] De Wette, *Introduction*, p. 315.

Though the conscious "design of the author" is the object in view, the final sentence suggests that the author's bias has something to do with his being a priest and is as such an expression of the *conventional* bias of the priests, or (to put it in more contemporary terms), the ideology of the priestly classes who presumably dominated the "theocratic kingdom" of the Persian period. More than that, de Wette does not say.

Ewald was the first critic to explore in any sort of detail the relationship between Chronicles and its historical context and to ascribe an apologetic purpose to the Chronicler.[37] The Chronicler's particularism, in Ewald's view, did not arise primarily from the inner degeneration of Hebrew religion (de Wette) but from the general historical and political context. The "problem" with the Chronicler's context, that which makes for inferior (i.e. particularistic) history writing, as Ewald sees it, is the fact that the nation of Israel is not autonomous, it is not free. The Chronicler was "not in a position to look straight at things; nor has he scope to look freely around him either, when his nation, driven into utmost straits, falls more and more under the influence of vague and faithless fears."[38] The decline of Israelite historiography as witnessed to by Chronicles is thus "an inherent necessity" brought on by the decline of the nation.

In particular he notes how the Chronicler's history, which begins with a universal scope, rapidly contracts and focuses on the history of only one nation, and, narrower still, on the history of a single city. Thus,

> The shortest and at the same time most accurate name for the work would be "Chronicle of Jerusalem," . . . [I]n this catalogue little notice is taken of the inhabitants of the surrounding country. And the author not only entirely passes over the history of the rival city of Samaria,

---

[37] H. Ewald, *History of Israel* (trans. R. Martineau; London: Longmans and Green, 1867).

[38] Ewald, *History*, p. 170. This emphasis on freedom and autonomy at the national level and its affects on the individual is very much in line with Hegel's view of history and the role of nations within history. For Hegel the process of history was the progressive development of freedom or the autonomy of consciousness. Each nation had a particular role to play in the process of the rise of the nation state. Thus, the consciousness of the individual is shaped by his/her particular situation. When de Wette published his *Beiträge* Hegel was still working on the rough draft of *The Phenomenology of the Spirit* and the latter's philosophy of history proved more popular in biblical criticism than de Wette's Kantian-Friesian philosophy of the mind (Rogerson, *Criticism*, p. 49).

> when describing the new Jerusalem, but in the earlier period, before the destruction of the city, omits the history of the Northern Kingdom almost totally. . . .[39]

This isn't so much an examination of what the Chronicler said but rather an explanation as to why this history has this particular "shape" and Ewald addresses this issue from the point of view of its historical determination, not in terms of the conscious motives of an individual. Neither Israel nor the Chronicler can transcend their historical situation.

Ewald does, however, also speculate about the Chronicler's conscious motive as it relates to the immediate occasion for the work. He dates the work to the beginning of Macedonian rule,[40] and postulates that the motive of the Chronicler was to recount "the favours shown by the Persian kings to the Temple and its servants . . . [in order] to receive similar favour from the new rulers."[41] This apologetic no doubt had a polemical side as well vis-à-vis "the rival city of Samaria" though Ewald does not develop this point at all. This sort of reading represents an attempt to ascertain the indirect communicative intentions of the Chronicler, which in this case means inferring that references to the northern kingdom are allusions to the inhabitants of that same territory in the Chronicler's day.

Relating directly to this point is the theory of a larger Chronistic History encompassing Chronicles and Ezra-Nehemiah for it was at this time that both Ewald and Zunz[42] came to the conclusion that the Chronicler was responsible for all three books. This theory was largely taken for granted in Chronicles research until recent decades and still finds its supporters.[43] Of course, such a theory has a significant influence on how one interprets the purpose of Chronicles and indeed those who argue against an exclusivist interpretation have generally done so on the basis that Chronicles is a separate work.[44] On a more general level though, this particular mode of reading Chronicles, when combined with a synchronic comparison with Samuel-Kings,

---

[39] Ewald, *History*, p. 174.

[40] Ewald, *History*, pp. 171–3.

[41] Ewald, *History*, p. 175.

[42] L. Zunz, *Die gottesdienstlichen Vorträge der Juden, historisch entwickelt. Ein Beitrag zur Altertumskunde und biblischen Kritik, zur Literature und Religionsgeschichte* (Berlin: Asher, 1832).

[43] J. Blenkinsopp, *Ezra-Nehemiah* (Old Testament Library; Philadelphia: Westminster, 1988), pp. 47–54.

[44] See H. G. M. Williamson, *Israel in the Books of Chronicles* (Cambridge: Cambridge University Press, 1977), pp. 1–4.

has meant that the slightest variation on the part of the Chronicler (over against Samuel-Kings) can be taking to imply a post-exilic stance, attitude or concern that is expressed more directly in Ezra-Nehemiah. This is not to suggest, however, that the exclusivist interpretation is necessarily dependent on the theory of a larger Chronistic History for the texts cited in its favour are from Chronicles. What it does do is transform an interpretation of the Chronicler's indirect intentions into an interpretation of his direct intentions.

Excursus on the Date of Chronicles

The relative date of Chronicles in the context of the Old Testament was the interest of the first generations of critical scholars. Following Wilhelm de Wette it is still generally agreed that the Chronicler used Samuel-Kings as his main source and hence post-dates those books. Besides Samuel-Kings it can be demonstrated that the Chronicler used parts of the Pentateuch and Joshua. This is most obvious in the genealogies where the lists of names and places, beginning with Adam and extending out from him to all the nations of the world and from Israel (Jacob) to "all Israel," are derived from lists found in Genesis, Numbers and Joshua. The Chronicler also presupposes Pentateuchal (Priestly and Deuteronomic) legislation in his historical treatment of the cult,[45] though he does exercise a degree of independence in ascribing cultic legislation to David (as it relates to the Levites in particular). Chronicles, thus, post-dates both the Pentateuch and the Deuteronomistic History; in other words, Chronicles is post-exilic.

The date assigned to Chronicles, relative or absolute, also depends on one's view of the composition history of the book. If one does not assume the unity of the work as it stands the whole dating procedure becomes more complex. The variety of literary material—genealogy, lists and narrative—incorporated in the final form of Chronicles is susceptible to source and redaction critical analyses.[46] The hypothesis of a larger Chronistic History incorporating Chronicles,

---

[45] De Wette and Wellhausen stressed the Chronicler's dependence on P, whereas von Rad and Noth demonstrated dependence on D. See also J. Shaver, *Torah and the Chronicler's History Work* (Atlanta: Scholar's Press, 1990). This question also dominated Chronicles research in the 19th century: see, M. P. Graham, *The Utilization of Chronicles in the Reconstruction of Israelite History in the Nineteenth Century*, SBLDS 116 (Atlanta: Scholars, 1990).

[46] J. W. Rothstein and J. Hänel, *Das erste Buch der Chronik* (KAT; Leipzig: Reichart, 1927) and A. C. Welch, *The Work of the Chronicler. Its Purpose and its Date* (London:

Ezra and Nehemiah complicates the picture even more with regard to the process of composition while at the same time narrowing the time frame for the composition of the final form. The notion of a Chronistic History necessitates at the earliest a late fifth century date for the final form if one takes the order of Ezra and Nehemiah's missions as given, or slightly later if one doesn't.[47] If, on the other hand, one posits a long process of composition reaching back in time beyond Ezra and Nehemiah then the Chronistic History hypothesis alone does not affect the terminus a quo. The trend in recent research, however, is to treat Chronicles as a relatively unified and independent work. If one accepts this as the starting point then the absolute date for the final form Chronicles can be established as falling between 400 and 200 BCE.

Regarding the *terminus a quo* the following data are relevant, starting with the earliest historical reference:

- 2 Chron. 36:20 refers to the beginning of Persian rule and 1 Chron. 9:1 refers to the exile of Judah.[48] The list of residents of Jerusalem that follows (1 Chron. 9:2ff) parallels the list found in Neh. 11:3–19 and while a good case can be made that the Chronicler used Nehemiah as his source, there is still the possibility that both depend on an earlier common source. These two texts bring us into the post-exilic period.
- 1 Chron. 29:7 mentions, anachronistically, ten thousand "darics" (אדרכנים) given for the service of the temple. The Persian daric was first minted by Darius I around 515 BCE to which one would have to add a certain amount of time for the daric to become widely used and for the Chronicler to refer to it in an anachronistic way; in other words, the early fifth century.[49]

British Academy, 1939) take this to the extreme by associating various redactions with different Pentateuchal sources.

[47] Along a similar line William Albright, following rabbinic tradition, argued that Ezra was himself the Chronicler ["The Date and Personality of the Chronicler," *JBL* 40 (1921), pp. 104–24].

[48] Japhet has recently defended the view that this list is intended to name residents of Jerusalem prior to exile and is, as such, a climax to the genealogies. Whilst the phrase in 9:2 translated "the first to live" is ambiguous, the notice concerning the exile in 9:1b points in the direction of those who would add "again", i.e. the returnees. Japhet, for her part, suggests that 9:1b is a gloss [S. Japhet, *I & II Chronicles* (OTL; London: SCM, 1993), pp. 206–8]. See the discussion in chapter three.

[49] For a full discussion see H. G. M. Williamson, "Eschatology in Chronicles," *TynBul* 28 (1977), pp. 123–6.

- A less direct and hence more controversial text brings down the *termius a quo* even further. The genealogy of Jehoiachin (1 Chron. 3:17–24) is, unfortunately, corrupt and may refer to anywhere between seven and ten generations after Zerubbabel. If we take the minimum of seven generations after Zerubbabel and multiply by twenty years per generation, the genealogy extends to the latter half of the fifth century, or c. 430 BCE.
- A late fifth century date has also been supported by Polzin's study of late biblical Hebrew. He puts the language of Chronicles in the same phase of development as Ezra, Nehemiah, Esther and Daniel, and showing the closest affinity to the Ezra and the non-Nehemiah Memoir material.[50]

Regarding the *terminus ad quem* the following data are relevant:

- Eupolemus, a Jewish historian of the mid-second century BCE relies more on Chronicles than on Kings in his account of Solomon and on one occasion cites the LXX of Chronicles.[51]
- Ben Sira's portrayal of David (Sir. 47:8–10) appears to be based on Chronicles. In particular the reference in verse 9 to David's placing singers before the altar corresponds with the Chronicler's account of the organization of the cult (1 Chron. 15–16). This would necessitate a late third century BCE date at the latest.[52]

The two main options within this two hundred year span from 400 to 200 BCE are the last century of Persian rule or the first century of Hellenistic rule. In last few decades only Peter Welten has tried to make a case for a Hellenistic date on the basis of what he felt was more or less concrete evidence. He cites, for example, details in the Chronicler's building reports which, he argues, necessitate a Hellenistic date on archeological grounds.[53] Welten also argues that the organization of the military divisions into heavy and light infantry

---

[50] R. Polzin, *Late Biblical Hebrew* (Missoula, MN: Scholars Press, 1976), pp. 27–84.

[51] The wording of Solomon's blessing in *Praeparatio Evangelica* 9.34 agrees with the LXX of 2 Chron. 2:11. For a translation of the Eupolemos fragments see J. H. Charlesworth (ed.), *Old Testament Pseudepigrapha*, vol. 2 (New York: Doubleday, 1985), pp. 861–72. On the historical-ideological significance of this connection between Eupolemus and Chronicles see chapter three, footnote 139.

[52] This is disputed by E. Ben Zvi, "The Authority of 1–2 Chronicles in the Late Second Temple Period," *JSP* 3 (1988), pp. 59–88.

[53] P. Welten, *Geschichte und Geschichsdarstellung in den Chronikbüchern* (Neukirchen-Vluyn: Neukirchner, 1973), p. 200.

(2 Chron. 14:7 [ET v. 8]) presupposes the military practice of the Greeks.[54] Both these arguments are unconvincing, however, in that (a) the archeology of pre-Hasmonean Jerusalem is fairly controversial to say the least, and (b) Greek mercenaries were used by both Egyptian and Persian armies since the sixth century.

His main argument, however, concerns the reference to some sort of defensive structure in 2 Chron. 26:15. Welten translates חשבנות as "catapults" for shooting arrows and large stones. The catapult was invented around 400 BCE and, to Welten's mind, would not have been widely known in Palestine until after Alexander's conquests.[55] This translation is, however, debatable. Yadin, for example, argues that this word refers to some sort of platform which facilitates the shooting of arrows and the dropping of large stones.[56] Thus, it would appear that no conclusive evidence is forthcoming from Chronicles which would allow us to decide in favour of the late Persian or early Hellenistic period. The lack of Hellenistic influence in Chronicles supports the former but some still argue for a Hellenistic dating.[57] In this study, I presuppose a Persian period dating but my proposal could be adapted to fit a Hellenistic date insofar as there was a degree of structural continuity in the relationship between the imperial power before and after Alexander.

It was Wellhausen who first suggested the link between the anti-Israel bias and the Samaritan problem, which was, supposedly, a major challenge facing the Chronicler's community. For the Chronicler, argues Wellhausen, "Israel is the congregation of true worship, and the last is connected with the temple at Jerusalem, in which of course the Samaritans have no part."[58] Wellhausen's minor insight was

---

[54] Welten, *Geschichte*, pp. 105–11.

[55] See Diodorus Siculus, XIV, 42, 1; and E. W. Marsden, *Greek and Roman Artillery* (Oxford: Clarendon, 1969), pp. 48–64.

[56] Y. Yadin, *The Art of Warfare in Biblical Lands in the Light of Archaeological Discovery* (London: Weidenfeld and Nicolson, 1963), pp. 326–7.

[57] See for example J. Kegler, "Prophetengeschtalten im Deuteronomistischen Geschichtswerk und in den Chronikbüchern: Ein Beitrag zur Kompositions- und Redaktionsgeschichte der Chronikbücher," *ZAW* 105 (1993), pp. 481–97; and most recently G. Stein, "Zur Datierung der Chronik: Ein neuer methodischer Ansatz," *ZAW* 109 (1997), pp. 84–92.

[58] J. Wellhausen, *Prolegomena to the History of Ancient Israel* (trans. W. Robertson Smith; Gloucestor, Mass: Peter Smith, reprint edn., 1973), pp. 187–8. By *Samarier*, here translated "Samaritans," Wellhausen might not be referring to the later Samaritan community associated with the sanctuary on Mt. Gerizim, but he does nonetheless

transformed by Torrey (and Noth) into the theory of an anti-Samaritan purpose,[59] a theory which came to dominate critical scholarship in this century.[60] The anti-Samaritan hypothesis concerns the author's motives and owes as much or more to Josephus's account of the Samaritan schism as it does to a "careful" reading of the text. Josephus (*Ant.* 9:277–91) claims that the Samaritan priesthood originated in Jerusalem and that the sanctuary on Mt. Gerizim was built at the beginning of the Greek period. Torrey can thus surmise that the Samaritans had as much of a claim to legitimacy as the priesthood in Jerusalem and were "the rightful heirs and the true church"; "were there any in Jerusalem who could show a clearer title?"[61]

Noth, like Torrey, follows Josephus's account of the Samaritan schism, but pays closer attention to the verbal meaning of the text and the intentions of the Chronicler. According to Noth, attention to genre and particularly "the overall plan of the work"[62] allows for a more accurate determination of the Chronicler's motive. Attending to the "overall plan of the work" concerns deducing what the Chronicler intended to say by looking at what he included in his

---

mean the inhabitants of Samaria in the post-exilic ("Judaistic") period. It is perhaps better to use the term "Samarians" for the inhabitants of this region prior to the definitive break between the two communities associated with the building of the sanctuary on Mt. Gerizim.

[59] C. C. Torrey, "The Chronicler as Editor and Independent Narrator," in *Ezra Studies* (New York: Ktav, reprint edn., 1970), p. 209. Torrey seems to suggest another plausible account of their origin when he states that "They could probably prove, in a great many instances, that not only individuals of priestly rank, but also whole priestly families, had migrated into the Northern-Israelite territory when Jerusalem was destroyed, and that their descendants were now pillars of the Samaritan church." No evidence is cited to support this supposition from the Persian period itself which makes it all the more likely that Josephus is behind this remark.

[60] A leading example would be Rudolph who follows the anti-Samaritan line of interpretation in his influential commentary. "Das Leitmotiv des Chronisten, daß das wahre Israel nur in Juda und Jerusalem zu finden sei, hat unverkennbar eine Spitze gegen die Ansprache der Samaritaner; so wird die Chr in der Tat "the first apology of Judaism" (citing R. H. Pfeiffer, *Introduction to the Old Testament* (New York: Harper, 1952), p. 806) [W. Rudolph, *Chronikbücher* (HAT; Tübingen: Mohr, 1955), p. ix].

[61] C. C. Torrey, "The Chronicler," p. 209. Torrey did not treat Second Temple Judaism as one undifferentiated unity but as a body of competing ideologies of which Jerusalem's was only one example. See R. P. Carroll, "Torrey, C. C.," in R. J. Collins and J. H. Houlden (eds.), *A Dictionary of Biblical Interpretation* (London: SCM, 1990), pp. 696–7.

[62] M. Noth, *The Chronicler's History*, JSOTS 50, trans. H. G. M. Williamson (Sheffield: 1987), p. 100. Of course, for Noth the "overall plan" included Ezra-Nehemiah but it must be said that the texts he cites in favour of his thesis are from Chronicles.

history and what he excluded (this time over against Samuel-Kings *and* the Pentateuch).

Noth reasons that if we observe what the Chronicler included in his history[63] we must come to the conclusion that his communicative intention (stated in positive terms) was "to demonstrate the legitimacy of the Davidic dynasty and of the Jerusalem temple as Yahweh's valid cult centre."[64] If, on the other hand, we observe that the Chronicler excluded those traditions which the Jews and Samaritans had in common (i.e. those contained in the Pentateuch, Joshua, and Judges) and that he neglects the history of the northern kingdom[65] we must conclude that his motive was to legitimate the Jerusalem temple in opposition to "the Samaritan community with a cult of their own on Mt. Gerizim."[66]

Excursus on the Samaritans

There are a number of historical problems which make Noth's anti-Samaritan thesis untenable. There are difficulties in identifying the Samaritans, in distinguishing them from the Jews of various periods,

---

[63] In other words, that the Chronicler begins his historical narrative with David and emphasizes the divine nature of his kingdom. David's kingdom is in fact the kingdom of God on earth, citing 1 Chron. 17:14 and 2 Chron. 9:8 (p. 101). Israel is no longer just the elected people of God, but the kingdom of the Davidides as well (2 Chron. 13:4ff; cf. 1 Chron. 28:4).

The other side of his Davidic interest, and closely linked with it, is the interest in the legitimate cult centre in Jerusalem: "the association of this sanctuary with the Davidic kingdom was so important that he really could not imagine that the founder of the dynasty did not regard concern for the building of the sanctuary to be his most important task." (p. 103) The legitimate cult and the legitimate cult personnel were in Jerusalem alone.

[64] Noth, *Chronicler's History*, p. 100. Noth's stress on the "overall plan" was directed against von Rad's view that the Chronicler's purpose in writing his history was to support the claims of the Levites.

[65] Noth does mention sporadic ties between Jerusalem and people of the north (2 Chron. 15:9; 30:1, 5, 10, 11, 18, 25; 34:9). These "counter-indicators" do not upset Noth's analysis of the "overall plan" and hence the communicative intention of the book. He explains their presence by claiming that they reflect contemporary relations between inhabitants of Samaria-Galilee and Jerusalem. Other texts, which assume that Judah's kings have some sort of authority over the North, suggest some sort of contemporary claim to northern territory, citing 2 Chron. 19:4; 31:1; 34:6 [Noth, *Chronicler's History*, p. 104].

[66] Noth, *Chronicler's History*, p. 101. A recent advocate of the anti-Samaritan thesis is R. Albertz who uses the same basic argument Noth uses regarding the "overall plan" vis-à-vis the Pentateuch and the Former Prophets, *A History of Ancient Israelite Religion in the Old Testament Period*, vol. 2, *From the Exile to the Maccabees* (trans. J. Bowden; London: SCM), pp. 544–56.

and in determining what the basis of this distinction was. There are two accounts of their origins. 2 Kings 17:24–41 claims that the inhabitants of Samaria are the descendants of colonists brought there by the Assyrians and made into nominal Yahwists. The point of view found in Ezra 4 corresponds to the one found in 2 Kings 17. The leaders of the community of returnees reject the offer of the inhabitants of Samaria ("the adversaries of Judah") to participate in the rebuilding of the Temple, even though they claim to be Yahwists. Consequently, the Samaritans oppose the temple project and, later on, the rebuilding of the wall of Jerusalem (that is, of course, if Sanballat's opposition equals Samaritan opposition).[67]

The Samaritans themselves claim that they are the descendants of the northern tribes of Israel. The twenty thousand odd deportees from the region, as recorded in the inscription of Sargon II (*ANET*, pp. 284–5), confirms, negatively, the view that the bulk of the northern Israelites remained in the land. The Elephantine Papyri contain a fifth century letter addressed to the Samaritan and Jewish priests (*AramP* 30) which assumes some sort of religious and/or ethnic link between all three communities.

Josephus claims that the Samaritan priesthood originated in Jerusalem and that the sanctuary on Mt. Gerizim was built in with Alexander's permission (*Ant.* 9:277–91).[68] But recent archeological excavations on Mt. Gerizim have demonstrated that the origin of the sanctuary on Mt. Gerizim is to be dated to the early second century BCE at the earliest.[69] It is also commonly accepted that the conflict between Jews and the inhabitants of Samaria intensified in the Hasmonean period, culminating in the destruction of the sanctuary and Shechem by John Hyrcanus (128 and 107 BCE, respectively).[70] We should not,

---

[67] R. Pummer, "Antisamaritanische Polemik in jüdischen Schriften aus der intertestamentarischen Zeit," *BZ* NF 26.2 (1992), pp. 224–42.

[68] H. Kippenberg accepts Josephus' account of the origins of the Samaritan priesthood [*Garizim und Synagoge: Traditionsgeschichtliche Untersuchungen zur samaritanischen Religion der aramische Periode* (RVV; Berlin: Walter de Gruyter, 1971), pp. 50–9]. However, in Samaritan tradition Alexander is remembered as an oppressor who forbade them to look at Mt. Gerizim when they worshipped.

[69] Y. Magen, "A Fortified Town of the Hellenistic Period on Mt. Gerizim," *Qadmoniot* 19.3–4 (1986), pp. 91–101; idem, "Mt. Gerizim, A Temple City [Hebrew]," *Qadmoniot* 23.3–4 (1990), pp. 69–96; and idem, "The Temple of Zeus on Mt. Gerizim [Hebrew]," in *Proceedings of the Twelfth Archeological Congress* (Jerusalem: Israel Exploration Society, 1986), pp. 14–15.

[70] R. T. Anderson, "Samaritans," in D. N. Freedman (ed.), *The Anchor Bible Dictionary* (New York: Doubleday, 1992), vol. 5, pp. 940–7. For further bibliography

therefore, read the Jewish-Samaritan conflict of the later Second Temple period back into the Persian period.

A somewhat more subtle approach is the tradition-historical study of von Rad.[71] In his analysis of the use of the term "Israel" he observes that the Chronistic history (i.e. Chronicles-Ezra-Nehemiah) contains different and conflicting ideas about Israel, some of which can be ascribed to the Chronicler himself and some to his "sources". Thus, the various viewpoints reflect different contexts and traditions incorporated in the text and do not all reflect the Chronicler's own views on the matter. In substantive terms, the conflicting views reflect the clash between theory and reality; the ideal of Israel as made up of the twelve tribes of Jacob clashing with the historical reality of the post-exilic community of Judah, Benjamin and Levi.[72] Of particular note is the use of the words "Jews"[73] and "Israel"[74] in the non-Chronistic material in Ezra and Nehemiah.[75] The former is used in political and organizational contexts whereas the latter is used in religious contexts. Von Rad concludes from this that the post-exilic community appropriated for itself, that is for Judah and Benjamin, the name "Israel" and the promises inherent in it.[76] Such is the self-understanding of the Chronicler's contemporaries and of the Chronicler himself.

In the Chronistic material in Ezra-Nehemiah the word "Jew" is not used. The emphasis is entirely on the continuity between the community of returned exiles and the Israel of old. The same viewpoint is also found in the genealogies of Chronicles (1 Chron. 1–9) where we find an enumeration of all the tribes of Israel.[77] But this

---

see: A. D. Crown, *A Bibliography of the Samaritans* (Metuchin, NY/London: American Theological Library Association, 2nd edn., 1993); and A. D. Crown, R. Pummer, and A. Tal (eds.), *A Companion to Samaritan Studies* (Tübingen: Mohr (Siebeck), 1993).

[71] G. von Rad, *Das Geschichtsbild des Chronistischen Werkes* (BWANT 54; Stuttgart: Kohlhammer, 1930).

[72] Von Rad, *Geschichtsbild*, p. 18. Even in the genealogy which, on the surface at least, attests to the twelve tribe ideal, the three "faithful" tribes stand out [von Rad, *Geschichtsbild*, pp. 25–6].

[73] Neh. 1:2; 2:16; 3:33, 34; 4:6; 5:1, 8,17; 6:6; 13:23.

[74] Ezra 2:59; 6:17; 7:28; 8:25, 35; 9:1; 10:1ff, 5, 10; Neh. 8:1; 9:2; 13:18.

[75] The "memoirs" of Ezra and Nehemiah in particular are taken to be largely authentic sources which gives us a direct insight into the Chronicler's era [von Rad, *Geschichtsbild*, p. 19].

[76] Von Rad, *Geschichtsbild*, p. 24.

[77] Von Rad, *Geschichtsbild*, p. 29. Von Rad also notes the more lenient view of intermarriage.

ideal concept of Israel does, in von Rad's view, eventually come into conflict with the narrower definition in the story of the divided kingdom, a definition rooted in the self-understanding of the Chronicler's community. Von Rad argues that when the Chronicler speaks, for example, of "all Israel in Judah and Benjamin" (2 Chron. 11:3) he means to say that the kingdom of Judah (and the post-exilic "remnant" of that kingdom) is the *true Israel*.[78] The northern kingdom is completely illegitimate and has, as it were, excluded itself from salvation history.

Torrey and Noth represent the Chronicler as one who welcomes, if not actively promotes, this narrower definition of Israel. Their interpretations of Chronicles are tied to a particular understanding of his motives. If you are going to argue, as they do, that the Chronicler is a polemicist you cannot have a polemicist at odds with himself over such a fundamental issue. Von Rad's interpretation, though dealing with the same issue in terms of what the text says (about Israel), speaks more to *theological intentions* (the ideal) than *political motive* (the reality). The Chronicler's history was not an ordinary secular history but the history of salvation, a history of the people of God. "Israel" is first and foremost a theological idea and this "allows" the Chronicler to equivocate in his use of it, according to von Rad. This difference in approach can be seen in von Rad's interpretation of those texts in 2 Chronicles 10ff which suggest either a more sympathetic attitude towards the people of the north (e.g. 2 Chron. 14:7ff) or extend the sphere of influence of the Davidides into the north (e.g. 2 Chron. 31:1). Whereas Noth explains their presence by claiming that they reflect contemporary relations between inhabitants of Samaria-Galilee and Jerusalem or perhaps a contemporary claim to northern territory,[79] von Rad also sees in them a theological commitment to a particular idea.[80] His work thus stands as a contribution in the area of intentions, theologically understood, rather than in the area of the contextual function of Chronicles. He allows for textual meanings and contextual functions which were not "intended" by the author and which, consequently, should not be incorporated into a reconstruction of the Chronicler's theology (or ideology as in worldview). The exclusivist interpretation put forward by von Rad is thus more positive and theological in orientation than

---

[78] Von Rad, *Geschichtsbild*, p. 31.
[79] Noth, *Chronicler's History*, p. 104.
[80] Von Rad, *Geschichtsbild*, p. 33.

Torrey's or Noth's and he enters into the Chronicler's theological world in a sympathetic, emic way. But from the point of view of the plurality of interpretative interests, it is possible that the narrower and broad views of Israel are different sides of the same coin, one at the level of direct communicative intention and the other at the level of contextual functions (if not motive). I will, of course, be examining this possibility in greater detail in chapters three and four.

Inclusivist?

Those who argue that the Chronicler is an inclusivist have much in common with von Rad.[81] Both Japhet[82] and Williamson,[83] for example, are particularly interested in the "all Israel" emphasis throughout Chronicles and in the "positive" notices about the North which contrast sharply with the line taken in Ezra-Nehemiah.[84] Again, in line with von Rad, both scholars think the Chronicler takes this position because he is an "idealist" and conversely that he is not pursuing a political agenda. The difference between von Rad and the "inclusivists" is that the latter reach different conclusions as to the relative weight this textual evidence should have in the interpretation of the communicative intentions of the Chronicler. Their reassessment of the communicative intentions in turn necessitates, in their view, a reappraisal of the Chronicler's motive which is to be assessed independently from Ezra-Nehemiah.[85]

---

[81] The inclusivist interpretation was previously put forward by Welch in *Work of the Chronicler*. Welch argued that the emphasis on the unity of Israel under David and Solomon and the efforts toward unity of Hezekiah and Josiah predates the Return and reflects the viewpoint of those who never went into exile (pp. 13ff). Unfortunately, Welch uses a now thoroughly out-dated method of establishing this context. He associates each of the two main redactional layers of Chronicles with a different Pentateuchal source. Since each Pentateuchal source had its own unique period of dominance the two redactions of Chronicles can be dated fairly accurately. Because the original redaction of Chronicles relies on Deuteronomy, Welch dates the Chronicler's compositional activity to the period before the Return (the period of the Deuteronomist). Had the Chronicler been a part of the Return, reasons Welch, his use of a law code which was superseded by the Priestly code would be quite impossible. "The Chronicler can only have belonged to the community which had never been in the exile" (p. 157).

[82] Japhet, *Ideology*.

[83] H. G. M. Williamson, *Israel in the Books of Chronicles* (Cambridge: Cambridge University Press, 1977).

[84] Von Rad also notes this contrast, especially in relation to intermarriage [von Rad, *Geschichtsbild*, p. 29].

[85] According to Japhet and Williamson, the literary argument is crucial, but (as noted above) the exclusivist position is not absolutely dependent on the view that Chronicles-Ezra-Nehemiah are one work.

Japhet examines the use of the phrase "all Israel" in Chronicles[86] and concludes that texts which apply this phrase to Judah and Benjamin are referring to the southern *kingdom*, not just Judah and Benjamin. For example, a text such as 2 Chronicles 12:1—"When Rehoboam was established ... he abandoned the LORD, he and all Israel with him"—is to be understood in the context of 2 Chronicles 11:13–17 which describes how priests and Levites from "all the tribes of Israel" (v. 16) were represented in the "southern kingdom."[87] According to Japhet, the Chronicler does not maintain the distinction between the ten northern tribes and the one southern tribe as does the Deuteronomistic historian (1 Kgs 11:35–36). Contrary to von Rad, Judah and Benjamin specify *geographical* regions in the phrase "all Israel in Judah and Benjamin" (2 Chron. 11:3).[88] And what about the Chronicler's attitude towards the northern kingdom? What about the texts which condemn the northern kingdom as illegitimate (e.g. 25:7)? Japhet's answer is simple: The condemnation applies only to the northern *kingdom* and not to the people of the North for "the northern kingdom, for all its sins, is an integral part of the people of Israel."[89] It is this attitude which, according to Japhet, contrasts sharply with the attitude to the inhabitants of the north in Ezra-Nehemiah. Whereas Ezra 4:1–2 (following 2 Kings 17:24ff) emphasizes the foreign origins of the inhabitants in the North who are said to have been brought there by the Assyrians, the Chronicler continues to speak of Israelites in the North after the Assyrian invasion. Hezekiah's Passover celebration includes "the whole assembly that came out of Israel and the sojourners who came out of the land of Israel" (2 Chron. 30:25). These interpretations have to do with the verbal meanings of the text and the direct intentions of the author.

Williamson's *Israel in the Books of Chronicles* is a study of the use of

---

[86] 1 Chron. 11:4; 13:6; 21:1–5; 2 Chron. 1:2–3 are Chronistic additions for the sake of special emphasis, where as 1 Chron. 14:8; 2 Chron. 7:4–6; 10:16; 11:3 are added for stylistic reasons only [Japhet, *Ideology*, pp. 272–4].

[87] Japhet, *Ideology*, p. 277.

[88] Japhets also discerns a steady expansion of the kingdom of Judah into the North. The reign of Asa (see 2 Chron. 15:8–9), according to Japhet, marks the beginning of this *geographic* expansion which gains pace in the reigns of Hezekiah and Josiah reaching as far as Zebulun (2 Chron. 30:11) and Naphtali (2 Chron. 34:5–7) [Japhet, *Ideology*, pp. 295–8].

[89] This is underscored by the use of the term "brother" (2 Chron. 11:4; 19:10 and 28:8).

the word "Israel" in Chronicles. Williamson contends, also against von Rad, that when the term "Israel" is applied to the southern kingdom it is not done in an exclusivist way.[90] For example, when the Chronicler applies the term "all Israel" to Judah in 2 Chronicles 11:3, he is merely levelling the score between the North and the South, for the term "all Israel" had already been applied to the northern kingdom (2 Chron. 10:16). The Chronicler wanted to show that the term "all Israel" could be used for either kingdom.[91] In extending its usage to include Judah, the Chronicler did not wish "to exclude or contrast with the Northern Kingdom, but to make a positive point that there was to be found in Judah an unbroken continuation of the Israel of earlier days."[92]

In a more recent essay, Williamson extends this thesis with regard to the temple theme in Chronicles.[93] Williamson argues that "the temple in Chronicles is not a litmus test of an orthodoxy that would exclude the non-conformist but rather a focus of unity for the people of Israel as a whole."[94] Taking his cue from modern ecumenical theory, he suggests that the Chronicler (like any good ecumenist) links the Temple to the period before the divisions in Israel occurred. These "physical ties of unbroken continuity" make the Jerusalem temple "a focus of continuity with the nation's earliest history and one that should therefore override more recent differences."[95]

These "more recent differences" relate to the contemporary implications of what the Chronicler says. As regards motives, Williamson contends that the Chronicler wants to steer a middle course between "assimilationists" and "separatists", two competing factions within the post-exilic community. "On the one hand, there can be no doubt about his unswerving loyalty to the Jerusalem cult . . . reconciliation with rebels could only be based on their return to complete allegiance

---

[90] 2 Chron. 11:3 reads "Say to Rehoboam son of Solomon king of Judah, and to all Israel in Judah and Benjamin. . . ." The parallel text in Kings reads "all the house of Judah and Benjamin and the rest of the people" (1 Kgs 12:23). Williamson disagrees with von Rad's claim that "Juda und Benjamin sind jetzt das wahre Israel" [von Rad, *Geschichtsbild*, p. 31].

[91] Williamson, *Israel*, p. 109.

[92] Williamson, *Israel*, p. 107.

[93] H. G. M. Williamson, "The Temple in the Books of Chronicles," in W. Horbury (ed.), *Templum Amicitiae: Essays on the Second Temple Presented to Ernst Bammel* (JSNTS 48; Sheffield: JSOT Press, 1991), pp. 15–31.

[94] Williamson, "Temple," p. 21.

[95] Williamson, "Temple," pp. 24–5.

to the authority of this cult."[96] On the other hand (and more importantly), the Chronicler is trying to reach out to all Israel on the basis
of his belief in the unity of the twelve: "a faithful nucleus does not
exclude others, but is a representative centre to which all the children of Israel may be welcomed if they will return."[97] The Chronicler's
presentation of the Temple was intended positively, unlike the temple polemic in Ezra 1–6 or in the Samaritan Pentateuch.[98] Both
sides, the assimilationists and the separationists, are at fault for making religion the servant of lesser social aims. The assimilationists
seemingly ignore religious boundaries as they pursue other interests,
though Williamson does not tell us what these aims are because,
presumably, the sources do not tell us what they are.

The contribution of Japhet and Williamson comes by way of
offering a different interpretation of the Chronicler's communicative
intentions giving due weight to those texts which offer a "broader"
view of Israel. In their opinion this precludes the idea that the
Chronicler was an exclusivist (in terms of motive) on the order of
Ezra-Nehemiah. A different understanding of the Chronicler's communicative intentions requires a different understanding of motive.
Having argued that we can't paint the Chronicler with an Ezra-
Nehemianic brush they reach for what appears to be the only alternative: the Chronicler must have been an inclusivist. But even at
the level of communicative intentions, these proposals present as
many problems as they solve. What does one do, for instance, with
those texts which do present a narrower understanding of Israel?
Japhet's geographical solution is not really a solution for although

---

[96] Williamson, *Israel*, p. 139 [emphasis mine].

[97] He expands on this further claiming that "the temple in Chronicles is not a
litmus test of an orthodoxy that would exclude the non-conformist but rather a
focus of unity for the people of Israel as a whole" [Williamson, "Temple," p. 21].
Taking his cue from modern ecumenical theory, he suggests that the Chronicler
(like any good ecumenist) links the Temple to the period before the divisions in
Israel occurred. These "physical ties of unbroken continuity" make the Jerusalem
temple "a focus of continuity with the nation's earliest history and one that should
therefore override more recent differences" [Williamson, "Temple," pp. 24–5].

[98] The main polemical feature of the Samaritan Pentateuch are the changes made
to the text that designate Mt. Gerizim as the sole legitimate place of worship: Deut
27:4 (altar to be built on Mt. Gerizim not Mt. Ebal); Exod. 20:17 (passage inserted
from Deut. 11:29–30 and 27:2b–3a, 4–7 saying that the altar is to be build an altar
on Mt. Gerizim); and Exod. 20:24 ("in the [not every] place where I have caused
[not I will cause] my name to be remembered") [B. Waltke, "Samaritan Pentateuch,"
in D. N. Freedman (ed.), *The Anchor Bible Dictionary* (New York: Doubleday, 1992),
vol. 5, pp. 932–40].

the text does clearly recognize that there are representatives from all Israel in Judah the point surely is that *Judah's* territory is the representative centre of Israel.

And at the level of motive one encounters even more difficulty.[99] Assuming, for the sake of argument, that "it is clear that there were at least two groups in Jerusalem," why are certain priests associating with "outsiders" and why do they have the same interests as the aristocracy?[100] Their use of religion for sectarian ends is matched by other separatist factions who make it serve their own exclusivist ideology. Ideology as used here describes the improper use of religion for social ends. The Chronicler is not being ideological for his is a voice which rises above these earthly squabbles and attempts to bring everyone together by means of the correct definition of Israel—an inclusive and loyal to God-Jerusalem-temple Israel. Why not include the Chronicler with the assimilation-minded priests who were no doubt loyal to the Temple and inclusivist in their "foreign policy"? Is Williamson reluctant to do this because the sources condemn these assimilationists? In Williamson's interpretation (as in other interpretations) the Chronicler is a surprisingly non-partisan individual in his approach and uninfluenced by his context. He is someone who, despite his predominant interest in the validity of Jerusalem and her temple, is able to act as broker between two rival groups. The Chronicler is thought of as interacting with his social context but still as master of his own ideas, intentions and motives. As we saw in the first part of this chapter, in order to address the full range of contextual questions which are associable with the concept of ideology one cannot limit oneself to the conscious intentions and motives of the Chronicler. There are difficulties too on the substantive level. The main subject of the Chronicler's history was a contemporary institution with enormous social, economic and political significance. We have to ask, with Noth and others, about the role of the Temple in Judean society and how the ideology expressed by the Chronicler functioned in relationship to that role? To answer this questions it is necessary, I would argue, to go beyond the model of the author who is in control of the meaning of his or her work.

---

[99] This applies only to Williamson because Japhet does not address the Chronicler's context.

[100] Ezra 9:1–2; Neh. 13:28.

Theocrat?

The theocratic interpretation of the Chronicler's "purpose" espoused by Rudolph is a positive (and perhaps more theologically palatable) restatement of the anti-Samaritan thesis. The Chronicler's theocratic theology may have emerged in the context of ideological conflict with the Samaritans, but, according to Rudolph, the Samaritan polemic is not its "guiding principle."[101] The issue the Chronicler wanted to address was how to understand the manner of God's rule in his particular context. What is the purpose (*der Zweck*) of the uniquely Chronistic material? The Chronicler wanted to portray the realization of the theocracy in the land of Israel as founded on the choseness of Israel, Judah and Jerusalem (communicative intention). To the post-exilic community this could only mean that it now embodied the theocracy (the indirect communicative intention).[102] In other words, the Chronicler wanted to show how God's rule was still effective in his own day while one pillar of this theocracy, the Temple, yet remained.

The Chronicler could hardly ignore the other pillar of theocracy—the house of David—in relating the history of God's rule from beginning to end, yet, in Rudolph's opinion, it had very little independent historical significance.[103] The Chronicler was by no means someone dissatisfied with the present state of affairs nor longing for the overthrow of Persian tyranny and the restoration of the Davidic monarchy. Rudolph concludes that, for the Chronicler, the failure of the

---

[101] The guiding principle of a work is, presumably, more like the communicative intention as opposed to motive. Noth had already pointed to the Chronicler's concern to establish that the rule of God on earth operates via David and his successors, in Jerusalem and in its temple and this point is developed further by Rudolph.

[102] Rudolph, *Chronikbücher*, pp. viii–ix.

[103] N. Poulssen, *König und Tempel im Glaubenszeugnis des Alten Testaments* (SBM 3; Stuttgart: 1967), also argues that the David theme is subordinated to the overall concern with the kingdom of God—the theocracy. God is the king and the Davidide is but a key functionary in the theocracy, something like a governor or representative. Poulssen interprets the changes introduced by the Chronicler to the Nathan prophecy as a theocratization of the dynastic promise (1 Chron. 17:14): Solomon will rule over *Yahweh's* house and kingdom. "Der Chronist betrachtet nämlich das Heiligtum als königliche Burg" (p. 173). "Das persönlichere Verhältnis von König und Tempel führt dazu, daß beim Chronisten die göttlich Statthalterschaft der idealen Könige überwiegend im Bereich des Heiligtums sichtbar wird, wo dem König trotz einiger Zugeständnisse an die privilegierte Stellung der Priesterschaft in nachexilischer Zeit schließlich doch die Vorrangstellung zukommt" (p. 182).

Davidic dynasty "ließ sich verschmerzen, solange die zweite Säule
der Theokratie, der Tempel in Jerusalem, so feststand, wie Gott es
derzeit dadurch, daß er die Herzen der Perserkönige lenkte, gefügt
hatte. . . ."[104]

Rudolph's theocratic interpretation of Chronicles was adopted by
O. Plöger in his influential book *Theocracy and Eschatology* and extended
into a full-blown theory about the socio-religious situation in post-
exilic Judah.[105] Plöger argues that the Jews of this period were divided
into two opposing groups, each with a different view of eschatology.
The Chronicler represents the official line of the theocratic party
whereas the eschatological voice is heard in Isaiah 24–27, Zechariah
12–14, Joel and later Daniel. Thus, "the Chronicler's work of history
is influenced not only by an outward looking anti-Samaritan aim
but also by an inward looking anti-eschatological point of view."[106]
Nothing new is on offer here; simply a more thorough-going reconstruction of the context and hence significance of the Chronicler's
theocratic ideology.[107]

Royalist?

Over against the theocratic interpretation one finds a number of
proposals which can be gathered under the heading "royalist."[108] The
common thread linking them all is the emphasis on David in Chronicles
which is taken as a sign of the continuing interest in the destiny of
the Davidic line. In other words, it is a matter of correctly assessing
the indirect communicative intentions of the Chronicler, taking into
consideration the context in which he was writing. What did the
Chronicler *mean by* concentrating on David? What relative weight
should be given to this "theme" over against the temple theme?

According to von Rad, the Chronicler, in common with the Israelite
understanding of history in general, saw the rule of God at work in

---

[104] Rudolph, *Chronikbücher*, p. xxiii.

[105] O. Plöger, *Theocracy and Eschatology* (trans. S. Rudman; Oxford: Blackwell, 1968),
pp. 37–43.

[106] Plöger, *Theocracy*, p. 40.

[107] Plöger's sociological distinction has been adopted (with some changes) by
P. Hanson, *The Dawn of Apocalyptic: The Historical and Sociological Roots of Jewish Apocalyptic Eschatology* (Philadelphia: Fortress, revised edn., 1979). He uses Mannheim's
definitions of ideology and utopia to distinguish between the theocratic and eschatological views, respectively [Hanson, *Dawn*, pp. 209–28).

[108] The term is Williamson's [see "Eschatology"].

the course of Israel's history. Therefore, it was important to work out just how this rule was established and by what means Israel's salvation was guaranteed. Von Rad argues that, for the Chronicler, David was *the* guarantor of God's salvation; a role Moses himself could not fulfil.[109] Von Rad goes on to suggest that such a view of David is evidence of the Chronicler's interest in the messianic debate within post-exilic Judaism.[110] He points to a number of changes made within the so-called dynastic oracle (1 Chron. 17 // 2 Sam. 7) which seem to support this view by extending the promise beyond Solomon to all of David's descendants.[111] The intentions embodied in these changes, so the argument seems to go, is to assert the applicability of the promise to David right down to the Chronicler's time. The motive behind this intention is, presumably, to foster messianic hope.

The determinative factor in this interpretation is, in the first instance, knowledge of the context; specifically the importance of the messianic theme in the post-exilic period. With that in mind von Rad then approaches the text with a view to discerning the Chronicler's intentions. This is a difficult task to be sure given the uncertainty of ascertaining the intention embodied in a complex work the size of Chronicles. Again, the way in which this problem is handled by interpreters is to pay ever closer attention to the details of the text (verbal meaning) and especially the synoptic details as a window onto the intention of the Chronicler. Criticisms of von Rad's proposal typically address either the details of the argument (verbal meaning and direct intentions) as read off of the parallel passages, or the plausibility of the indirect intentions at the macro-level.

Another "royalist" interpretation, championed in various forms by Freedman, Cross, and Newsome, links the centrality of David directly with the political situation at the time of Zerubbabel.[112] The pur-

---

[109] Von Rad, *Geschichtsbild*, p. 136.

[110] Von Rad, *Geschichtsbild*, p. 121.

[111] The three changes made by the Chronicler to the Nathan prophecy in 2 Sam. 7 are: (1) the omission of the passage which says that the descendents of David could fall into sin and would be punished (2 Sam. 7:14). In Chronicles we have an absolute abstract ideal statement that Yahweh will not withdraw his grace from the Davidides (1 Chron. 17:13). The throne is secured on Yahweh's grace alone and as such is eschatalogically oriented; (2) the tone of the Chronicler's "of your sons" (v. 11) looks beyond Solomon as the recipient of the promise, whereas the Samuel passage is the less futuristic "who will come forth from you" (v. 12); and (3) in Samuel, Solomon will rule over David's house and kingdom whereas in Chronicles it is Yahweh's kingdom [von Rad, *Geschichtsbild*, 124–6]. These conclusions are contested.

[112] D. N. Freedman, "The Chronicler's Purpose," *CBQ* 23 (1963), pp. 436–42;

pose of the Chronicler's work was to support the re-establishment of not only the Temple but also the Davidic dynasty. This theory has not been well received not least because of problems with its literary critical presuppositions and with the early dating of the hypothetical "first version" of Chronicles.[113]

Williamson presents a moderate eschatological interpretation of Chronicles.[114] Again, his emphasis lies in clarifying the communicative intention of the Chronicler.[115] He prefers to call the Chronicler's attitude towards the Davidic dynasty "royalist" with just a hint of realized eschatology; in other words, the Chronicler did not look exclusively to the future, nor see in the present the fulfilment of God's rule over Israel. It is somewhat ironic, however, that in attempting to put the theocratic interpretation of Chronicles to rest, Williamson succeeds in solving Rudolph's problem of relating the Davidic theme to the temple theme. Rudolph merely suggests that the Davidic promise was mentioned for the sake of historical completion and did not have independent historical significance. Williamson contends that it is much more important than that; that it is integral to the Chronicler's theology. But, in suggesting a way to reconcile these "royalist" ideas with the temple theme, he has in fact offered a much better argument for the theocratic interpretation than Rudolph's own arguments. What is *the* condition of the promise as found in 1 Chron. 17? The building of the Temple! How is this promise maintained or realized in the Chronicler's own time? By Israel's loyalty to the Temple! Does this add up to a refutation of Rudolph's basic premise? It doesn't. Again, it is a question of establishing intentionality by making a judgement as to the relative "weight" of these themes, the role they play in the "overall plan" of the narrative, and the contextual implications of this. There are, of course, eschatological overtones

---

F. M. Cross, "A Reconstruction of the Judean Restoration," *JBL* 94 (1975), pp. 4–18; and J. Newsome, "Towards a New Understanding of the Chronicler and His Purpose," *JBL* 95 (1975), pp. 201–17.

[113] For a lengthy critique of this position see Williamson, "Eschatology," pp. 120–30.

[114] Williamson, "Eschatology," pp. 115–54.

[115] D. Murray tries to do the same in a recent article on the subject and comes to a different conclusion. After examining four key texts (2 Chron. 7:12–22; 29:5–11; 30:6–12; and 36:11–21), he concludes that although the Chronicler is interested in the Davidic promise "a hope for the future restoration of the Davidic dynasty was not an important item of belief for our author, and clearly not one which he was seeking to commend to his readers" ["Dynasty, People, and the Future: The Message of Chronicles," *JSOT* 58 (1993), p. 90].

here and there in the text but one could reasonably argue that these are drowned out by a theocratic drum-beat from all sides.[116]

Leviticist?

The final proposal has to do with the prominent place of the Levites in the Chronicler's narrative. As noted by de Wette, the Chronicler's "Levitizismus" is evident in the amplification or embellishment of narratives to include details relating to the Levites. The Chronicler introduces Levitical singers, music, and praise to the temple dedication ceremonies (2 Chron. 5:11–14 and 7:5–10). During his reforms, Jehoida reinstates the Levitical priests (according to Mosaic and Davidic patterns) and the gatekeepers to keep out the unclean, all of this again accompanied by rejoicing and singing (2 Chron. 23:17–20). 2 Kings 11:18–19 describes the reform but says nothing about these measures. The Chronicler also expands the account of Josiah's Passover, in which the Levites feature prominently, from three verses (2 Kgs 23:21–3) to twenty verses (2 Chron. 35:1–19).[117]

Von Rad postulated a far-reaching historical connection between the Chronicler's Leviticism and his context; indeed, he went so far as to make the Levites the central concern of Chronicles.[118] In von Rad's treatment the Levitical *Tendenz* also takes on a different content than it had with de Wette.[119] For de Wette the Chronicler's Leviticism is "meaningful" with reference to a new priestly ideology (as in system of ideas)[120] whereas for von Rad it is "meaningful" with reference to the historical context. The Chronicler's Leviticism is related to the conflict between priests and Levites over responsibilities and prerogatives in the temple. He works from the basic historical premise that the centralization of worship in Jerusalem lead to a diminished role for the Levites, especially in the key area of sacrifice.[121] The struggle between priest and Levite continued in the

---

[116] Williamson's viewpoint is supported by B. Kelly, *Retribution and Eschatology in Chronicles* (JSOTS 211; Sheffield: Sheffield Academic Press, 1996) and will be discussed at greater length in chapter six.

[117] De Wette, *Introduction*, pp. 277–282.

[118] Von Rad, *Geschichtsbild*, p. 119.

[119] A major reason for this is a difference in method: de Wette concentrated on parallel sections while von Rad concentrated on the non-parallel sections.

[120] These changes were part of the Chronicler's attempt to correct Israel's historical traditions in light of a new understanding of religion (i.e. Pentateuchal religion).

[121] He sees a struggle between these two groups which is reflected in the differing conceptions of the place of the Levites citing Ezek. 44:10–14 versus Mal. 2:4.

early post-exilic period even though the Levites were clearly distinguished from the priests and, according to the sources, their numbers were low.[122] The Levites were not satisfied with the Aaronide domination of the cult and strove to participate in the main cultic activities just short of sacrificing on the altar.[123] If the Levites were to have an important role in the cult it would have to be connected with the offering. According to the Chronicler, the Levites accomplished this through the office of cult singer (a task they took on subsequent to the deposition of the ark in the Temple). The theme of the ark, so central to the historical presentation of the Chronicler, is thereby connected to the contemporary issue of the status and role of the Levites in the Second Temple.[124] Von Rad concludes, therefore, that. . . .

> In die Sprache der nachexilischen Levitenbewegung übersetzt heißt nun das Ganze: die Lade und die vor ihr postierten Leviten haben von Jahwe gleiche Bestätigung erhalten wie die legitime Stiftshütte, ja sie hatten in der heiligen Stadt göttlich sanktionierten Dienst, längst ehe die Aaroniden in den Tempel einzogen.[125]

In his approach to understanding the "purpose" of Chronicles, von Rad is combining a view to what the Chronicler said (the foregrounding of the Levites, etc.) with a sense of what the Chronicler meant by what he said (the place of the Levites is divinely sanctioned via David) and with a particular understanding of the historical context (the conflict between Levites and priests) in order to arrive at a hypothesis as to conscious motive (to champion Levitical rights).

As a counter-point to this proposal one might mention Noth's comments on von Rad's thesis. In addition to his literary-critical arguments (whereby much of the "Levitical" material such as 1 Chron. 23–27 is said to be secondary), Noth was unimpressed by von Rad's

---

[122] Ezra 2:40. Von Rad notes the absense of the singers in P and asks, ". . . antwortet P auf die Aspirationen dieser Gruppe mit einem stillschweigenden Boykott, so, wie der Levitenstolze Chronist seinerseits die Netinim totschweigt? Wahrscheinlich fand P infolge theologischer Gründe keine Stelle für den kultischen Gesang. Alle bei ihm vorgesehenen Kulthandlungen atmen einem überaus ernsten und düsteren Geist. Die kultische Freude, ein wichtiger Bestandteil der deuteronomischen Feste, hat in dem opferwesen des P, das so einseitig den Sühnegedanken betont, keinen platz" [von Rad, *Geschichtsbild*, p. 84].

[123] The Chronicler calls the Levites קדש in 2 Chron. 23:6 and 35:3.

[124] Von Rad, *Geschichtsbild*, pp. 99–100.

[125] Von Rad, *Geschichtsbild*, p. 101.

arguments for making the Levites the central concern of Chronicles.[126] If the "overall plan" of the work is decisive in determining the communicative intention of the work, the Levitical *Tendenz* is no real candidate. The Levites are, at best, the supporting cast in a play with David, Solomon and the Temple playing the leads. Nor is this Leviticism to be thought of as a conscious motive or (to use Noth's term) an intentional bias. The Chronicler is merely operating according to the social conventions of his day which included certain ideas about who should do what in the cult. It is "not a question of catching him pursuing some particular "bias" but simply of the readily intelligible influence of an author's own times on his historical presentation."[127] Noth's criticism of von Rad is a rare example of an interpreter of Chronicles differentiating between conscious motive and the "unconscious" influence of historical circumstances.

Conclusion

Noth's contribution to the discussion of the Chronicler's "purpose" is an appropriate point on which to conclude this chapter for he is one of the few to differentiate between different aspects of "purpose" in the interpretation of Chronicles. Once we separate off motives, intentions and contextual functions there seems to be a general consensus about what the book is saying in terms of verbal meaning. Most would agree that the communicative intentions of the Chronicler included an interest in the South and the North, an interest in David, and an interest in the Levites. All would agree that the Temple and its cultus is the most recurrent theme. The disagreements about the Chronicler's intentions and motives have rather to do with different assessments as to the relative weight of various themes. Beyond that, fundamental disagreements about "purpose" stem from fundamental differences in the way intentions and motives are related to context. It is in this area in particular that a proper theoretical treatment of ideology can make a contribution to the way we conceptualize and reconstruct this relationship. Only rarely do we see a sensitivity to the issues involved, and again, Noth is exemplary; but von Rad,

---

[126] It is not surprising to find Noth arguing this way because he was arguing for an anti-Samaritan polemic. Noth's criticisms are not, however, merely a case of special pleading on behalf of his anti-Samaritan polemic theory.

[127] Noth, *Chronicler*, p. 84.

Ewald and indeed de Wette were also aware of the contextual functions of the text which cannot, as it were, be filtered through the conscious motives of the author.

On the substantive side, this survey calls for a re-assessment of the Chronicler's purpose and in particular a re-assessment of the exclusivist and theocratic proposals. It is my view that they were much closer to the truth as regards the contextual function of Chronicles than the "inclusivist" and "royalist" proposals were. The latter interpretations are, in my view, important corrective manoeuvres especially in terms of a more adequate assessment of communicative intentions, but the questions still remain as to the function of Chronicles in its context. What is the ideology of the Chronicler? To what extent do his motives and intentions cohere with the contextual functions of this text?[128]

---

[128] Whether or not these questions can be answered satisfactorily given the limited amount of evidence for this period is another matter entirely. I will address this issue in the body of the text but even then some idea as to what the evidence might relate to is required.

CHAPTER TWO

IDEOLOGY AND INTERPRETATION

Introduction

In the last chapter I adopted Geuss's map of ideology as a way of differentiating between various definitions of ideology and in doing so touched on a number of important theoretical issues that are directly relevant to this study. I will now address some of these issues at greater length with a view to articulating as clearly as possible the social theoretical perspective and concept of ideology adopted in this study. The approach argued for is, broadly-speaking, hermeneutical in orientation drawing on the work of Ricoeur, Eagleton, Giddens and Habermas.

In his *Lectures on Ideology and Utopia*[1] Ricoeur presents an original (if not well known)[2] exposition and hermeneutical reconstruction of the concept of ideology. Rather than viewing ideological distortion as a separate issue, Ricoeur notes significant interconnections between the different functions of ideology relating to distortion, legitimation and integration. He uncovers these interconnections via a "regressive phenomenology" beginning with Marx's understanding of ideology as systematically-distorted consciousness and ending with a discussion of the integrative function of ideology which he believes is the fundamental function of ideology.

As is well known, Ricoeur's hermeneutical philosophy attempts to transcend the opposition between understanding and explanation, hermeneutics and science, especially as it relates to the so-called human sciences. The various modes of explanation, from the structuralist approaches to language and text to the explanatory moves of sociology and psychoanalysis, are retained as one axis within

---

[1] P. Ricoeur, *Lectures on Ideology and Utopia* (ed. G. H. Taylor; New York: Columbia, 1986).

[2] There is no reference to this book in T. Eagleton, *Ideology: An Introduction* (London: Verso, 1991), or M. Zizek (ed.), *Mapping Ideology* (London: Verso 1994), let alone a serious engagement with his work even though Ricoeur and Eagleton's theories of ideology have a lot in common.

Ricoeur's hermeneutical philosophy. The goal of hermeneutics—to reach an understanding of a person, text, or culture—may require what Ricoeur calls "explanatory detours" in order to overcome systemic distortion in communication, that is, a hermeneutic of suspicion as well as a hermeneutic of retrieval. Thus, ideological criticism, as one of a number of "explanatory detours", has a significant role to play in hermeneutics (biblical hermeneutics included). In terms of Geuss's map, Ricoeur would define social criticism, insofar as it is critical of ideology from the point of view of how society really works, as a mode of explanation and locate it within the broader hermeneutical agenda of anthropology.

From Marx to Ricoeur

Marx's contribution to the understanding of the concept of ideology remains foundational, as well as controversial. I begin, therefore, with an brief sketch of Marx's understanding of ideology (and one prominent derivation thereof) before moving on to consider Ricoeur's critical reconstruction of it.

Ideology as Socially-Determined Thought

"Life is not determined by consciousness, but consciousness by life."[3] This most famous of Marx's propositions is the mother of all theories of ideology. It is found in *The German Ideology*, the aim of which is to make the case for historical materialism in terms of a critique of German idealism. The basic premise of *The German Ideology* is that all thought, all consciousness, is socially-determined. Thus, "what men say, imagine, conceive," all the products of consciousness, are but the "ideological reflexes and echoes of this life process." The juxtapositioning of "consciousness" and "life" for the sake of his argument (and for rhetorical effect) has led to a rather mechanistic understanding of human existence as implied in the base-superstructure model of society where causal priority is assigned to the economic base over the ideological superstructure. But if we isolate this state-

---

[3] Commenting on the selected texts from *The German Ideology* in K. Marx and F. Engels, *Basic Writings on Politics and Philosophy* (ed. L. S. Feuer; New York; Anchor Books, 1959), pp. 246–60. All subsequent citations from this text are found on p. 247 of this work.

ment from its rhetorical context, these "ideological reflexes" can be defined as but "one part of the socio-cultural system" (to use Geuss's terms) though not the "basic" or "determinative" part. That is to say (and continuing in this vein) the definition of ideology we find here is to be located on the "anthropological" side of Geuss's map with "ideology" (as in our thoughts, beliefs, and ideas) on one side of the socio-cultural system and "what is really going on" on the other. In short what we have here is a *materialist* anthropology which need not involve a false consciousness.

But this definition of ideology as socially-determined thought does, of course, have a negative correlate. The specifically *German* ideology is the idealism of early nineteenth century German philosophy, particularly that of Hegel and Feuerbach. This idealism is, according to Marx, a form of consciousness which doesn't recognize its own historicity, that it is determined by the social context of early nineteenth century Germany and is powerless to change society and the course of history. "In politics the Germans have thought what other nations have done."[4] German idealism is also a false consciousness in that it inverts the base-superstructure model and denies social determinism.[5] It is considered false from the point of view of a particular theory of how society works. Its "falseness" is not simply a local epistemological error but an error at the level of fundamental premises. In its quest to understand and hence to change life

---

[4] K. Marx, "A Contribution to the Critique of Hegel's 'Philosophy of Right'," in, *Critique of Hegel's "Philosophy of Right"* (ed. J. O'Malley; trans. A. Jolin and J. O'Malley; Cambridge: Cambridge University Press, 1970), p. 137 [quoted in Ricoeur, *Lectures*, p. 26].

[5] Marx's concepts of *life* and *consciousness* parallel Hegel's objective and subjective mind. But it is here that Marx applies Feuerbach's reversal. For Marx, the state is not the objective embodiment of the absolute idea of freedom; the reality of the Prussian state at that time—the reality of censorship and torture—told him otherwise. The subject of reality is not Absolute Mind (as grasped by subjective mind) and the predicate is not civil society, family, circumstance (the objective moments of the idea). "Family and civil society are the presuppositions of the state; they are the really active things; but in speculative philosophy it is reversed" [Marx, "Contribution," p. 9]. Feuerbach and Marx both held to the idea that inversion results in human alienation . . . critique in emancipation, but Marx's concept of emancipation differs from Feuerbach's. For Feuerbach the goal of emancipation was still the full autonomy of consciousness [Ricoeur, *Lectures*, pp. 29–30]. For Marx, however, alienation arises primarily in the "real life" process of labour. To highlight this Marx opposed consciousness and real life, but it is important to remember that Marx did not take issue with the idea that humans are conscious beings whose thoughts and feelings are constitutive of what they do. He took issue, rather, with the idea of the *autonomy* of human consciousness.

for the better it presents "reality" upside-down by asserting the priority and autonomy of consciousness.

This analysis of the "German ideology" was in the first instance an historical analysis of a particular historical situation but, in the history of Marxism, this doctrine and the base-superstructure model have been understood universally as applying to all societies past and present. If, however, we leave the orthodox Marxist dogmas to one side we are left with what has become a central tenant of sociology—the social-determination of consciousness—and the central problem of social theory—the nature of social-determination. All theories of ideology are thus either neo-Marxist or post-Marxist.

Ideology as Systemically-Distorted Consciousness

Another rather more complex understanding of ideology is found in Marx's essay on "The Fetishism of Commodities and the Secret Thereof."[6] This essay is foundational for understanding the concepts of reification and alienation. In order to make sense of this concept of ideology, a small digression into the theory of the commodity form is required.

A commodity is defined in terms of its *use-value* and its *exchange-value*. *Use-value* is the qualitative aspect of a commodity. A thing is a useful thing only with regard to particular physical qualities and in the context of its being used in a particular way. *Exchange-value*, on the other hand, is a quantitative relation: "the proportion in which use-values in use of one sort are exchanged for those of another sort."[7] Commodities are *social* use-values, that is use-values for others that are transferred by means of exchange. In light of the fact that the use-values of different commodities are inherently unique, the exchange between two commodities is a seemingly arbitrary determination of equivalence: x amount of A = y amount of B. This equation tells us that in two different things (A and B) with two different use-values there exists equal quantities of something common to both (C): x of A = C and y of B = C. What is common to all commodities *as commodities* is simply labour in general, labour in the abstract. Labour has been expended on them and is therefore somehow embodied in them. The magnitude of the exchange

---

[6] K. Marx, *Capital;* vol. 1, *A Critical Analysis of Capitalist Production* (New York: International Publishers, 1967), pp. 76–87.

[7] Marx, *Capital*, p. 44.

value of a commodity as determined by the market is measured by the quantity of *abstract labour* embodied in it. Abstract labour is the total labour-power of a society as embodied in the sum total of commodities produced. Units of abstract labour are all the same and correspond to the socially-necessary or average amount of labour needed to produce a commodity. Thus, the commodities produced by an idle, unskilled worker are not less valuable than those of a hard-working and skilled labourer. It is the social average that counts.

Marx cites as an example the influence of the introduction of the power-loom on exchange values. With the introduction of the power-loom the amount of *labour in general* required to produce a quantity of linen was halved. Thus, one hour post-powerloom labour produced a certain exchange-value of linen (e.g. x of linen = y of coal). For those still using the hand-loom, however, one hour *real labour* was equivalent to only one half hour *labour in general* or *abstract labour* and thus produced only one half of x. The exchange-value of the product produced by *real labour* is thus reduced at a stroke without any change in the effort or skill of the worker or in the use-value of the linen.

In an exchange economy the two-fold nature of commodities thus finds its correlate in the two-fold character of labour. The exchange of one commodity for another is in reality a social interaction between labourers, but in a market economy this *social* relationship escapes human control. The exchange value of a thing is mistaken for the real or inherent value of a thing.[8] "A commodity is therefore a mysterious thing, simply because in it the social character of men's labour appears to them as an objective character stamped upon the product of that labour. . . ."[9] Marx calls this the fetishism of commodities. As the value of commodities fluctuates on the market so too does the value of labour even though the particular quality of productive labour may stay the same. Something inhuman, the market system, determines human life resulting in alienation whereby "human powers, products and processes escape the control of human subjects and come to assume an apparently autonomous existence."[10]

It is only within such a system that capital can have the appearance of productivity. To use the example cited, the capital that owns

---

[8] Geuss's definition II.a: "an epistemological mistake" but of systemic proportions.
[9] Marx, *Capital*, p. 77.
[10] Eagleton, *Ideology*, p. 70.

the powerloom benefits from the apparent productivity of the power-loom itself. In reality, of course, only the worker is productive but in the capitalist system the labourer has lost control over the means of production and hence over the value of his or her labour. The worker who does not have control over the means of production, who does not own capital, must sell his labour to capital in order to survive. He puts his life into the object which he makes, but having exchanged it for a wage, his life no longer belongs to him. It belongs instead to the object. Labour gives capital the power over that which actually generates it.[11] The fetishism of commodities is thus an ideology, a functionally false consciousness, which masks social contradictions of the capitalist mode of production. But it is at the same time a necessary part of this system in that the social illusions of capitalism are anchored in real contradictions and are somehow structurally-necessary to this specific social order. The falsehood is real.[12]

This understanding of ideology moves beyond the paradigm of ideology as conscious thought as found in *The German Ideology*. Here ideology is treated not so much in terms of what is thought or said (ideology in terms of its discursive aspect and manifest content) but in terms of what ideology does and the social structures in which it is embedded (ideology in terms of its functional properties). Tackling this "falseness" is not simply a matter of changing one's thinking from say an idealist position to a materialist one for the social consciousness of the capitalist mode of production as a whole is distorted.

Althusser

Marx's understanding of ideology as systemically-distorted consciousness is taken up and elaborated by Althusser in terms of an affective (versus cognitive) and structuralist theory of ideology which sharpens the deterministic thrust of this definition of ideology. Two of Althusser's propositions interest me in particular.

The first proposition is that *ideology has a material existence*. By "materiality" Althusser means that "the 'ideas' of a human subject exist in his actions"[13] which are inserted into practices and these practices

---

[11] Ricoeur, *Lectures*, pp. 35–48.
[12] Eagleton, *Ideology*, p. 84.
[13] Althusser, "Selected Texts," in T. Eagleton (ed.), *Ideology* (London: Verso),

are inscribed within the material existence of the institutional apparatuses of the state. "This existence is material."[14] Although the modality of this material existence is not the same as that of a stone, it can nonetheless be described as "material" at the level of social structures as a whole.

This understanding of ideology applies specifically to the capitalist mode of production. Following Marxist-Leninist theory, Althusser sees the modern state as an instrument of repression which contains two bodies: the *Repressive State Apparatus* or RSA's (government, army, police, and courts) which ultimately function by violence and the *Ideological State Apparatuses* or ISA's (religious, educational, family, legal, political, trade-union, communications, cultural institutions) which function by ideology. That which unites these ISA's is that beneath them all is the ruling ideology of the ruling class. Since ideologies in particular always express class position, "a theory of ideologies depends . . . on the history of social formations, and thus of the modes of production combined in social formations, and of the class struggles which develop in them."[15] Thus, the materiality of ideology in Althusser is cast in terms of an Marxist economic determinism referring "in the last instance to the relations of production."[16]

The second proposition, that *ideology interpellates or summons individuals as subjects* specifies the main task of ideology at this higher level. By this Althusser means that ideology is a particular organization of signifying practices which constitutes us as social subjects. Just as we are named by our parents and called by name a thousand times over so too are we "named" by society and made subjects of the state. Like our own name, we take our status as subjects as obvious; to be a subject is to immediately recognize oneself and be recognized without considering how recognition is possible. According to Althusser, the "taken-for-grantedness" of our subjectivity is but an effect of an ideological process. Ideology is a reality insofar as it is embodied in social practices but it is nevertheless the reality of something which is illusory: "What is represented in ideology is . . . not the system of real relations which govern the existence of individuals,

---

p. 105. The selected texts are from L. Althusser, *For Marx* (London: New Left Books, 1965), pp. 232–4, and *Lenin and Philosophy* (London: New Left Books, 1971), pp. 136–65.

[14] Althusser, "Selected Texts," p. 104.
[15] Althusser, "Selected Texts," p. 99.
[16] Althusser, "Selected Texts," p. 104.

but the imaginary relations of those individuals to the real relations in which they live,"[17] thus, the fundamental illusion of ideology is the illusion of subjectivity. For Althusser, to recognize oneself as subject is to be recognized by the State as subject to and as object of the State: *all recognition is miscognition.*

These two propositions signal a radical break with the philosophy of consciousness; something which Marx himself was unable to do. In Althusser, the notion of consciousness is replaced by the notions of discourse and practice. Discourse has a distinct advantage over consciousness in that it implies both a meaning and a materiality, resolving in the process the ambivalence of the Marx's life-consciousness dichotomy. Althusser's variation on Marx's understanding of ideology as socially-determined thought has influenced literary critics such as Jameson and Eagleton as well as discourse theory where the emphasis is on the social determination of language rather than on the language usage of individuals as in speech-act theory.

Ricoeur on Marx and Althusser

Unlike Althusser, Ricoeur pursues a humanistic interpretation of Marx retaining the dialectical tension between individual and society, consciousness and discourse, autonomy and determinism. What he recovers from Marx is a sense of "individuals living in definite conditions" as opposed to the notion of "the individual as simply contingent with regard to its conditions."[18]

Ricoeur's theory of ideology builds on a third definition of ideology found in *The German Ideology* which stands in tension with the two definitions discussed above. Marx seems to allow for a "basic" pre-distorted level of consciousness and communication when he states that "[t]he production of ideas, of conceptions, of consciousness is at first directly interwoven with the material activity and the material intercourse of men, the language of real life."[19] Thus, "[c]onsciousness can never be anything else than *conscious existence*, and the existence of men is their actual life process."[20] This consciousness, and indeed one could say this level of ideology, is an intrinsic aspect of the socio-cultural system as distinct from but also intertwined

---

[17] Althusser, "Selected Texts," p. 103.
[18] Ricoeur, *Lectures*, p. 100.
[19] Marx, *German Ideology*, p. 247.
[20] Marx, *German Ideology*, p. 247.

with productive activity and not simply a "reflex" or "echo" of this activity.

Ricoeur links this understanding of consciousness with an earlier statement of Marx about language. In the *Manuscripts* Marx states that "[l]anguage is as old as consciousness, language *is* practical consciousness that exists also for other men, and for that reason alone it really exists for me personally as well; language, like consciousness arises from need, the necessity, of intercourse with other men."[21] According to Ricoeur, "Marx's whole description of language here does not belong to a theory of class but to a fundamental anthropology, because all human beings speak, and they all have a language."[22] From this Ricoeur seeks to recover a non-idealistic anthropology from Marx while at the same time preserving his insight into "human existence under certain conditions." To use the base-superstructure model against itself, if human existence is irreducibly linguistic, even as it relates directly to material activity, then language and indeed ideology belong to the base.

This interpretation of Marx is, of course, difficult to achieve in that Marx argued so vigorously against idealist philosophy which stressed the autonomy of consciousness. We have in Marx the first materialist answer to the philosophy of consciousness and in trying to grasp his critique we fail to see his positive definition of consciousness. "The ideology criticized [in The German Ideology] claims that in order to change people's lives, it is enough to change their thoughts."[23] The German philosophers come in for criticism because they didn't inquire into the connection between their own philosophy and German

---

[21] K. Marx, *The Economic and Philosophic Manuscripts of 1844* (ed. D. J. Struik; New York: International Publishers, 1964), pp. 50–51. Marx's positive concept of consciousness is actually quite Kantian. Consciousness is the capacity for projecting objects, for organizing an objective world in representation, and for reality-testing. Reality-testing is not an autonomous capacity but rather a part of the whole process of the living individual [Ricoeur, *Lectures*, p. 80]. This, as Ricoeur indicates, has important implications for social theory. Premises are inevitable for the social scientist since he/she cannot start by merely looking at the things-in-themselves. "In sociology, we cannot proceed by means of the naked eye alone. Instead, we must have such notions as forces and norms, and these are not given in reality but are constructs" [Ricoeur, *Lectures*, p. 82]. The question then for Marxist sociology has been this: to what real basis is the ideological process reduced? Is class structure a construct or a "basic" reality? Ricoeur identifies two traditions in Marxist sociology: the objectivist/structuralist interpretation of Marx (the ideology versus science approach described above) and the individual "real life" interpretation.

[22] Ricoeur, *Lectures*, p. 83.

[23] Ricoeur, *Lectures*, p. 71.

reality, the material conditions of their life. But for Marx, material conditions are always defined within a sphere of human activity; there is a reciprocity between humanity and material context. Even if one goes along with the idea that history is a development of productive forces, these productive forces do not have an autonomous existence outside relations of production as embodied in social and judicial institutions, forms of property and so on.[24] According to Ricoeur,

> ... the great discovery of Marx is the complex notion of the individual under certain conditions.... We may bracket out the individual and start from the conditions and contend that the conditions are the causes. In doing so, however, we do not destroy the dialectic between individual and condition, because the individual always exists in a certain condition or under a certain condition.[25]

It is here that Althusser and Ricoeur part company. Althusser turns away from anthropological concepts such as consciousness and representation and turns instead to the "science" of the forces of production—reality in terms of autonomous forces. In the objectivist/structuralist tradition, the individual disappears. Ricoeur, however, is critical of this move. To say, for example, that ideology represents the "imaginary relations" of individuals as opposed to the "system of real relations which govern the existence of individuals"[26] still implies a pre-distorted constative function of the imagination and consciousness. If everything is distorted and if all recognition is miscognition, then nothing is distorted. If there is no symbolic structure *from the start* then there is nothing to distort. Althusser, however, ignores this primary anthropological level of imagination and representation and thus shifts from the language of representation to that of apparatus; the imaginary, not in terms of its anthropological aspect and symbolic structure, but in terms of its incorporation into the State Apparatus. Ricoeur on the other hand distinguishes between recognition and miscognition for it is not a question of either/or but rather a question how to disentangle the two.

I will discuss the implications of Ricoeur's critique of Althusser as it applies to legitimation and integration but before doing so will seek to broaden the social theoretical foundations of this approach

---

²⁴ Ricoeur, *Lectures*, pp. 73–4.
²⁵ Ricoeur, *Lectures*, p. 101.
²⁶ Marx, *German Ideology*, p. 247.

via Giddens and Habermas. The point of this exercise is to outline
a social theory which complements Ricoeur's approach to ideology.

Between Action and Structure

Giddens, like Ricoeur, has proposed a way of transcending the dichotomy between the autonomous individual and the determined
individual and thereby reconciling the action-oriented and structure-
oriented approaches in sociology. He begins by considering the common sense perception of human agency. A distinctive trait of human
experience is that we normally know what we are doing and why
we are doing it. This "knowing" involves, necessarily, knowledge of
the institutional context in which our actions take place, and of
the social conventions which serve as patterns for our actions. As
agents we feel free to decide what course of action to take in light
of our knowledge of ourselves, our context and the possible outcomes.[27]
This sense of autonomy is the strength of the idealist case, but is
this sense of autonomy an irreducible notion?

Giddens offers a few observations from the perspective of sociology which relativize this sense of autonomy. The first concerns the
nature of the participant's knowledge of the social conventions which
guide our actions. Not only does knowledge of social conventions
vary within a particular group, but it is often only practical and ad
hoc knowledge. Even though we know what we are doing, we can't
necessarily put it into words or say exactly what it means. We know
the conventions but we are not entirely aware of them. We know
the language, but we cannot describe the grammatical rules. This
creates a grey area between emics and etics in that the sociologist
in his or her attempt to understand a socio-cultural system is likely
to have to resort to social scientific metalanguage in order to get at
this non-discursive dimension of human activity.[28]

His most important observation, however, relates to the consequences of our actions. Our actions have consequences we do not intend and these unintended consequences do not just affect the limited
world of the individual, they affect the structure and reproduction of

---

[27] A. Giddens, *Social Theory and Modern Sociology* (Stanford: Stanford University
Press, 1987), pp. 2–3.

[28] Giddens, *Social Theory*, pp. 5–7.

society itself.[29] Unintended consequences may be perverse. We may decide, for example, to withdraw our money from the bank, but if everyone decided to do the same thing at the same time the bank would collapse. None of those debiting their account need have intended to break the bank but the consequences are nonetheless real and socially significant. Unintended consequences may also be positive. The fact that we lodge our money in banks at all and trust them to take care of it has the unintended consequence of allowing banks to exist in the first place. Most of us, however, do not feel that we have "created" banks or that we sustain their existence (unless, of course, we are paying exorbitantly high mortgage rates). The claims to trustworthiness made by banks (and the word "trust" is often right in the name of a financial institution) is like a self-fulfilling prophecy. It is trustworthy because it secures the trust of every individual depositor, not because it has a high security safe. All of us are involved in social orders we as individual human agents did not intentionally establish, and in following established conventions we reproduce these institutions. Our actions constitute and reconstitute the institutions which in turn are the institutional orders for others. Giddens calls this the "recursive nature of social life."[30]

Durkheim makes a similar observation about social conventions but is led thereby to deny the very sense of social agency that all of us properly have. In the opening paragraphs of *The Rules of Sociological Method*, Durkheim writes,

> The system of signs that I use to express my thought, the system of currency I employ to pay my debts, the instruments of credit I utilize in my commercial relations, the practices followed in my profession, etc., function independently of the use I make of them. Thus there are ways of acting, thinking, and feeling which possess the remarkable property of existing outside the consciousness of the individual.[31]

Giddens argues that society does not exist outside individual consciousness and that there is an important relationship between small-scale punctiliar action of individuals and large-scale social structures. "The complex conventions we observe in day-to-day life are not just a superficial gloss upon large-scale institutions, they are the very stuff of their continuity and fixity."[32] The implication of this view of human

---

[29] Giddens, *Social Theory*, p. 10.
[30] Giddens, *Social Theory*, pp. 8–11.
[31] E. Durkheim, *The Rules of Sociological Method* (New York: Free Press, 1964), p. 2.
[32] Giddens, *Social Theory*, p. 14.

agency for sociological method is that we cannot make a hard and fast distinction between meaningful action and functional behaviour. All human "behaviour" is charged with meaning; that is to say, all human behaviour is action.

> The subjects of study in the social sciences and the humanities are concept-using beings, whose concepts of their actions enter in a constitutive manner into what those actions are. Social life cannot be accurately described by a sociological observer, let alone casually elucidated if the observer does not master the array of concepts employed (discursively and non-discursively) by those involved.[33]

Habermas is also interested in incorporating "meaning" into sociological analysis and thus in reconciling the "hermeneutical" and "scientific" schools of sociology. He constructs a theory of meaningful action in terms of a theory of communicative action. In Habermas's model of communicative action, the participant is outfitted with the same interpretative capacities as the observer. The interpretative activity of participants concerns itself in the first instance with situation definitions.

> A definition of a situation establishes an order. . . . A situation definition by another party that prima facie diverges from one's own presents a problem of a particular sort; for in the cooperative processes of interpretation no participant has a monopoly on correct interpretation. For both parties the interpretative task consists in incorporating the other's interpretation of the situation into one's own in such a way that . . . the divergent situations can be brought to coincide sufficiently.[34]

The sociologist cannot therefore claim the neutral status as observer, for he/she has to deal with these very situation definitions and, indeed, must enter into the situation as a virtual participant, understanding the validity claims of the actual participants on the basis of familiarity with the situation itself or from comparative contexts. The reasons participants give for their actions can only be understood as reasonable if they are in fact reasonable to the observer. Thus, the object domain of social inquiry is always already constituted by the interpretative activity of its members.[35]

---

[33] Giddens, *Social Theory*, p. 18.

[34] J. Habermas, *The Theory of Communicative Action*; vol. 1, *Reason and the Rationalization of Society* (trans. T. McCarthy; Cambridge: Polity, 1984), p. 100.

[35] Habermas, *Communicative Action*, vol. 1, p. 107. See A. Giddens, *New Rules of Sociological Method* (London: Hutchinson, 1976), p. 158.

This does not mean, however, that the sociologist as virtual participant gives up the capacity for critique for "[i]t is [the] potential for critique built into communicative action itself that the social scientist, by entering into the contexts of everyday action as a virtual participant, can systematically exploit and bring into play outside these contexts and against their particularity."[36] Habermas's hermeneutics, like Ricoeur's, is a *critical hermeneutic* as distinct from Gadamer's hermeneutics of understanding.

> If in the performative attitude of virtual participants in conversation we start with the idea that an author's utterance has the presumption of rationality, we not only admit the possibility that the interpretandum may be exemplary *for us*, that we may learn something from it; we *also* take into account the possibility that the author could learn *from us*. Gadamer remains bound to the experience of the philologist who deals with classical texts: "The classic is that which stands up in the face of historical criticism." [*Truth and Method*, p. 255] The knowledge embodied in the text is, Gadamer believes, fundamentally superior to the interpreter's.[37]

Habermas also recognizes, of course, that social reality is not exhausted by the ideas consciously held by individual participants. Ideas, beliefs and attitudes change in response to forces and factors that cannot be explained solely in terms of the inner logic of communication. Giddens approaches this side of social existence when he speaks of unintended consequences whereas Habermas uses the concepts of lifeworld and system.

The concepts of lifeworld and system correspond to the two sides of action, the intended meanings and the unintended consequences at the level of society as a whole. One could say that the sum total of meaningful action, including social conventions, is the lifeworld and the sum total of action consequences is the system. At the heart of this proposal is the distinction between social integration and system integration: "mechanisms of coordinating action that harmonize the *action orientations* of participants from the mechanisms that stabilize nonintended interconnections of actions by way of functionally intermeshing *action consequences*."[38]

---

[36] Habermas, *Communicative Action*, vol. 1, p. 121.

[37] Habermas, *Communicative Action*, vol. 1, p. 134.

[38] J. Habermas, *The Theory of Communicative Action*, vol. 2, *Lifeworld and System* (trans. T. McCarthy; Cambridge: Polity, 1987), p. 117.

LIFEWORLD	SYSTEM
social integration	system integration
action orientations	action consequences
intention/goals/motives	unintended consequences
communicative action	functional maintenance of the system
culture and language	material environment

Interpretative sociology or anthropology limits itself to the perspective of the self-interpretation of the culture under investigation. This screens out anything that inconspicuously affects the lifeworld from the outside and therefore is blind to causes and consequences of actions that lie beyond the horizon of the lifeworld.

> In fact, however, goal-directed actions are coordinated not only through processes of reaching understanding, but also through functional interconnections that are not intended by them and are usually not perceived within the horizon of everyday practice.[39]

On the other hand, a purely system theoretical approach to society is also inadequate because

> ... the structural patterns of action systems are not accessible to [purely external] observation; they have to be gotten at hermeneutically, that is, from the internal perspective of participants. The entities that are to be subsumed under systems-theoretical concepts from the external perspective of an observer must be identified beforehand as the lifeworlds of social groups and understood in their symbolic structures.[40]

The significance of Habermas's theory of communicative action and Giddens's structuration theory for this study is that they offer a way of conceptualising the socio-cultural system which recognizes the dialectical tension between conscious motives and meaningful action on one side and functional interconnections and systematic distortion on the other.

Ideology and Legitimation

As discussed above, Althusser defines ideology as an illusion at the heart of the State which permeates society at the level of subjectivity itself: "all recognition is miscognition." Althusser therefore speaks

---

[39] Habermas, *Communicative Action*, vol. 2, p. 150.
[40] Habermas, *Communicative Action*, vol. 2, p. 150.

of Ideological State Apparatuses and forces of production from a "scientific" point of view as opposed to asking how ideology as an symbolic system "works" on the inside. Ricoeur is critical of this position not least because it fails to explain how one can describe an ideological discourse as illusory without also implying that there is a non-illusory discourse within which the distortion arose. If all recognition is miscognition then there is no such thing as miscognition. According to Ricoeur a systemically-distorted discourse is still a symbolic system of linguistic signs and meaningful practices that requires interpretation: "[w]e must make sense of their meaning before considering their use."[41] The objective of ideological criticism is to disentangle recognition from miscognition or, as Taylor puts it, "to distinguish between objectification—the positive transformation of values into discourses, practices and institutions—and alienation— the distortion of these values, the reification of discourses, practices and institutions."[42]

The practical implication of this insight as it relates to the relationship between ideology and power is that one cannot simply correlate ruling ideology and ruling class with an economic interest providing the causal link. If one wants to understand systems of domination and the role of ideology within them one has to look at the way ideologies of legitimation work on the inside seeking to determine where distortion is "anchored" in the lifeworld. The link between ruling ideology and ruling class, between power structures and economic interests, is in the first instance the individual self-conscious ruler and the self-conscious work of legitimation that the ruler performs.[43] Ricoeur therefore turns to Weber's motivational model as an alternative way of modelling systems of domination or authority and attendant modes of legitimation.[44]

Weber identifies three different systems of authority classified on the basis of type of motivation embodied in each:

- bureaucratic, legal authority   instrumental motivation
- charismatic authority   value-rational motivation
- traditional authority   traditional motivation[45]

---

[41] Ricoeur, *Lectures*, p. 154.

[42] G. H. Taylor, "Editor's Introduction," in Ricoeur, *Lectures*, p. xxvii.

[43] M. Weber, *Economy and Society: An Outline of Interpretive Sociology* (eds. G. Roth and C. Wittich; Berkeley: University of California Press, 1978).

[44] Ricoeur, *Lectures*, p. 184.

[45] Weber, *Economy*, pp. 941ff. See Ricoeur, *Lectures*, p. 186.

Authority or domination has to do with the probability that a command with a specific content will be obeyed by a given group. Other than using or threatening to use force, those in authority can claim legitimacy in various ways with the hope of motivating individuals to act in a certain way. Because all claims to *legitimate* authority presuppose a legitimate order, an ideology that legitimates must not only speak to the issue of who rules but also to the issue of who we are (as in the unity which embraces both ruler and ruled). In other words, ideologies of legitimacy must not only address the question of the ruler's identity as established on the basis of certain legitimate *claims* but must also address the *beliefs* people already have about who they are. An ideology of legitimation must incorporate an ideology of identity which integrates the group and provides for the mutual orientation of action for the members of the group.

One can see this most clearly perhaps in traditional forms of authority where the most important issue is the continuity of the social order through time. Social relationships are ordered according to the idea that what comes from the past has more legitimacy than that which has come about in the present. But the same thing can be said of any kind of authority; a political body like the modern democratic state is governed not only via the instrumental criteria of bureaucratic efficiency but also by the way in which it identifies itself among other groups. The first function of ideology is to preserve the groups identity through time . . . to connect past, present and future.[46] In traditional authority the gap between claim and belief is small. Recognition of who rules is tightly bound up with recognition of who we are and is all but taken for granted. But in other forms of domination where legitimation requires a more conscious effort on the part of the ruling class, the gap between claim and belief is more significant.

Ricoeur's main thesis with regard to the ideology of legitimation is that ideology fills this gap between claim and belief. His thesis rests on a concept of surplus value now linked to power, not work. According to Marx's analysis of capitalism, the capitalist employer steals the surplus-value produced by the worker by exploiting the two-fold character of labour as it exists within a market economy. The capitalist makes an investment at the level of abstract labour (as in the powerloom example cited above) and can on this basis

---

[46] Ricoeur, *Lectures*, p. 210.

claim the surplus "produced by" his investment. In the capitalist system the real source of productivity, the labourer, is not recognized. Applying this concept of alienation to power, one could say the ruler makes an ideological investment which disguises the real source of power. There is always more in the claim to legitimacy of a given system of authority than the normal course of legitimation can satisfy, that is to say, there is a supplement of belief provided by an ideological system.[47]

Charismatic authority is a good example of this.[48] Recognition of who rules is decisive in this system of authority for if people don't believe in the claims of the charismatic leader, his or her leadership would end. In this form of authority the leader is completely dependent on the belief of the people, yet the leader cannot make his claim to authority in these terms (i.e. that he/she needs belief) but rather has to state them in ideological terms, that is, in terms of his or her exceptional qualities. These sort of claims are the ideological investment made by the charismatic leader and when successful pay a dividend in terms of what Ricoeur calls a surplus of belief. Charismatic leaders seek out, via ideology, this surplus of belief but they can never admit that they rely on this belief. This is the point at which recognition (beliefs concerning who we are and who should rule) becomes miscognition. One is encouraged to believe but can one disbelieve? The danger with the ideology of legitimation is that recognition becomes a duty. In this way the true origin of power is stolen, for once belief is given one cannot get it back. Ricoeur argues that this lack of reciprocity between claim and belief is a potential source of distortion within all ideologies of legitimation.[49]

This analysis of the potential for distortion within ideologies of legitimation is still a matter of a functionally-false consciousness operating at the level of political discourse. The ideas and beliefs that the participants hold about who they are and who should rule are part of everyday discourse within the horizon of the lifeworld but when the actions of individuals are taken on aggregate they have systemic consequences that extend beyond this horizon. These unintentional

---

[47] Ricoeur, *Lectures*, pp. 201–2.

[48] Indeed, Ricoeur asks if charismatic authority the kernel of all power. All political power demands a decision-maker, someone "qualified to lead" hence all political power preserves the charismatic element.

[49] Ricoeur, *Lectures*, pp. 211–12.

consequences also have a "pre-history" in the social conventions and institutions of the lifeworld within which these actions takes place. These social conventions are, as it were, at the back of participants who may not understand the conventions by means of which they orient their action and lives. That is to say, to understand the conventions of power and authority and the role of ideology within them requires explanatory moves which address the distortion at the systemic level beyond the lifeworld perspective of participants.

Ideology and Integration

We have not yet addressed the question of how ideology works to integrate social groups. In answering this question, Ricoeur builds on Geertz's treatment of ideology within the framework of semiotics. This is the final stage in Ricoeur's three-stage "regressive phenomenology" of ideology.

The first stage was ideology as distortion as defined by Marx; the fundamental concept was "ruling class expressed by ruling ideas". One approached this concept via the concept of interest, applied an attitude of suspicion and proceeded to dismember this distortion using the base-superstructure model. In the second stage, Ricoeur asked how one might make sense of the idea that a distorting thought is "caused" by class structure. One way of making sense of it is to recognize that implied in the concept of ruling class is the concept of authority. Ideology is thus not merely related to class interest, but to all forms of authority. Ricoeur locates ideology in the gap which separates the leader's claims to legitimacy and the follower's belief in that legitimacy. The attitude here is that of a value-free observer who classifies different forms of social organization according to their motivational framework and in terms of ideal types.

The third stage of Ricoeur's regressive analysis is ideology as integration. Here the attitude is that of the anthropologist in conversation with the subject and the model of study is semiotics. It is at this point that Ricoeur picks up the point he made contra Althusser that it takes a system of symbols to have a system of distorted symbols.

These three stages can be summarized as follows:
1. Distortion

   Key concepts:
   * interests of the ruling *class* expressed by ruling ideas
   * systematic distortion

Approach:
  - that of the critic
  - applying an attitude of suspicion
  - causal dismantlement of distortion

Model:
  - base-superstructure

2. Legitimation

Key concepts:
  - authority, as implied in *ruling* class and *ruling* ideas
  - forms of legitimate authority
  - the gap between claims and beliefs

Approach:
  - that of the value-free sociologist
  - motivational framework

Model:
  - ideal types

3. Integration/Identity

Key concept:
  - symbolization

Approach:
  - that of the anthropologist
  - an interpretative attitude
  - conversation

Model:
  - semiotics

Geertz is critical of theories of ideology which merely state that ideologies are the representation of certain interests. There is an assumption here which isn't understood by those making it, namely, how a material interest is expressed as an idea. We first have to know how symbols symbolize something else . . . how they mediate meaning. "With no notion of how metaphor, analogy, irony, ambiguity, pun, paradox, hyperbole, rhythm, and all the other elements of what we lamely call 'style' operate . . . [we cannot construe] the import of ideological assertions."[50] Geertz's semiotic approach allows one to compare ideology to the rhetorical devices of discourse. What is needed is a semiotic approach which treats ideology in terms of its rhetorical capacities.

---

[50] Geertz, *Interpretation*, p. 209. Ricoeur, *Lectures*, p. 257.

Geertz cites the example of an American labour law which trade unionists called the "slave labor law." The rhetorical meaning of this phrase, in the context of the Cold War, called to mind the slave labour camps of Siberia. This sort of rhetoric was designed to counter, at a politically-effective level, a law which was aimed at abolishing of the "closed shop". The terms in which the law was framed did not address the potential consequences it would have on the working class and so, in order to address these more fundamental issues, the language used by the trade unionists transcended the legislative language. The rhetoric of "slave labor" though literally incorrect was nonetheless commensurate with the ideological struggle between government, industrialists and trade unionists. This is an example of the integrative function of rhetoric which served at that time to integrate political opposition to a potentially oppressive law. He goes on to argue that this small example is a model of the integrative function of ideology as a whole. According to Geertz, ideology gives participants a coherent, if systematically over-simplified, orientation for action.[51] "Whatever else ideologies may be ... they are, most distinctly, maps of problematic social reality and matrices for the creation of collective conscience."[52]

Geertz recognizes, however, that ideology is also about power and is for reason susceptible to distortion: "The function of ideology is to make a politics possible by providing the authoritative concepts that render it meaningful, the suasive images by means of which it can be sensibly grasped."[53] Ricoeur adds,

> The notion of the authoritative is a kernel concept, because when the problem of integration leads to the problem of a system of authority, the third concept of ideology sends us back to the second. It is not by chance that a specific place for ideology exists in politics, because politics is the location where the basic images of a group finally provide rules for using power. Questions of integration lead to questions of legitimation, and these in turn lead to questions of distortion. We are therefore forced to proceed backwards and upwards in this hierarchy of concepts.

---

[51] Ricoeur, *Lectures*, pp. 257–8.
[52] Geertz, *Interpretation*, p. 220.
[53] Geertz, *Interpretation*, p. 218. Ricoeur, *Lectures*, p. 259.

The Goal of Critique

I conclude this discussion of Ricoeur by briefly considering the orientation and goal of critique. Ricoeur argues that the realization of the integrative character of ideology helps us to preserve the appropriate level of critique, the goal of which is not to destroy the adversary but to reach an understanding of the other.[54] But how is this done? From what point of view can this be done? What sort of criteria can one use to judge an ideology which stands in the way of understanding? Is it some transcendental viewpoint? Is it a matter of contrasting ideology with "reality" or with a "scientific" knowledge of humanity? Ricoeur argues that

> we must assume that the judgment on ideology is always the judgment from a utopia. This is my conviction: the only way to get out of the circularity in which ideologies engulf us is to assume a utopia, declare it, and judge an ideology on this basis. Because the absolute onlooker is impossible, then it is someone within the process itself who takes the responsibility for judgment. . . . It is to the extent finally that the correlation ideology-utopia replaces the impossible correlation ideology-science that a certain solution to the problem of judgment may be found. . . .[55]

At the level of integration, ideology functions to preserve the order whereas utopia puts into question what presently exists and represents an awareness of the contingency of social order. At the level of legitimation, ideology serves to maintain systems of domination whereas utopia challenges authority, providing an imaginative variation on the nature of power and represents an awareness of the credibility gap that exists in all systems of legitimation. And at the level of distortion, ideology reifies and alienates whereas utopia is mere escapist fancy with no link between the future and the present.[56] Thus, one

---

[54] Ricoeur, *Lectures*, p. 263.

[55] Ricoeur, *Lectures*, pp. 172–3. Mannheim introduced the useful comparison between ideology and utopia which he describes as two forms of noncongruence. But his comparison of ideology and utopia is limited: "Mannheim [unlike Geertz or Ricoeur] has no notion of a symbolically constituted order; hence an ideology is necessarily the noncongruent, something transcendent in the sense of the discordant or that which is not implied in humanity's genetic code" [Ricoeur, *Lectures*, p. 174].

[56] F. Jameson also proposes a dual hermeneutic of ideology and utopia. Dialectical criticism, as he calls it, includes "utopian thinking, which compares the existing reality with possible alternatives and finds utopian hope in literature, philosophy an other cultural texts" [quote from R. Fowler, *Literature as Social Discourse: The Practice of Linguistic Criticism* (London: Batsford, 1981), p. 425].

"breaks" with ideology by exploiting the critical self-reflective and distantiating potential of social imagination. The task of critique is to disentangle recognition from miscognition from the vantage point of a utopia of total recognition and from a "deep-rooted interest in the plenitude of individual existence."[57]

Conclusion

I began this chapter by looking at Marx's definition of ideology as socially-determined thought and as systematically-distorted consciousness. The key issue has to do with the relationship between the individual, consciousness and action on one side and social structures and forces on the other. I outlined two basic directions one can take Marx as represented by Althusser and Ricoeur. Althusser was seen to be representative of the structuralist tradition which views ideological distortion in terms of the autonomous forces which give rise to it. In the objectivist/structuralist tradition, the individual disappears. Ricoeur represents the humanistic tradition in which ideological distortion is treated as distortion within a system of symbols which implies that there is a pre-distorted level of communication and consciousness. Ricoeur's "regressive phenomenology" is an attempt to uncover the pre-distorted levels of ideological activity as they relate to legitimation and integration. In the humanistic tradition the individual does not disappear though the reality of systemic distortion is still recognized.

I supported Ricoeur's approach from the social theoretical side with reference to Giddens's structuration theory and Habermas's lifeworld and system distinction. Both social theories attempt to model (at two different levels) the dialectical relationship between individual action as it takes place in the context of the lifeworld and the functional interconnection of action at the level of social structure and system.

In the following chapters, I will use Ricoeur's three-stage analysis of ideology as a pattern for studying the Chronicler's ideology, though moving in the opposite direction. I begin with an examination of the Chronicler's ideology of *identity*—the understanding of Israel which the book projects (chapter three). I then explore the

---

[57] Ricoeur, *Lectures*, p. 153.

social implications of this ideology of identity as it relates to the organization of power both in terms of *legitimation* (chapter five) and *distortion* (chapters five and six). These three readings of Chronicles constitute an "explanatory detour" on the road to a better understanding of Chronicles. The perspective adopted is informed by the conviction that ideology is always. . . .

> on the brink of becoming pathological because it has a conservative function in both the good and the bad senses of that word. Ideology preserves identity, but it also wants to conserve what exists and is therefore already a resistance. Something becomes ideological—in the more negative meaning of the term—when the integrative function becomes frozen, when it becomes rhetorical in the bad sense, when schematization and rationalization prevail. Ideology operates at the turning point between the integrative function and resistance.[58]

---

[58] Ricoeur, *Lectures*, pp. 265–6.

CHAPTER THREE

EXILE AND IDENTITY

Introduction

In this chapter I compare and contrast the ideologies of identity of
Chronicles and Ezra-Nehemiah as they relate to the "memory" of
exile. In both Chronicles and Ezra-Nehemiah the exile plays a significant role in their respective understandings of what Israel is and
ought to be. For both writers the exile was an event of the distant
past which means that the way in which the exile is remembered
and the purpose for which it is remembered will be of some interest.

For the sake of the argument I will treat the two writers as contemporaries living under similar circumstances in Judah in the fourth
century. In order to establish the social dynamics of their ideologies
I will broaden the inquiry by looking at the Persian imperial context within which the theocratic community of the Second Temple
emerged. From this point of view the exile is also significant as an
experience which determined, to a greater or lesser extent, the nature
of the community. That is to say, the exiles who returned in both
the sixth and fifth centuries seem to have brought with them social
patterns and practices that defined the community in Judah. There
is, therefore, some justification in calling the theocratic community
of the Second Temple the "post-exilic" community, even with reference to the fourth century.

Beginning with the Ending (2 Chronicles 36)

Some people read the conclusion to a novel first. Is it out of simple curiosity, impatience or is it perhaps wanting to know where the
author is taking one, rather than being led through the plot blindly?
Whatever the motive may be, beginning with the ending transforms
how we read the rest of the book and can, among other things,
serve to focus our attention on the way in which the plot is constructed. As I see it, the difference between your average punter and

a literary or biblical critic is the fact that the critic reads books more than once. The second time around the critic (like the person who reads the conclusion first) knows where the story is going and can pay attention to other things; that is to say, the second time around the reader is a critic, a judge, a master of the text. Reading the ending first is simply a shortcut to a critical reading of the text.

The End of the Judean Kingdom in Chronicles

Both Chronicles and Kings end, roughly speaking, with the defeat of Zedekiah, the destruction of Jerusalem and the exile of people of Judah bringing to a close in both cases an account of the kingdom of Judah from the glory days of David and Solomon to its final igno-minious end. But apart from these basic similarities the two accounts of the end of the Judean kingdom differ substantially both in their treatments of the end of Zedekiah's reign, the destruction of Jerusalem and in their concluding postscripts. Very little in fact is "taken over" into Chronicles from the account in 2 Kgs. 24:18–25:21. 2 Chron. 36:11–12a follows 2 Kgs. 24:18–19 with a number of characteristic omissions. The omission of "just as Jehoiakim had done" is of par-ticular interest because it relates to the Chronicler's overall theodicy. The Chronicler does not, generally speaking, adopt the view that the reason for the punishment of exile is the accumulation of the sins of the kings of Judah in general (2 Kgs. 23:37b), and Manasseh (24:3) or Jehoiakim (24:19) in particular. These judgements which follow the formula כְּכֹל אֲשֶׁר עָשָׂה "according to all that he [as in Manasseh etc.] had done" are not made in the Chronicler's evaluations of the kings of Judah.[1]

In a relatively long section with no parallel in the book of Kings (36:12b–21) the Chronicler spells out, among other things, his unique understanding of the reason for Judah's punishment. He begins with Zedekiah whose offences relate to his attitude towards God and his spokesmen, the prophets: "He did not humble himself [כנע] before Jeremiah the prophet who spoke from the mouth of the Lord" (v. 12b); ". . . he stiffened his neck and hardened his heart against turning [שוב] to the LORD, the God of Israel" (v. 13b); and he was also unfaithful [מעל] with regard to the cult.

---

[1] This formula is used positively by the Chronicler in an his evaluation of Uzziah with reference back to Amaziah (2 Chron. 26:4), of Jotham with reference back to Uzziah (27:2), and of Hezekiah with reference back to David (29:2).

The culmination of this indictment against Judah (vv. 14ff) is, however, directed against the people and their leaders.[2]

> And all the leading priests[3] and the people were also *exceedingly unfaithful* (הרבו למעול מעל), following all the abominations of the nations; and they polluted the house of the LORD that he had consecrated in Jerusalem.

The people themselves are to blame for their fate on account of their "exceeding unfaithfulness" (the Chronicler's standard negative evaluation doubled). Their chief offence, apart from polluting the Temple, is that they ignored the LORD's warnings via the prophets whom they mocked, despised and scoffed instead. God's capacity for mercy was consumed and in his wrath against them their fate was sealed.[4]

But what sort of fate does the Chronicler have in mind? The final verses of this section describe the destruction of Jerusalem and its temple concluding with this statement:

> He took into exile in Babylon those who had escaped from the sword, and they became servants to him *and to his sons until the establishment of the kingdom of Persia*, to fulfil the word of the LORD by the mouth of Jeremiah, *until the land had made up for its sabbaths*. All the days that it lay desolate it kept sabbath, *to fulfil seventy years* (2 Chron. 36:20–21).

There are a number of notable features that set this text apart from 2 Kings which simply concludes "So Judah went into exile out of its land." Firstly, the emphasis is on Jerusalem, not on Judah as a whole.[5] It is Jerusalem that is destroyed (36:17–19) and it is the survivors of the destruction of Jerusalem who are exiled.[6] Secondly, no

---

[2] In line with what has been described by Riley as a "democratizing" tendency in Chronicles [W. Riley, *King and Cultus in Chronicles: Worship and the Reinterpretation of History* (JSOTS 160; Sheffield: Sheffield Academic Press, 1993), p. 92]. Unlike in 2 Kings, we do not hear of Zedekiah's ultimate fate [S. Japhet, *I & II Chronicles* (OTL; Louisville, KY: Westminster/John Knox, 1993), p. 1073].

[3] A possible textual problem: LXX has "all the leaders of Judah and the priests."

[4] The idea that the Chronicler believes in "immediate retribution" [R. B. Dillard, "Reward and Punishment in Chronicles: The Theology of Immediate Retribution," *WTJ* 46 (1984), pp. 164–72] needs to be tempered somewhat for, according to Kelly, the Chronicler *does* have a sense of an accumulating guilt [B. Kelly, *Retribution and Eschatology in Chronicles* (JSOTS 211; Sheffield: Sheffield Academic Press, 1996), pp. 108–9]. Kelly cites 2 Chron. 22:7–8, 28; 32:25 and 34:26–28 (esp. v. 28). He thus argues, contra Japhet, that 36:15–16 refers to the whole history of the Judean monarchy. For more on the question of retribution see chapter six.

[5] Throughout Chronicles Jerusalem is representative of all Israel, the heart and soul of Israel. See the discussion in chapter four.

[6] The notion of "survivors" or "remnant" is, of course, an important theological

mention is made of those who remained behind in Judah (cf. 2 Kgs. 25:22; Jer. 39:10). Thirdly, and most importantly, *the period of exile is limited* to the period of Neo-Babylonian rule: ". . . and they became servants to [Nebuchadnezzar] and his sons, *until the establishment of the kingdom of Persia*" (v. 20). The exile had a definite time limit, which is not simply a retrospective statement of fact but is more importantly a prior, divinely-imposed, time limit which fulfils "the word of the LORD by the mouth of Jeremiah, until the land had made up for its sabbaths. All the days that it lay desolate it kept sabbath, to fulfil seventy years" (v. 21).

This view of the exile is a combination of the theological interpretations of the exile found in Jeremiah and Leviticus.[7] The reference to Jeremiah at the beginning and at the end of this Chronistic section underscores the link between the fate of Zedekiah and Judah and the word of God as announced by this prophet. And this together with the use of the "seventy years" motif illustrates the Chronicler's indebtedness to Jeremiah, though the final treatment is still his own. In Jer. 25:11 the seventy years emphasizes the *extent* of God's wrath, not its limitation. For seventy years "these nations [i.e. Judah and its neighbours] will serve the king of Babylon" after which time the Babylonians themselves will be made to drink "this cup of the wine of wrath" (v. 15).[8] In Jer. 29:10, on the other hand, the end of the seventy years will indeed mark the end of the exile and a return to the land, but in the context of Jeremiah's letter to the exiles the seventy years signifies a long period of time in comparison to other shorter time-estimates (Jer. 28:3; 29:8).[9]

---

concept for the exiles and indeed for Judah after the Assyrian invasion. See the article on שאר by R. Clements in *TWAT*, vol. vii, cols. 933–50. In the Deuteronomistic History it is used with reference to Judah, sole survivor of the Assyrian invasion (2 Kgs. 17) and of Jersualem as surviving remnant (2 Kgs. 19). In Jeremiah it is used to refer to the survivors of 597 who are not the lucky ones (24:8–10), the "rest" that are exiled and those who remain behind (42:10–17). According to Ezekiel only the remnant in exile has hope (Ezek. 11:16; and 36:24); the remainees do not have a claim to the land (33:29). In contrast to the exclusivity of Ezekiel, the Chronicler refers to the "remnant" in the North after the Assyrian invasion (2 Chron. 30:6; 34:9, 12). But in Ezra-Nehemiah the "remnant" is used with reference to the exiles or returnees only (Ezra 1:4; 3:8; 9:8, 15; Neh. 11:20).

[7] On the ideology of land in Leviticus 25–26 see most recently N. Habel, *The Land is Mine: Six Biblical Land Ideologies* (Minneapolis: Fortress, 1995), pp. 97–114.

[8] R. P. Carroll, *Jeremiah* (OTL; London: SCM, 1986), p. 558.

[9] W. Holloday, *Jeremiah 2: A Commentary on the Book of the Prophet Jeremiah Chapters 26–52* (Hermeneia; Minneapolis: Fortress, 1989), pp. 139–40; Carroll, *Jeremiah*, pp. 493–6.

The seventy years in Jeremiah may be interpreted in a number of ways. It may refer to a literal seventy years such as 587/6–516/5 (from the destruction of the temple and its rebuilding) or 605–539 (from the beginning of Nebuchadnezzar's reign to the end of the Neo-Babylonian dynasty, rounded up for good measure). Seventy years may also be symbolic of a life-span. Whatever the case may be in Jeremiah, the Chronicler has interpreted this seventy years with reference to Lev. 26:33–35, and 43 which sees the removal of the people from the land as an opportunity for the land to "enjoy its sabbath years."[10] This text, like Jeremiah 29, holds out a note of promise that God will again remember the land. In the Chronicler's treatment, however, the restoration is seen, not so much as a promise, but as an inevitability. The exile has been emptied of a good deal of its force as marking the loss of nationhood, the suspension of the covenant and the reversal of the promise of land.[11] In this concluding chapter the exile is a gap in the story of Israel that is immediately overcome (somewhat like the gap between chapters, nothing more).[12] The "positive" significance of the exile as dealt with elsewhere in Chronicles will be explored further below (and in chapter six) but I will first "follow the link" between Chronicles and Ezra-Nehemiah that is established by the concluding postscript found in 2 Chron. 36:22–23.

From 2 Chronicles 36 to Ezra 1

The books of Chronicles end by quoting a number of verses from the so-called "Edict of Cyrus" as found in Ezra 1:1–4 thereby linking the pre-exilic history of Chronicles and the post-exilic history of Ezra-Nehemiah. I am not at this point concerned about the literary historical issues relating to the originality of these verses or indeed

---

[10] Note also that the land can be healed (2 Chron. 7:14) and purified (34:3, 8); see Kelly, *Retribution*, p. 182. This sacralization of the land works hand in hand with the Chronicler's autochthonous *Tendenz*: see S. Japhet, "Conquest and Settlement in Chronicles," *JBL* 98 (1979), pp. 205–18.

[11] According to Kelly, "The Chronicler is not so much concerned as the Deuteronomist was, in accounting for the exile and loss of land, as he is with stressing the fact of the resumption of Yahweh's saving activity towards Israel, and what the people's appropriate response should be" [Kelly, *Retribution*, p. 182].

[12] One notes in this connection that the *story* of the experience of the exile (as distinct from the stories set in the exile such as Daniel and Esther) is not an integral part of "the story" of Israel as told in Genesis through 2 Kings or Chronicles through Nehemiah.

to the theory of a larger Chronistic History. I am treating Chronicles as an independent work (over against Ezra-Nehemiah) and I am interpreting Chronicles in its final form which includes these final verses. And even if these verses have the hallmarks of "a later addition" they do fit nicely in the context and could for that reason have been placed there by "the Chronicler" himself.[13] As we saw above, the end of the neo-Babylonian empire at the hands of the Persians (as predicted by Jeremiah, according to the Chronicler's view of things in verse 21) is already mentioned in verse 20 which means that the addition of a short extract from the "Edict" simply reinforces that particular line of thought.

A comparative glance at these two texts indicates a couple of small changes in Chronicles over against Ezra.

2 Chron. 36:22–23	Ezra 1:1–4[14]
In the first year of King Cyrus of Persia, in fulfillment of the word of the LORD spoken by Jeremiah, the LORD stirred up the spirit of King Cyrus of Persia so that he sent a herald throughout all his kingdom and also declared in a written edict: "Thus says King Cyrus of Persia: The LORD, the God of heaven, has given me all the kingdoms of the earth, and he has charged me to build him a house in Jerusalem, which is in Judah. Whoever is among you of all his people, *may the LORD his God be with him*! Let him go up.	In the first year of King Cyrus of Persia, in fulfillment of the word of the LORD spoken by Jeremiah, the LORD stirred up the spirit of King Cyrus of Persia so that he sent a herald throughout all his kingdom and also declared in a written edict: "Thus says King Cyrus of Persia: The LORD, the God of heaven, has given me all the kingdoms of the earth, and he has charged me to build him a house in Jerusalem, which is in Judah. Whoever is among you of all his people, *may his God be with him*! Let him go up ... to Jerusalem in Judah, and rebuild the house of the LORD, the God of Israel—he is the God who is in Jerusalem; and let all survivors, in whatever place they reside, be assisted by the people of their place with silver and gold, with goods and with animals, besides the freewill offerings for the house of God in Jerusalem.

---

[13] I.e. the "author" responsible for the bulk of the book could have been his own final editor. But this is to place too much emphasis on the author's conscious intentions, as if one can and should differentiate between the thought of the author and the thought of a final redactor.

[14] Slightly modified from the NRSV to bring out the parallels.

The only interesting change is the shift from "may his god be with him" (Ezra 1:3) to "may the LORD his God be with him" which may be construed as removing the pagan notion of many people— many gods. The Chronicler also pulls up short, ending on the jussive ויעל "let him go up." More importantly, however, is the way this text confirms and strengthens the Chronicler's notion of exile as something that was overcome or bridged straightaway in the interests of the on-going story of Israel in its land. The reader is not left to ponder the catastrophe of 587/6 and the seventy year exile but is rather hurried along into the Persian period and the restoration beyond exile.

One could say that 2 Chron. 36:22–23 is really no ending at all but rather a textual link between these two books, stories, and periods of time, and hence a directive to keep reading (elsewhere).[15] And this is exactly what I propose to do in the following section; that is, I will follow this link from Chronicles to Ezra-Nehemiah, reading the one in light of the other. The *way* in which I "take up" this directive to keep reading elsewhere is of course a crucial factor in my interpretation but one could argue that a *contextual* reading of Chronicles with reference to the post-exilic period in general and Ezra-Nehemiah in particular is exactly what the Chronicler had in mind.

If we consider this from the point of view of intentionality one could argue that in order to understand what the Chronicler *meant by* what he said (the communicative intentions of the Chronicler) or even the contextual implications of this move (the indirect intentions) requires that one read Chronicles and Ezra-Nehemiah together; and not just the books of Ezra and Nehemiah but also the history of the post-exilic community to which it refers.[16] What is *meant by* this link must surely involve the notion that there is a link between the story of Israel before and after exile and between the author's past and the author's present. In other words, this textual link to Ezra-Nehemiah is also at the same time a link to the historical *and* ideological context in which, roughly speaking, the book was written. Ezra-Nehemiah is not

---

[15] J. Miles, *God: A Biography* (New York: Vintage, 1996), pp. 391–6, describes the effects of this link and the "displacement" of Ezra-Nehemiah to its current location in the Hebrew Bible just before Chronicles as a perpetual round (as in round song). This link sends the reader back to Ezra and Nehemiah and from there to Adam at the beginning of Chronicles, through David to the end of Chronicles and back again. I discuss this idea further in chapter six.

[16] For the distinction between communicative intention and verbal meaning see chapter one.

just the main historical account of this period but is also in itself an important fragment of the ideological fabric of that same community. Asking about the role of exile in the ideology of the Chronicler leads thus to the question of the role of the exile in the ideology of identity in Ezra-Nehemiah. One could say that Chronicles has its very own context—textual, historical and ideological—appended to it.[17]

Exile and Restoration in Ezra 1–6: An Outside Initiative

The books of Ezra-Nehemiah tell the story of the restoration of the post-exilic community in terms of a collaborative outside initiative involving Jewish exiles and the Persian authorities at the highest level, though originating in the realm of the LORD "in fulfillment of the word of the LORD spoken by Jeremiah" (Ezra 1:1).[18] As an "outside initiative" the restoration parallels, or is made to parallel, the story of the exodus from Egypt. That the writer of Ezra 1 is dependent on Deutero-Isaiah in this regard is indicated in a number of ways. The "stirring up (עור, hi.) of the spirit of Cyrus," for example, suggests not only Jer. 51:11, "the LORD has stirred up (עור, hi.) the spirit of the kings of the Medes," but also Deutero-Isaiah's description of the role of Cyrus in the purposes of God:

> Who has roused [עור, hi.] a victor from the east, summoned him to his service? (41:2)

> I stirred up [עור, hi.] one from the north and he has come, from the rising of the sun he was summoned by name (41:25).

> I have aroused him [עור, hi.][19] in righteousness, and I will make all his paths straight; he shall build my city and set my exiles free, not for price or reward, says the LORD of hosts (45:13).

Unlike Pharaoh who at first refused to let Israel go up to worship their god and then only reluctantly, Cyrus willingly permits the Jews to go up.

---

[17] This blurring of the textual and the historical may be disquieting to the strict historical critic on the one hand and to the pure literary critic on the other, but it is the very thing which interests the ideological critic who shares with the New Historicists a "reciprocal concern with the historicity of texts and the textuality of history" [L. Montrose, "Professing the Renaissance: The Poetics and Politics of Culture," in H. Aram Veeser (ed.), *The New Historicism* (London: Routledge, 1989), p. 20].

[18] Keeping the translation that we quoted above which is that found in 2 Chron. 36.

[19] Referring to Cyrus. NRSV inserts "Cyrus" here on the basis of Isa. 45:1.

That the author of Ezra-Nehemiah is dependent, to a certain extent, on Deutero-Isaiah's understanding of the restoration is confirmed later in this chapter. In Deutero-Isaiah the return from exile is portrayed as a second Exodus:

> Do not remember the former things, or consider the things of old. I am about to do a new thing; now it springs forth, do you not perceive it? I will make a way in the wilderness and rivers in the desert.[20]

The prophet not only announces the immanent and mighty intervention of the LORD on behalf of the people against the Babylonians with Cyrus as his instrument of wrath, but urges the people to respond with renewed confidence in their God (for the gods of the Babylonians are mere idols) and to "Go out from Babylon, flee from Chaldea, declare this with a shout of joy, proclaim it, send it forth to the end of the earth; say, 'The LORD has redeemed his servant Jacob!'" (Isa. 48:20).

The response of the people to Cyrus's edict is described in Ezra 1:5–11 and what was probably a series of returns is here presented as one return.[21] Just as the LORD "stirred up" Cyrus so too are the exiles (or at least representatives from every section of the community, lay, priestly and levitical) "stirred" by the spirit of God to return and rebuild the temple (v. 5), as if also in response to Deutero-Isaiah's charge. They are supported by their neighbours with vessels of silver and gold (v. 6) just as the Israelites were supported by their Egyptian neighbours (Exod. 3:21–22; 11:2; 12:35–36), a text which finds its echo also in Isa. 45:14.[22] They also returned with the temple treasures "the vessels of the house of the LORD that Nebuchadnezzar had carried away from Jerusalem and placed in the house of his gods" (v. 7). The temple vessels are an important theme in the narrative of the return, both here and elsewhere, as a tangible symbol of continuity between the First and Second Temples.[23] Of particular interest in this regard is Isa. 51:11 which links the new Exodus and the temple vessels:

---

[20] Isa. 43:18–19.

[21] Williamson argues that the author of Ezra 1–6 had only the Cyrus edict and the inventory of temple vessels from which to construct an account of the return [H. G. M. Williamson, "The Composition of Ezra i–vi," *JTS* 34 (1983), pp. 1–30].

[22] "Thus says the LORD: The wealth of Egypt and the merchandise of Ethiopia, and the Sabeans, tall of stature, shall come over to you."

[23] P. R. Ackroyd, "The Temple Vessels—A Continuity Theme," *VTS* 23 (1972), pp. 166–81.

> Depart, depart, go out from there! Touch no unclean thing; go out from
> the midst of it, purify yourselves, *you who carry the vessels of the LORD.*

The final echo of the exodus in this passage is found in Ezra 1:11
which concludes this chapter: "All these [vessels] were brought up,
when the exiles were *brought up* from Babylonia to Jerusalem." The
verb עלה is, of course, the same verb used in the "Edict of Cyrus"
and in the book of Exodus with regard to the Israelites "going up"
out of Egypt to the land promised to the patriarchs (3:8, 17; and 33:1).

This presentation of the return, and especially the use of Deutero-
Isaiah and the "Return as exodus" motif, reinforces the idea that
the community of the post-exilic period was constituted from the
very beginning as a *community of exiles.* Just as Israel first became a
nation in Egypt and the people of God through the experience of
the exodus so too was this Israel born in a new exodus out of captivity. The particularity of the portrayal of the exile in Ezra-Nehemiah
can be clarified further with reference to Chronicles. Whereas the
Chronicler's perspective in 2 Chronicles 36 is "exile as something to
be overcome," the perspective in Ezra-Nehemiah is "exile as something to be remembered." The exile is remembered as the defining
experience for the people of God in the post-exilic period. This may
sound like a tautology but only because historians have taken over
the periodization of history into pre-exilic, exilic, and post-exilic periods that we find in the biblical narratives. And while it is probably
true that the community centred in Jerusalem in the Persian period
was indeed founded by returnees under the sponsorship of the Persians, it is the way in which this event is remembered and to what
end these events are remembered which is significant.[24] The act of
remembering is fundamental to the ideology of identity.

The stress on the *exilic* identity of the Jewish community in Persian
Judah is maintained beyond Ezra 1. Ezra 2 (which has its parallel

---

[24] Willi has recently argued that we must distinguish between the early Persian
period and the later period with regard to both politics *and* religion and culture
[T. Willi, *Juda, Jehud, Israel: Studien zum Selbstverstandnis des Judentums in persischer Zeit*
(Tübingen: J.C.B. Mohr (Paul Siebeck), 1995), pp. 34–9: noting Stern's archeological evidence for continuity in material culture up to the mid-fifth century]. In the
literature of the late sixth century, namely Haggai and Zechariah 1–8, one has a
sense of continuity with monarchic Judah which one does not find in Ezra-Nehemiah.
Just as the missions of Ezra and Nehemiah transformed (or are said to have transformed) the community in the late fifth century, so too does the book Ezra-Nehemiah
represent a radical transformation of the self-understanding of the community.

in Nehemiah 7) purports to be a list of "the sons of the province who came from the captivity of the exiles" (Ezra 2:1/Neh. 7:6). It is organized according to the divisions of the people into the laity (literally בני ישראל), priests, Levites and lesser temple staff. These groups are followed by a list of those who "could not prove their families or their descent, whether they belonged to Israel" (Ezra 2:59). Within these divisions the returnees are enumerated according to "the sons of x" or "the men of y" which together comprise "the whole assembly (קהל)" (v. 64). These groups are also known individually as בית אבות or "house of the fathers" (as distinct from the בית אב). I will come back to this text (and its ideological import) in chapter five, but for now simply emphasize the way in which the one side of the claim—that the restoration was an outside effort of the returnees and the Persian emperor—is made in Ezra. Not only is this claim narrated as such but official documents are supplied to prove it, or rather, a narrative thread is wound around a whole series of official documents in these opening chapters of Ezra.[25]

In the narratives in the remainder of Ezra[26] the description of the community as comprised of former exiles occurs again in Ezra 4:1 which sets these returned exiles over against "the adversaries of Judah and Benjamin." In this text, as in 6:19–21 (where the returned exiles celebrate the completion of the temple together with those who had "separated themselves from the pollutions of the nations of the land) and 9:4 (where the returned exiles are castigated for their unfaithfulness, מעל, in intermarrying with "the peoples of the lands") we see how remembering the exile is portrayed as essential for group identity. At this point I am simply noting the ideological drift of these texts as they relate to the question of exile and identity and will look at the socio-historical implications of these claims below.

The other side of the "outside initiative" claim has to do with the role of the Persians as portrayed in the narrative and in the official Persian documents incorporated into the narrative. We are, of course, dealing with a range of questions at a number of levels relating to

---

[25] See T. Eskenazi, *In an Age of Prose: A Literary Approach to Ezra-Nehemiah* (SBLMS 36; Atlanta, GA: Scholars Press, 1988), pp. 75 7.

[26] גולה occurs only once in Nehemiah 7:6 which is parallel to Ezra 2:1. Elsewhere we find the expression "those who had returned from the captivity" but this is in Nehemiah 8 which relates Ezra's reading of the law.

the structure of the narrative of Ezra 1–6 and the authenticity of these "documents." Regarding the former, one must bear in mind the degree to which the narrative of Ezra 1–6 is an ideological construct written a century if not two centuries after the events to which it refers and one of the "tendencies" of this narrative is its pro-Persian stance.[27] Regarding the Persian documents incorporated in the narrative, the question of their authenticity is still debated[28] but for the sake of my argument I will assume that they are largely genuine. More to the point is the fact that a claim to Persian sponsorship is being made and backed-up with documentary evidence. According to Eskenazi, the "veneration of the written word" is one of the main "themes" of Ezra-Nehemiah. "From one perspective, Ezra-Nehemiah describes the ways divinely initiated written texts— the decree of Cyrus and the Torah of Moses—are fulfilled. For God's messages are transcribed into written texts to be actualized by the community."[29]

The initiative for the restoration may ultimately rest with Yahweh but the fulfilment of his word follows an imperial chronology (see also Hag. and Zech. 1–8). The portrayal of Cyrus draws on, as we have seen, the portrayal of Cyrus found in Deutero-Isaiah, especially Isaiah 44 and 45. Deutero-Isaiah stresses throughout his book that the LORD is still in control and that he will act on behalf of his chosen people for his name sake by rebuilding Jerusalem and restor-

---

[27] Japhet notes a number of tendencies in Ezra 1–6 which explain to a certain degree the problematic treatment of Sheshbazzar and Zerubbabel [S. Japhet, "Sheshbazzar and Zerubbabel," *ZAW* 94 (1982), pp. 66–98].

[28] The authenticity of the "Edict of Cyrus" which is found in Ezra 1:1–4 *and* 6:3–5 (the latter version is usually considered to be the official written version) has been defended by E. Meyer [*Die Entstehung des Judentums: Eine historische Untersuchung* (Halle: Niemeyer, 1896), pp. 7–81], E. J. Bickerman ["The Edict of Cyrus in Ezra 1" in *Studies in Jewish and Christian History*, vol. 1 (Leiden: Brill, 1976), pp. 72–108] and more recently H. G. M. Williamson [*Ezra, Nehemiah* (WBC; Waco, TX: Word, 1985), pp. 8–15, and 80–81]. C. C. Torrey, *The Composition and Historical Value of Ezra-Nehemiah* (1896); A. H. Gunneweg, "Die aramäische und die hebräische Erzählung über die nachexilische Restauration—ein Vergleich," *ZAW* 94 (1982), pp. 299–302; and L. Lebram, "Die Traditionsgeschichte der Esragestalt und die Frage nach dem historischen Esra," in H. Sancisi-Weerdenburg, A. Kuhrt, and J. W. Drijvers (eds.) *Achaemenid History*, vol. 1, *Sources, Structures, and Synthesis* (Proceedings of the Grönigen 1983 Achaemenid History Workshop; Leiden: Nederlands Instituut voor het Nabije Oosten, 1987), pp. 103–38, deny its authenticity. The argument hinges on language, theological concepts used, and the degree to which the "Edict" parallels contemporary Persian records.

[29] Eskenazi, *Age of Prose*, p. 189.

ing the cities of Judah (44:26). Cyrus is called by name and described as "my shepherd" (44:28) and as "my anointed whose right hand I have grasped" (expressions which all have clear royal and Davidic overtones).[30] This Cyrus will rebuild Jerusalem and lay the foundation of the temple (44:28). In Ezra-Nehemiah the author has given this forward-looking theological interpretation of Israel's place in the world a thoroughly political (and now also retrospective) spin, claiming in the process "first-year" priority.[31]

Ezra 5:1–6:18 essentially confirms this notion of an imperially-sanctioned community and indeed develops further the idea of co-sponsorship. It underlines the consistency of policy from Cyrus to Darius, citing both a shorter Aramaic version of the "Edict of Cyrus" (6:3–5) and Darius's own edict (6:6–11) which specifies in greater detail what is to be done in having the temple rebuilt. Darius's decree commits the empire financially to this project and specifies that, in return, the Jews "offer pleasing sacrifices to the God of heaven, and pray for the life of the king and his children," the "God of heaven" providing a suitable religious middle ground from a Persian and Jewish perspective.

The two sides of the "outside initiative" theme are brought together in Ezra 4:1–3,[32] where Cyrus's edict is used as the legal basis for excluding the non-returnees from the temple project: "You shall have no part with us in building a house to our God; but we alone will build to the LORD, the God of Israel, as King Cyrus of Persia has commanded us" (4:3). The narrative of Ezra 4–6, which chronicles the opposition to the returnees, is chronologically confused as it now stands though not thematically confused. The themes brought together in this section of Ezra—the returnees in conflict over the initiative to rebuild the temple with the backing of Persian empire—are part

---

[30] P. R. Ackroyd, "The Biblical Portrayal of Achaemenid Rulers" in H. Sancisi-Weerdenburg, A. Kuhrt, and J. W. Drijvers (eds.), *Achaemenid History*, vol. 5, *The Roots of the European Tradition* (Proceedings of the Groningen 1986 Achaemenid History Workshop; Leiden: Nederlands Instituut voor het Nabije Oosten, 1990), pp. 2–3.

[31] Ackroyd, "Biblical Portrayal," p. 4.

[32] Williamson distinguishes between Ezra 4:1–3 and 4:4–5. The former is to be dated to the reign of Darius, not Cyrus, and provides a context for Tattenai's visit in 5:3. The latter text follows on from the dedication of the foundation of the temple and provides an explanation for the delay in the building of the temple. Ezra 5:6–23 is a digression, chronologically and thematically speaking (it deals with the *city* not the temple being rebuilt), and so 5:3 find its continuation in 5:24 [*Ezra, Nehemiah*, pp. 43–5].

of the larger thematic and literary structure of Ezra-Nehemiah thereby demonstrating that the "outside initiative" perspective is maintained throughout Ezra-Nehemiah and is for that-reason central to
it. Williamson, for example, divides the book into four main sections, each of the first three dealing with a main aspect of community life (Temple, Law, City) and observes a similar pattern within
each section:

I. Ezra 1–6	Temple	a) Persia as divine agent b) return of exiles c) external opposition/danger d) opposition/danger overcome e) celebration
II. Ezra 7–10	Law	a) Persia as divine agent b) return of exiles c) external opposition/danger d) opposition/danger overcome e) no celebration
III. Neh 1–7	City	a) Persia as divine agent b) return of exiles c) external opposition/danger d) opposition/danger overcome e) no celebration
IV. Neh 8–12		Suspended climax to I–III Jerusalem repopulated Walls rededicated

In each of the three main sections dealing with the "construction"
of the institutions of the post-exilic community we find Persia and
returned exiles playing a prominent role. The community they construct and which they call "Israel" is a conception of Israel that
unites those who returned to the land with those in the diaspora
within the imperial framework. In order to examine the contextual functions and ideological import of this particular account of origins, it
is necessary to consider the larger social, political and ideological
context. The argument to be advanced is that this account which
concerns the very foundation of the Jewish community in Judah represents one "voice" in an ideological debate (if not conflict) about
the nature and identity of the Jewish community within the Persian
empire.

The Restoration from the Persian Perspective

The texts we have looked at so far present the restoration of Jerusalem in the Persian period as an outside effort involving returned exiles and outside sponsorship. How is this to be understood with reference to the Persian context? Assuming for the sake of argument that the imperial documents in Ezra-Nehemiah are authentic, why did the Persians allow for the return of exiled Jews and the re-establishment of the Jerusalem Temple? Most historians conclude that the Persians' intention was to create a loyal enclave in an area far from the administrative centres of the empire (Susa, Persepolis, Ecbatana, Babylon) yet close to Egypt and hence of strategic importance. But this conclusion is too general to be of much use to us and leaves a number of questions unanswered. Against this view one might well ask why the Persians would take an interest in a city lying in ruins and high in the hills well off the beaten path between Mesopotamia and Egypt. Furthermore, if they were keen on restoring Jerusalem, why allow the *exiles* to return and rebuild the Temple? Why not allow the remainees to restore Jerusalem? Perhaps the remainees were not interested in rebuilding the Temple (although the writer of Ezra-Nehemiah says otherwise: Ezra 4:1–3). One wonders if they anticipated the kind of conflict that seems to have occurred in the process of the creation of this community. And related to that one might ask about what sort of entity the Persians intended to create? I will seek to answer these questions by looking at the administrative policy and imperial ideology of the Persian as far as can be made out.

The Cyrus Cylinder

I begin, as is usual, with a look at the Cyrus Cylinder which provides the closest parallel to the Cyrus edict. The Cyrus Cylinder is a dedicatory inscription connected with the restoration/rebuilding program undertaken by Cyrus in Babylon following his "peaceful" conquest of the city. The Cyrus Cylinder begins with an historical preamble setting Cyrus's invasion in context.[33] Marduk and the gods were angry with Nabonidus for his violation of proper cult practices, for removing images to Babylon, and "on account of (the fact that) the

---

[33] This is a typical feature of Neo-Babylonian inscriptions; see "Nabonidus Inscription XI" in *ANET*, pp. 309–11.

sanctuaries of all their settlements were in ruins[34] and the inhabitants of Sumer and Akkad had become like (living) dead" (ll. 10–11).[35] Upon seeing this Marduk, the chief god of Babylon, "scanned and looked (through) all the countries, searching for a righteous ruler" (l. 12). Having found the man he wanted, "he pronounced the name of Cyrus, king of Anshan, and declared him (lit.: pronounced [his] name) to be ruler of all the world" (l. 12). The Cylinder goes on to describe how Cyrus took Babylon without bloodshed. Cyrus begins speaking in the first person at line 20:

> I am Cyrus, king of the world, great king, legitimate king, king of Babylon, king of Sumer and Akkad, king of the four rims (of the earth), son of Cambyses, great king, king of Anshan, grandson of Cyrus, great king, king of Anshan, descendent of Teispes, great king, king of Anshan, of a family (which) always (exercised) kingship; whose rule Bel and Nebo love, whom they want as king to please their hearts.[36]

In the desire to establish the legitimacy of his rule, Cyrus uses epithets in accordance with ancient Mesopotamian tradition and asserts his legitimate descent from a long-established family of kings. Berger concludes from this and from the negative evaluation of Nabonidus's reign that the priests of Marduk (though working at the behest of Cyrus) produced this inscription using the language and conventions of royal inscriptions established in the first instance by the Sumerians.[37] In other words, this is standard ancient Near Eastern royal ideology and not an original piece by Cyrus himself.[38]

The measures enacted in the Cylinder are described as follows:

> (As to the region) from . . . as far as Ashur and Susa, Agade, Eshnunna, the towns of Zamban, Me-Turnu, Der, as well as the region of the Gutians, I returned to (these) sacred cities on the other side of the Tigris the sanctuaries which have been in ruins for a long time, the images

---

[34] This translation of line 11 is disputed. P.-R., Berger, "Der Kyros-Zylinder mit dem Zusatzfragment BIN II Nr. 32 und die akkadischen Personennamen im Danielbuch," *ZA* 64 (1975), p. 197, translates "deren Wohnstätte aufgegeben war." J. N. Postgate [via personal conversation with Williamson: *Ezra, Nehemiah*, p. 13] also argues that it refers to abandoned settlements.

[35] Citing the *ANET* translation with line numbers from Berger.

[36] Lines 20–22.

[37] Berger, "Kyros-Zylinder," p. 217.

[38] Berger, "Kyros-Zylinder," p. 218. It does not follow then that since the language (such as "the LORD, the God of Israel"; v. 3) and conceptuality of the Cyrus edict in Ezra 1 includes Jewish elements its authenticity must be suspect [Berger, "Kyros-Zylinder," p. 219].

which (used) to live therein and established for them permanent sanctuaries. I (also) gathered all their (former) inhabitants and returned (to them) their habitations.[39]

The returning of gods to their sanctuaries along with their inhabitants is often cited as providing the closest parallel to the actions taken by Cyrus vis-à-vis the Jews. We must, however, clearly distinguish between what this text *demonstrates* and what it *suggests* about Persian imperial policy vis-à-vis religious/ethnic groups like the Jews. First of all, the Cylinder demonstrates that the Persians worked closely with the clerical leaders in Babylonia in order to support the rule of the Persians ideologically with a view to "harnessing the interests and energies of the local elite."[40] From the Persian perspective this was a matter of *co-opting* local religious institutions for their own purposes. From the Babylonian perspective, or at least from the perspective of the ruling elite in Babylon, Cyrus was probably a welcome change in their fortunes, making *co-operation* a prudent and pragmatic choice.

I would argue from this that the Jews in Babylon were in an analogous situation. They were, in all likelihood, broadly familiar with Persian objectives and, as an exiled elite, were probably more easily convinced of the benefits of Persian rule, or (to put it differently) were in a position to see how their interests and the interests of the Persians coincided. But whatever the motive, they were thereby participating in this political and ideological act as much as the Persians. There must also have been enough overlap in their religious world views to allow these monotheistic Jews[41] to imaginatively participate in Persian ideology to the point of offering "pleasing sacrifices to the God of heaven,[42] and [to] pray for the life of the king and

---

[39] Lines 30–32.

[40] C. Tulpin, "The Administration of the Achaemenid Empire," in I. Carradice (ed.), *Coinage and Administration in the Athenian and Persian Empires* (BAR Int'l Series 343; Oxford: B.A.R., 1987).

[41] Judging by Deutero-Isaiah.

[42] Williamson argues that the expression "God of Heaven" is to be seen as Jewish accomodation to Persian administrative policy [*Ezra, Nehemiah*, p. 12]. The phrases "God of Heaven," "Ya'u the Lord of Heaven" and "Ya'u the God of Heaven" are also used in AramP 30, a letter addressed to Bigvai, governor of Judaea [see A. Cowley (ed.), *Aramaic Papyri of the Fifth Century* (Osnabrück: Otto Zeller, reprint edn., 1967), p. 113]. The Persian god Ormazd was "a celestial god portrayed with a winged sun-disk in the heavens and acknowledged as creator of heaven and earth" [R. Bowman, *Interpreter's Bible*; cited by Williamson]. Most of the OT occurrences of the expression (Ps. 136:26; Gen. 24:3, 7; Jonah 1:9; Neh. 1:4, 5; 2:4, 20) are

his children" (Ezra 6:10). One could well imagine that Cyrus's edict was drafted on the basis of a request by leading Jews in Babylon.[43] All this explains the "outside initiative" emphasis in Ezra-Nehemiah in terms of historical plausibilty (if not probability).

Returning to the Cylinder, the text also suggests a tolerance on the part of Cyrus and the Persians and a new interest and concern for the plight of various ethnic groups within the empire. But this is only suggested, not demonstrated. Kuhrt, in particular, has argued that this was not a unique act of tolerance on the part of the Persians nor did it establish a new tolerant, federalist policy in the ancient Near East. We must not be fooled by Herodotus (3:90) and the writers of the Old Testament into thinking that Cyrus was a great humanitarian. The Cyrus Cylinder is specifically related to Babylon and surrounding area and the text itself fits the age-old Babylonian genre of "building texts." This is definitely not evidence for Cyrus's personal convictions nor for an official policy of tolerance. The Persians also destroyed temples and deported peoples (Herod. 5:13–16; 4:204; 6:20).[44]

Persian Administrative Policy

Cyrus was, of course, only the first in a long line of Persian emperors (of the Achaemenid line) whose rule eventually extended far beyond that of any empire before them. Although Cyrus's rule doesn't inaugurate a sudden change in administrative policy,[45] the Persians under Darius did ultimately develop a new administrative style and ideological practice to cope with the incredible diversity within the empire. After sketching out the basic features of this new administrative system, I will look more closely at the ideological practice that accompanied it.

Empires are by definition multi-ethnic or multi-national entities established by conquest wherein centripetal forces of administrative

---

late and most occur contexts in which there is official contact with the Persians or foreigners in general.

[43] Williamson, *Ezra, Nehemiah*, p. 11.

[44] A. Kuhrt, "The Cyrus Cylinder and Achaemenid Imperial Policy," *JSOT* 25 (1983), pp. 83–97.

[45] Hoglund discusses the administrative developments of the Neo-Assyrian, Neo-Babylonian and Persian empires [K. Hoglund, *Achaemenid Imperial Administration in Syria-Palestine and the Missions of Ezra and Nehemiah* (SBLDS 125; Atlanta, GA: Scholars Press, 1992), pp. 1–28].

control and taxation conflict with the centrifugal forces of intra- and extra-territorial trade and local political, religious, and social endeavour and interaction. The Assyrian empire represented one end of this continuum with its policy of radical centralization using mass deportation to increase the agricultural production of under-developed regions of the empire. This policy not only benefited the imperial economy, generating greater surpluses for the centre, but also facilitated the control of conquered populations who, when isolated from their homelands and concentrated geographically, were less of a threat to internal security.[46] The whole empire was divided into provinces which were ruled by representatives of the empire. While these provinces corresponded in many cases to the pre-existing political entities, very little scope was given for the incorporation of local forms of leadership. The Assyrian empire differentiated among various ethnic groups in terms of their status with the imperial system.[47] The Neo-Babylonian empire (and, for the Levant, the intervening period of Egyptian domination) represented somewhat of a hiatus whereby certain territories reverted to the traditional hereditary forms of government they had prior to Assyrian domination. The Neo-Babylonians did, however, re-impose provincial government on provinces that revolted.[48]

When the Persians conquered the Neo-Babylonian empire they merely took over the existing administrative structures. But this rather

---

[46] The mass deportations during the Assyrian and Neo-Babylonian periods thus accelerated the ethnic interaction which obtained in Mesopotamian the Persian period. In the late 7th c. BC, Babylonian ethnic groups aligned themselves into broad kin-based groups tracing their descent to a common eponymous ancestor [J. A. Brinkman, *Prelude to Empire*, (Occasional Papers of the Babylonian Fund; Philadelphia, 1984), p. 11]. Ethnic groups also included occupationally-specific "ethnic" groups. In the Persian period, one third of the names found in Babylon are foreign. Generally speaking, the interaction of ethnic groups led to synchretism, but in some cases ethnic groups maintained their identity and lived in their own quarters in the city. The Achaemenids also founded ethnically-based military colonies such as the Jewish colony at Elephantine [M. Dandamaev, "Politische und Wirtschaftliche Geschichte," in G. Walser (ed.), *Beiträge zur Achämenidengeschichte* (Historia Einzelschriften 18; Wiesbaden: Harrassowitz, 1972), pp. 56–8]. Kümmel also speaks of "erblicher Berufstraditionen" in all vocations in the Neo-Babylonian period. This type of social structure is an adaptation of the kinship structure to meet the demands for greater system differentiation. One also encounters occupationally-defined kinship groups in Neh. 3:8 [see H. M. Kümmel, *Familie, Beruf und Amt in spätbabylonischen Uruk: prosopographische Untersuchungen zu Berufsgruppen des 6. Jahrhunderts v. Chr. in Uruk* (ADOG 20; Berlin: Mann, 1979)].

[47] Hoglund, *Achaemenid*, pp. 11–12.

[48] Hoglund, *Achaemenid*, pp. 15–19.

loose arrangement was too weak for Darius who came to power in
the midst of the uprisings following the death of Cambyses. Darius
reorganized the satrapies and separated civil from military administration, which up to that point had been concentrated in the hands
of the satrap.[49] Along with maintaining the provincial entities within
the satrapies, many of which resembled former kingdoms, Darius
retained various types of local autonomous units within the satrapies
and indeed encouraged the development of local powers (Judah being
a prime example). The administrative regions and units of the empire
were, therefore, a mixture of central institutions—the satrapies and
provinces—and locally-defined administrative units such as the *poleis*
and kingdoms of Asia Minor, the temple and city communities of
Asia Minor and Mesopotamia and tribal groups on the fringes of
the empire.

Darius's administrative changes were also aimed at the systemati-
zation of the tax system. All the land was assessed as to its productive capacity and tribute levels for the satrapies were set accordingly.
Tribute was paid in silver and in kind. A portion of the silver tribute was stored in the large treasuries in Mesopotamia and Persia
while the rest stayed in the satrapies. Taxes in kind were used to
pay for the operation of the bureaucracy and military garrisons. The
satrap was a tax-collecting unit and so too was the province, but
the way in which taxes were collected at the provincial level, and
below that at the level of the city, varied greatly.[50]

Persian Imperial Ideology

Given the lack of uniformity in the administrative and taxation system,
one has to wonder at the ability of the Persians to maintain this
large empire for two centuries. The fundamental means of control
was, of course, the threat of force and the Persians were not averse
to acting on this threat if need be. What is more interesting (and
problematic) though are the means they used to control this vast empire other than force. What was the difference between Persian rule
and Assyrian or Neo-Babylonian rule? What image of empire did
they develop and project? In short, what sort of imperial ideology
did they produce and for whom did they produce it?

---

[49] Hoglund, *Achaemenid*, p. 24.
[50] Tulpin, "Administration," pp. 137–58. It appears, for example, that Nehemiah
was free to invent new taxes beyond those required by the Persians.

As we saw in chapter two, beyond merely threatening coercive action, the state seeks to co-ordinate the activity of its subjects by "taking hold of" their action orientations, by encouraging a belief in their legitimacy, by securing an advance in trust; in short, by developing an ideology which will do these very things. As Tulpin puts it, maintaining control is "partly a matter of . . . manipulating high status local interest groups and taking advantage of low status groups' indifference to the identity of the ruling power,"[51] and of harnessing "the energies and interests of native dominant classes to their own ends."[52] The first objective of Persian ideology would have been the indoctrination of its own ruling classes but beyond that its objective would have been the indoctrination of the (former) ruling classes of the peoples within the conquered territories.[53] The subtleties of the ideology (written or visual) would, of course, be lost on the majority of the population, but the audience of the ideology had to be broad enough and the correspondence between ideology and the realities of their administration had to be close enough in order for it to keep this select group of subjects imaginatively participating in the imperial order.

The degree to which Persian imperial ideology represents something new in terms of ancient Near Eastern imperial ideology can be ascertained by comparing the epithets used of Assyrian kings and those used of Persian rulers (both before and after Cyrus). I begin with an inscription by Darius which enunciates in a very straightforward way the key elements of a uniquely Persian ideology.

> A great god is Ahuramazda, who created this earth, who created yonder sky, who created man, who created happiness for man, who made Darius king, one king of many, one lord of many (lines 1–8).[54]

This text asserts the unity of the cosmos and society as the work of one creating god, Ahuramazda. Koch notes the non-mythological quality of the language, the lack of anthropocentrism and the idea

---

[51] Tulpin, "Administration," p. 109.

[52] Tulpin, "Administration," p. 112.

[53] M. Liverani, "The Ideology of the Assyrian Empire," in M. Trolle Larsen (ed.), *Power and Propaganda: A Symposium on Ancient Empires* (Mesopotamia 7; Copenhagen: Akademisk Forlag, 1979), p. 302. Some of Liverani's comments apply to empires in general.

[54] DNa (or the first inscription of Darius found at Naqs-i-Rustam, which is some miles north of Persepolis) as translated by R. G. Kent [*Old Persian: Grammar, Texts, Lexicon* (AOS 33; New Haven, CO: Yale, 2nd edn., 1953), p. 138].

of the sonship of the king. It was by the will of Ahuramazda and through his aid that Darius personally, and not just the Persians in general, became king.[55] The inscription continues,

> I am Darius, the great king, king of kings, king of countries containing all kinds of men, king in this great earth far and wide, son of Hystaspes, an Achaemenian, a Persian, son of a Persian, an Aryan, having Aryan lineage (lines 8–15).[56]

The opening formula "Great King, King of Kings" is based on a standard Assyrian formula, which in turn developed out of the Old Babylonian and Sumerian traditions.

> I, Assurbanipal, the great king, the mighty king, the king of the universe, the king of the four regions of the world, the king of kings, the unrivalled prince (Assurbanipal Stele S²).[57]

The expression "king of the four corners of the world" is equivalent to the Sumero-Akkadian "king of the world."[58] Its rough equivalent in Old Persian in the Darius inscriptions may be the phrase "king in this great earth far and wide." The earliest known use of the epithet "king of the world" is found in an Assyrian inscription by Zarriqum, an Assyrian governor, who uses it of his overlord Aram-Sin (Ur III).[59] The epithet "king of the universe" makes its first appearance in an inscription by Shamshi-Adad I (1726–1694).[60] Thus, the ancient Near Eastern tradition was passed down via the Assyrians to the Neo-Babylonians to the Persians.[61]

The discontinuity between the ancient Near Eastern tradition and Persian ideology is apparent in relation to the epithet "king of the universe/totality." In the Assyrian text the king is "king of totality"

---

[55] K. Koch, "Weltordnung und Reichsidee im alten Iran," in H. Frei and K. Koch, *Reichsidee und Reichsorganization im Perserreich* (OBO 55; Göttingen: Vandenhoeck & Ruprecht, 1984), p. 56.

[56] Kent, *Old Persian*, p. 138.

[57] D. D. Luckenbill, *Ancient Records of Assyrian and Babylon*, vol. 2, *Historical Records of Assyria: From Sargon to the End* (Chicago: University of Chicago Press, 1927), p. 375.

[58] It also occurs in the Cyrus Cylinder and is quoted above.

[59] A. K. Grayson, *Assyrian Royal Inscriptions*, vol. 1, *From the Beginning to Ashur-resha-ishi I* (Wiesbaden: Harrassowitz, 1972), p. 4.

[60] Grayson, *Assyrian*, p. 19.

[61] I have already noted continuity with this tradition in the Cyrus Cylinder, but two other inscriptions which pre-date Darius also illustrate this continuity: "Ariararamnes, the great king, king of kings, king of Persian" (AmH) and "Arsames, the great king, king of kings, king of Persia" (AsH) [Kent, *Old Persian*, p. 116].

whereas in the Persian text the king is "king of countries containing all kinds of men." Liverani argues that the concept of empire as found in Assyrian ideology is based on a "theory of qualitative diversities" or dualities: a duality of space (a central-imperial-civilized-cosmic zone versus a peripheral-chaotic zone); a duality of time (a time of disorder before "the creation," i.e. before the establishment of Assyrian rule); a duality of men (Assyrians versus foreigners); and a duality of goods (manufactured goods and even ideological goods such as order, justice and protection versus raw materials).[62] This ideology was intended for the Assyrian population who had be motivated "as if they were working in their own interest against the foreigners—whilst in fact they are working with the foreigners to the advantage of the ruling class."[63] Thus, the ideology of the Assyrian empire "matched" its administrative practices which, as we noted above, were highly centralized. The Persians, on the other hand, ruled over a humanity which is differentiated according to nationality: "king of countries containing all kinds of men." As Koch puts it, "Die Vielen sind nicht eine ununterscheidbare Masse, ein unübersehbares Sklavenheer, über das sich einsam der Monarch erhebt, sondern eine gegliederte Menge, deren jeweilige Besonderheit wohl zu beachten ist."[64] Every nation also has its appropriate place within the universal imperial order which was disrupted prior to the Persians.

> Ahuramazda, when he saw this earth in commotion, thereafter bestowed it upon me, made me king; I am king. By the favor of Ahuramazda I put it down *in its place*; what I said to them, that they did, as was my desire.[65] [Italics mine]

The same idea is found in Susa:

> Saith Darius the King: Much which was ill-done, that I made good. Provinces were in commotion; one man smiting the other. The following I brought about by the favor of Ahuramazda, that the one does not smite the other at all, *each one is in his place*. My law [*data*]—of that they feel fear, so that the stronger does not smite or destroy the weak.[66] [Italics mine]

---

[62] Liverani, "Ideology," pp. 305–14.
[63] Liverani, "Ideology," p. 299.
[64] Koch, "Weltordnung," p. 59.
[65] DNa, lines 30–37 [Kent, *Old Persian*, p. 138].
[66] DSe, lines 30–41 [Kent, *Old Persian*, p. 142].

And finally from the Behistun inscription:

> I reestablished the people on its foundation, both Persia and Media and the other provinces. As before, so I brought back what had been taken away. By the favor of Ahuramazda this I did: I strove until I reestablished our royal house on its foundation as (it was) before (lines 66–70).[67]

An integral part of this order as established by the Persians is the law (*data*) of the king, a concept which relates to a general legal order not a law code.

> Als Instrument der Weltregierung bezweckt es nach dem Kontext nicht, die Menschheit zu nivellieren und womöglich ein einheitliches Staatvolk zu schaffen, wie es wohl das Ziel assyrischer Herrscher war, sondern im Gegenteil, durch Wahrung der Verschiedenheit der Länder-Völker die Reichseinheit zu fördern. Hier scheint ein föderalistisches Prinzip durch, welches begreiflich macht, warum die Grosskönige jene kultische Toleranz betreiben und Gesetze sammeln lassen, welche den Landesbrauch aufgreifen . . .[68]

It is exactly at this point that, according to Koch and Frei, ideology corresponds to administrative reality. The administration of the empire was a combination of central and local authority, including various local/national legal codes within an overarching legal order. Frei cites a number of examples in which the central administration recognizes and sanctions local law, including examples in the Old Testament.[69] Frei concludes from this that the Persian administration entertained the concept of constitutionality (*Rechtsstaatlichkeit*). "Der Untertan war nicht Untertan, er war Reichsangehöriger."[70]

Frei's conclusions are supported by Nylander's study of Persian imperial art. In contrast to the "Machtkunst" of Assyria and Egypt emphasizing domination and humiliation, "the Achaemenid representations consistently show the personifications of foreign lands as free, dignified men who may even bear arms in the presence of the king. On Darius's so-called Suez Canal Stela the nations appear as fully grown, free men, a schema for which no prototypes seem to be

---

[67] DB, col. 1, lines 66–70 [Kent, *Old Persian*, p. 120].

[68] Koch, "Weltordnung," p. 63.

[69] H. Frei, "Zentralgewalt und Lokalautonomie im Achämenidenreich," in H. Frei and K. Koch, *Reichsidee und Reichsorganization im Perserreich* (OBO 55; Göttingen: Vandenhoeck & Ruprecht, 1984), pp. 8–43. The most important example is the "Trilingual [stele] of Letoon" in which Satrap Pixodaros endorses a local decree dealing with the establishment and maintenance of a local Carian god.

[70] Frei, "Zentralgewalt," p. 27.

known in Egypt."[71] Persian imperial iconography thus expresses "a specific set of emblems for kingship and empire, a vision using images of piety and harmony rather than those of conquest and control"; in short, a federalist "ideology of commonwealth."[72]

Whilst these conclusions may exaggerate the situation somewhat, in that for the majority of people membership in the Persian empire was just as oppressive as any other, the textual and visual evidence does demonstrate the way in which discursive space was created for the construction of an imperial practice and ideology which could and did include many nations and peoples. Reading the attitude toward the Persians that we find in Ezra-Nehemiah and the Persian evidence together, we see that from the historical-contextual perspective the "outside initiative" theory of the origin of the community as put forward in Ezra-Nehemiah is a plausible one. This involved, in my view, the collaboration of the Jews living in Babylon—especially the Jews of the former ruling classes in Judah who saw themselves as representing the heart and soul of Israel—and the Persian imperial administration. The restoration was probably not initiated from the Persian side but the administrative policies and ideological practices of the Persians were of the sort as to allow for positive Jewish participation.

The Nature of the Post-Exilic Community

Before leaving the historical questions as to the plausibility of the story of origin as told by the author of Ezra-Nehemiah we must consider briefly the nature of the community established by this "outside initiative." Two key issues need to be addressed: the external political status of the community and the internal social structure of the community.

Regarding the external political status of the community in the empire, there are two main positions on this issue: Judah was *either* reconstituted as a province by the Persians in the sixth century under Sheshbazzar and/or Zerubbabel *or* continued to be a part of the province of Samaria until Nehemiah's time (assuming that it was incorporated into the province of Samaria by the Babylonians).

---

[71] C. Nylander, "Achaemenid Imperial Art," in M. Trolle Larsen (ed.), *Power and Propaganda: A Symposium on Ancient Empires* (Mesopotamia 7; Copenhagen: Akademisk Forlag, 1979), p. 353.

[72] Nylander, "Achaemenid," pp. 355–6.

The first option is based largely on the texts which speak of "governors" (sg. פחה) prior to Nehemiah.[73] The use of פחה with reference to "governors of the province Beyond the River"[74] suggests that when the term is used with reference to leaders in the Judean community it should also be understood as referring to an official appointed by the Persians in charge of the "province" (מדינה)[75] of Judah.[76]

The second option, put forward by Alt[77] responds to those aspects of the text which suggest that the political status of Judah and the community of returnees was a matter of considerable political conflict prior to Nehemiah. For example, when Tattenai, the governor of the province Beyond the River, makes inquiries as the rebuilding of Jerusalem (Ezra 5:3ff) he does not address a governor such as Zerubbabel but rather negotiates with the "elders of the Jews" (Ezra 5:5). Furthermore, the opposition to the rebuilding of the temple involving the Samarians suggests that they had some sort of jurisdiction over what was going on in Jerusalem.

Needless to say, the historical and philological arguments in favour of Alt's thesis can be and have been countered. For example, Zerubbabel's appointment could have been made after Tattenai's visit. Nor is there any "positive" evidence in support of Alt's theory of a larger Samarian province. But the evidence doesn't allow us to be more precise about the external political status and jurisdiction of Judah.[78]

It would seem, however, that we can be more precise about the social structure of the community.[79] An alternative to the "external

---

[73] Neh. 5:15. In Hag. 1:1, 14; 2:2, 21, Zerubbabel is referred to as "governor." Mal. 1:18 also mentions "gifts" (taxes?) for the "governor."

[74] Ezra 8:36; Neh. 2:7 et al.

[75] Hag. 1:1 et al.

[76] M. Smith, *Palestinian Parties and Politics that Shaped the Old Testament* (New York: Columbia University Press, 1971), pp. 147–53; and H. G. M. Williamson, "The Governors of Judah under the Persians," *TynBul* 39 (1988), pp. 59–82, defend this view.

[77] A. Alt, "Die Role Samarias in der Entstehung des Judentums," in *Kleine Schriften zur Geschichte des Volkes Israel, II* (München: C. H. Beck, 1953), pp. 316–37.

[78] The archeological evidence relating to the existence of governors of Judah in inconclusive. On the basis of the occurrence of הפחואַ and הפחה with personal names, N. Avigad, *Bullae and Seals from a Post-exilic Judean Archive* (Jerusalem: Israel Exploration Society, 1976), has attempted to reconstruct a list of governors from bullae and seals from the Persian period. E. M. Meyers, "Shelomith Seal" *EI* 18 (1985), pp. 33–38, affirms this view.

[79] D. L. Smith, *The Religion of the Landless: The Social Context of the Babylonian Exile* (Bloomington, IN: Meyer Stone, 1989), p. 113.

status" approach is the citizen-temple community hypothesis of Weinberg.[80] According to Weinberg, the citizen-temple community is an intermediary formation which was not coterminous with the province of Judah but which eventually came to dominate the province.[81] The citizen-temple hypothesis addresses the same level of community organization as is addressed in the text as it relates to its institutional structures, its concepts of membership and forms of leadership. That is to say, the self-understanding of the community had much more to do with the issue of "citizenship" and access to the temple than with its external political status and the function of its governors. These latter issues are significant in the text insofar as leaders of the community are at the same time acting as Persian officials of one kind or another.

Weinberg's hypothesis is based on two types of evidence. Firstly, it is based on the genealogical texts of Ezra-Nehemiah which suggest, to Weinberg, demographic changes in the community. When the population numbers for the community found in Ezra 2//Nehemiah 7 and those in Neh. 11:25–36 are compared with each other and with the supposed total population of Judah (using pre-exilic texts as a guideline),[82] Weinberg notes an increase in the size of the citizen-temple community from 20–70% of the total.[83] The problem with this argument is that it is very difficult to take the figures in Ezra-Nehemiah at face value let alone to calculate the total population of Judah prior to the Babylonian exile. Neh. 11:25–36, for example, is an ideal portrayal of Judah based on Joshua 15–18.[84]

----

[80] J. P Weinberg, *The Citizen-Temple Community* (trans. D. L. Smith-Christopher; JSOTS 151; Sheffield: JSOT Press, 1992), pp. 34–48. He argues that because Nehemiah is called פחה but without a toponym he is not governor of the province of Judah.

[81] Although Weinberg holds to Alt's hypothesis as well, one could well imagine that the two entities co-existed from the sixth century.

[82] 2 Kgs. 24:14–15; 25:11, 19; Jer. 52:27, 30.

[83] Weinberg, *Citizen-Temple*, pp. 34–48.

[84] J. Blenkinsopp, "Temple and Society in Achaemenid Judah." in P. R. Davies (ed.), *Second Temple Studies*, vol. 1, *The Persian Period* (JSOTS 117; Sheffield: JSOT Press), pp. 42–4. An attempt has been made recently to firm up the demographics from the side of archeology. Carter has suggested that Judah was a relatively small and vulnerable community in the Persian empire. His evidence from archaeological surveys suggests that Judah was a small province of approximately 620 square miles (excluding the Shephelah and the coastal plain) with a population approximately 11,000 in Persian Period I (i.e. prior to Nehemiah's mission) rising to 17,000 in Persian Period II. These demographic figures are provisional at best but this does not lessen the fact that they contradict the much larger estimates of

The other type of evidence Weinberg appeals to is the comparative material from citizen-temple communities in the Neo-Babylonian, Persian and Hellenistic periods.[85] The one feature that these communities have in common, other than having a temple as a central institution, is the belief that the god is the owner of the land; though it must be said at the outset that this one ideologeme is used to justify quite different relations of production. Membership in these communities, which were organized along kinship lines, determined access to the cult and established one's right to land.[86] Weinberg classifies these communities in terms of the pattern of land ownership.

In group A-1, the temple is *de facto* the owner of the land. The land is divided among the members of the community, though some of the land is managed directly by the temple. In Uruk, for example, the affairs of the temple were administered by a city-temple assembly which was divided into ancestral houses. Membership in this assembly was limited to those who held property and by ethnic criteria. The land managed directly by the temple was sublet to dependent farmers who made up a large portion of the population. The temple was also the largest employer of slaves. Ethnic minorities had their own assemblies, but the main assembly of Uruk dealt with a wider range of issues, even those involving ethnic minorities.[87]

A similar pattern is found in Babylon (though this is not cited by Weinberg as an example). Full-fledged citizens in Babylon were members of one of a number of temple assemblies. Only full-fledged citizens held property in the communal district which was under the assembly's jurisdiction. The citizen body included high ranking offi-

---

the population of Yehud, such as Weinberg's 200,000, by a huge margin. The population in Jerusalem in Persian period II would have represented approximately ten percent of the total population or 1250–1500, which is "well within the 5 to 10 percent average of urban centres in the pre-industrial age. But this sort of demographic analysis is also controversial especially as it relates to the co-efficient used to get from settlement size to population size. These are based on contemporary population densities in the Middle East which may or may not be comparable with the ancient settlement patterns [C. Carter, "The Province of Yehud in the Post-Exilic Period: Soundings in Site Distribution and Demography," in T. Eskenazi and K. Richards (eds.), *Second Temple Studies*, vol. 2, *Temple and Community in the Persian Period* (JSOTS 175; Sheffield: JSOT Press, 1994), pp. 106–45].

[85] See M. Dandamaev, "Babylonia in the Persian Age," in *Cambridge History of Judaism*, vol. 1, *Introduction: The Persian Period* (Cambridge: Cambridge University Press, 1984), pp. 330–1.

[86] Cf. Ezek. 11:15–17 and Lev. 25:23. See J. Blenkinsopp, *Ezra-Nehemiah* (OTL; Philadelphia: Westminster Press, 1988), p. 60.

[87] I. Eph'al, "The Western Minorities in Babylonia in the 6th–5th Centuries BC: Maintenance and Cohesion," *Orientalia* 47 (1978), pp. 74–90.

cials, craftsmen, and peasants and the status of each of these groups was hereditary. The temple owned large tracts of land and irrigation canals which were leased to dependent farmers. The temple also owned slaves who were employed in tasks connected with the running of the temple or in manufacture. The citizens lived separately from the dependent farmers and other inhabitants of the city, such as foreign residents and slaves.[88] Elders played a prominent role in the running of the assembly. They were called upon to solve important local issues, often in conjunction with temple officials and governors of the city, relating to temple affairs, property disputes and the like. They also acted as representatives of the city before the king.[89]

A different social structure obtained in Comana in Cappadocia and Comana in Pontus, contradicting Weinberg's classification.[90] Unlike the previous two examples, in which full-citizens together with the temple clergy, administrated the affairs of the community and temple lands, it was the high priest of the temple (both dedicated to the moon-goddess Ma) who had immediate jurisdiction and was next in rank only to the king of Cappadocia (the high priest was usually a member of the royal family). The temples owned large estates and a large number of slaves (*hierodouloi*)[91] and the high priests enjoyed the surplus production from the temple estates.[92]

---

[88] Blenkinsopp, "Temple and Society," p. 33.

[89] M. A. Dandamaev, "The Neo-Babylonian Elders," in M. Dandamaev, et al. (eds.), *Societies and Languages of the Ancient Near East* (Festschrift I. M. Diakonoff; Warminster: Aris and Phillips, 1982), pp. 38–41. Sarkisian describes the relationship between temple and community in the Seleucid period as the "gradual merging of the temple personnel with the more or less well-to-do strata of the urban population.... Many members of the community, although not all, nor even the majority, occupied offices in the temples, but their service in a temple was not obligatory. Most of the members of the community were private persons independent of the temples, though connected with them by various ties.... But it was doubtless the political rights ensuing from one's membership in the civic-and-temple community that mattered most" [G. Kh. Sarkisian, "City Land in Seleucid Babylonia," in I. M. Diakonoff (ed.), *Ancient Mesopotamia. Socio-Economic History: A Collection of Studies by Soviet Scholars* (Moscow: Nauka, 1969), pp. 313–14].

[90] Weinberg simply names Comana without specifying which one he meant. Since they are virtually identical, though, it doesn't really matter. Weinberg also cites Zela (in Pontus) as an example of group A-1 but again it doesn't conform to his classification. Zela was built by the Persians and dedicated to the Persian goddess Anahita/Anaitis and was ruled by a high priest and temple servants made up the largest part of the population. See *Pauly-Wissowa*, Supplement XIV, for "Zela."

[91] In Comana of Pontus, the slaves could not be sold since they were attached to the land.

[92] See *Pauly-Wissowa*, vol. XI.1; and R. Stillwell (ed.), *The Princeton Encyclopedia of Classical Sites* (Princeton: Princeton University Press, 1976), pp. 233–4.

In group A-2, the temple is *de facto* owner of the land, but does not have direct role in its administration. Mylasa was the most important town in Caria and had a number of temples dedicated to Zeus. A sacred road sixty stadia long connected two of these temples and during a yearly festival a religious procession would move along it from one temple to the other. The town was of pre-Greek origin and was alternately dominated by Greece and Persia. The population was divided into *phylae* and *synagogae* each with a particular patronym. Each *phyla* had a particular god with its own temple and temple land. The enlargement and leasing of this temple land is the main topic of the inscriptions kept in the temple. Each *phyla* had its own elected administration (known as the "representatives of the gods") which was responsible for these land transactions. The city administration (*boule/demos*) was the highest authority and was also made up of elected members. Officers chosen from the assembly were called elders (*archairesiai*). The elders of the *boule* were made up of the elders of the *phyla* and priestly duties were connected with eldership. The high priesthood was probably acquired via purchase. Mylasa was involved in a religious association with Miletus and the main temple of Zeus Karios was located here. Judges for the region also came from Mylasa.[93]

According to Weinberg's hypothesis the citizen-temple community in Judah is the only example of group B ("group" is thus a misnomer) in which the temple doesn't own land. It can nonetheless be classified along with these other groups because the community was dominated by the temple and the land was "owned" by the god of that temple. In common with the citizen-temple communities of Mesopotamia, the affairs of the Judean community were administered by the assembly in which both priests *and* elders played a leading role. Indeed it would appear that the role of the elders in the community was crucial in maintaining identity "across" the pre-exilic, exilic and post-exilic periods.[94] That is to say, the citizen-temple community in Judah,

---

[93] See *Pauly-Wissowa*, vol. XI.1; and *Princeton Encyclopedia of Classical Sites*, p. 601.

[94] In the pre-exilic period the elders are leaders who had a role in the religious, political and judicial affairs of cities (cf. Jer. 19:1 and 26:17). In the exile they appear as the leaders of the community (see Jer. 29:11; and Ezek. 8:1; et al.) thus indicating some continuity of social structure in Babylon. According to Rost the elders were over the משפחה in the pre-exilic period and were replaced by the "heads" after the exilic. See Smith, *Religion*, pp. 94–8; and the discussion of the post-exilic "heads" in chapter five.

like its Mesopotamian counterparts, was a *theocratic community* in which the temple was the central institution, not a hierocracy ruled solely by priests (as in the two Comana's discussed above). Another point of contact with the Mesopotamian examples is that membership in the Judean citizen-temple community seems to have been determined by ethnic criteria (Ezra 9). That is to say, the citizen-temple community is a social entity in which social boundaries—and along with that the maintenance of ethnic identity—were all-important. And whilst there was no doubt considerable overlap between the citizen-temple community and the province of Judah in terms of "personnel" and leadership, the *political* status of the province would have been of secondary importance.[95] This does not, of course, solve the problem as to the status of the community prior to Nehemiah but whatever the actual relationship between the two aspects of the post-exilic community were, one has to take into account considerable development and variation over time. Weinberg himself argues that, although considerable progress was made in the sixth century (not least the rebuilding of the temple), it was only by the time of Nehemiah that the post-exilic citizen-temple community was fully established.[96]

Though doubts have been expressed as to "whether we are dealing with a quite distinct form of sociological organization, as the theory requires, or simply variations of a common [temple assembly] pattern" that had existed in Mesopotamia for millennia,[97] Weinberg's thesis has found qualified acceptance in so far as it is able to synthesize the temple-community-land dimensions of life as referred to in the sources and place this nexus within a broader socio-historical context. Blenkisopp's recent reconstruction, for example, is simply a qualified version of the citizen-temple community hypothesis. The community of the post-exilic period which described itself as "the assembly of the golah, the assembly of those who returned from captivity, and the assembly of God"[98] was a self-contained entity which

---

[95] Smith, *Religion*, pp. 107–8.

[96] Weinberg, *Citizen-Temple*, pp. 105–26.

[97] Blenkinsopp, "Temple and Society," pp. 29–30.

[98] Citing Ezra 10:8; Neh. 8:17; and 13:1, respectively. The references to קהל in Ezra-Nehemiah are as follows: קהל Ezra 10:1; Neh. 8:2; כל הקהל Ezra 2:64; 10:12, 14; Neh. 5:13; 7:66; 8:17; קהלה גדולה Neh. 5:7; קהל האלהים Neh. 13:1. The verb קהל is used four times in Samuel-Kings, two times in Ezekiel, fourteen times in Chronicles, and four times in Ezra-Nehemiah. The noun קהל is used nine times in Samuel-Kings, thirteen times in Ezekiel, thirty four times in Chronicles, and eleven times in Ezra-Nehemiah (a related noun, קהלה, one time).

defined itself over against its immediate neighbours in the area. "By assuming responsibility for the actual rebuilding of the temple, with the backing of the imperial authorities and to the exclusion of the native population (Ezra 4:1–3), they reserved to themselves control of the temple operations, which translated into a large measure of social control."[99]

And regarding the "exilic" origins of the post-exilic community, Blenkinsopp argues that the "assembly of the golah" replicated the more important features of their life in exile and is typologically comparable to the ethnic minority assemblies in Babylonia.[100]

> They reconstituted their own assembly (*puhru, qahal*), organized according to ancestral houses including, free, property-owning citizens and temple personnel, under the leadership of tribal elders and the supervision of an imperial representative, in a cohesive social entity which, while allowing for additional adherents, was jealously protective of its status and privileges.[101]

To summarize: The "outside initiative hypothesis" is an historically plausible account of the origin of the post-exilic community in light of both Persian policy and ideology and the comparative material for citizen-temple communities. Hence, the origin of the post-exilic Jewish community should be sought among the members of the exilic community in Babylonia. This exile community, which was a synthesis of the former ruling and priestly classes of Judah, developed community structures designed to maintain their religious and ethnic identity in the face of a dominant culture.[102] As such their situation was analogous to both the many ethnic minority communities in Mesopotamia, and to the larger temple assemblies which dominated the ancient cities of Mesopotamia (in memory and outlook if not in actuality).[103] This community, as an already distinct ethnic entity, could therefore envision and portray themselves to the Persians as a loyal citizen-temple community in waiting. When the opportunity arose to reclaim their past, their temple, and their land it was

---

[99] Blenkinsopp, "Temple and Society," p. 45.

[100] Blenkinsopp, "Temple and Society," pp. 51–3.

[101] Blenkinsopp, "Temple and Society," p. 53.

[102] See Smith, *Religion*, for a sociological treatment of the exilic community and its religion.

[103] Some have suggested the possibility of there being a Jewish temple in Babylonia. See the discussions of Ezra 8:17 in Williamson, *Ezra, Nehemiah*, p. 117; and Blenkinsopp, *Ezra-Nehemiah*, pp. 165–6.

not an opportunity to be missed. In the process of "restoration," the "exilic" identity of the community was maintained as the main criteria of membership in the citizen-temple community in the province of Judah. That is to say, the ethnic criteria which had served the purpose of maintaining identity in a minority situation in Babylon were transformed in the post-exilic setting and adapted for the purpose of establishing the social boundaries of, and social control over, the affairs in the *post-exilic* community which ultimately came to dominate the province of Judah.

Ezra-Nehemiah: A Vertical Ethnic Ideology

Having examined the historical plausibility of the "exilic" origins of the "post-exilic" community and the role this played in determining the nature of the community, we turn our attention to the way in which the question of the identity of the community is handled in Ezra-Nehemiah and Chronicles and the significance of exile within their distinct ideologies of identity. The point of interest, especially in dealing with Ezra-Nehemiah, is not the sociological realities to which the texts refers but the way in which the text presents them. Assuming for the sake of argument that intermarriage was an issue in the post-exilic community, what I want to examine is the way in which this issue is handled and what this may tell us about the writer's ideology of identity.

In the story of the restoration told by Ezra-Nehemiah, the specifically "exilic" identity of the assembly figures into every aspect of community life and most prominently in issues relating to inter-community conflict and boundary definition. The narrative articulates what I call a vertical ethnic ideology of identity and it does so in terms of the on-going struggle for survival as a distinct entity in the face of outside pressures and competition. Since the stories about intermarriage problems are prime expressions of this concern my analysis of the ideology of identity of Ezra-Nehemiah will focus on the narratives concerning intermarriage found in Ezra 9–10 and Nehemiah 13.

Excursus on the Vertical-Lateral Typology

In characterizing the ideologies of identity in Ezra-Nehemiah and Chronicles I use the typology of ethnic groups proposed by A. D. Smith. Smith uses the spatial metaphors "vertical" and "lateral" to describe the degree to which ethnic culture penetrates different ethnic groups (which he calls *ethnie*).

> As a first step, it is useful to distinguish between two processes in ethnic life: on the one hand, towards an extension of the *ethnie* in space at the cost of any social depth, and on the other hand, a social "deepening" of ethnic culture at the cost of its tight circumscription in space. The former process leads to what may be termed "lateral" *ethnie*, the latter to "vertical" *ethnie*.[104]

The prototypical vertical *ethnie* is the minority group or enclave which distinguishes itself from society at large.[105] The deep penetration of culture characteristic of this type of group results in a relatively unified, demotic and egalitarian society. It is assumed that everyone on the inside should think and act in the same way, but because it is governed by concensus and moral persuasion factional disputes are endemic and splits inevitable. The overriding concern within the enclave is for boundary maintenance and its greatest fear the loss of members. The "outside" is thus a threat to the community, but insofar as the enclave is dependent of the "outside" for resources and/or protection it must, paradoxically, reach an accommodation with it.

A lateral *ethnie*, on the other hand, is not a dependent community. It is best exemplified by the multi-ethnic state in which one group is dominant. Smith cites the Hittites as an example of a lateral ethnic group comprising a community of feudal nobles, priests and warriors who incorporated lesser communities as "partners" in an "unequal federalism" which was maintained in the political sphere by treaties and in the religious sphere by a "spiritual federalism."[106] The lateral *ethnie* is thus a hierarchical culture which incorporates groups of varying status and with different roles to play within a

---

[104] A. D. Smith, "The Politics of Culture: Ethnicity and Nationalism," in *Companion Encyclopedia of Anthropology* (London: Routledge, 1994), p. 713. The emphasis on ethnicity as *process* is characteristic of the approach to ethnicity pioneered by F. Barth, *Ethnic Groups and Boundaries: The Social Organization of Culture Difference* (Bergen: Scandinavian University Press, 1969). Barth was critical of the "cultural traits" approach to ethnicity which could not deal with the fact that ethnic "boundaries persis despite a flow of personnel across them." In his research he noted the way in which ethnic distinctions are maintained via a "process of exclusion and incorporation" [Barth, *Ethnic Groups*, p. 9].

[105] Mary Douglas's distinction between enclavist and hierarchical cultures complements Smith's typology. See M. Douglas [*In the Wilderness: The Doctrine of Defilement in the Book of Numbers* (JSOTS 158; Sheffield: JSOT Press, 1993), pp. 42–78].

[106] Smith, "Politics," p. 713.

well-defined social structure. Central in the ideology of a lateral ethnie is the "idea of an encompassing whole"[107] which embraces and
defines the diversity within.

The merit of this typology of social groups is that, unlike a strictly
etic approach, it takes in to account the way in which groups per-
ceive themselves (emics) but allows for a broadly etic classification
of the cultural strategies that underlie ideologies of identity. It can
also account for the fact that ideologies of identity are also the subject of internal debate and conflict which means that there is no
straightforward correlation between the classification of a group according to its social structures and institutions and a classfication of
its ethnic ideology or cultural strategy. Thus, although the post-exilic
community was an enclave, sociologically-speaking, this does not
mean that its "culture" was uniformly enclavist or that its ethnic
strategy was strictly vertical. Quite the opposite, for when viewed in
this way the contrast between the ideology of identity expressed in
Ezra-Nehemiah and the one put forward in Chronicles is rather stark.

Ezra 9–10

The problem of intermarriage is described in Ezra 9:1–2 as a failure on the part of "the people of Israel, the priests and the Levites"
to separate themselves (הבדיל) from "the peoples of the lands with
their abominations, from the Canaanites, the Hittites, the Perizzites,
the Jebusites, the Ammonites, the Moabites, the Egyptians, and the
Amorites." The result is that through intermarriage "the holy seed
has mixed itself with the peoples of the lands." The language used
to describe this "crisis" is heavily coloured by the language of the
Torah where it warns of the danger of intermarriage with the indige-
nous Canaanite population. According to Deuteronomy 7, Israel is
to destroy "the Hittites, the Girgashites, the Amorites, the Canaanites,
the Perizzites, the Hivites and the Jebusites" and not intermarry with
them because of the danger of idolatry.[108] This list of the deadly
seven nations is expanded via Deuteronomy 23 which states that
"No Ammonite or Moabite shall be admitted into the assembly of
the LORD. Even to the tenth generation, none of their descendants
shall be admitted to the assembly of the LORD. . . ." The assembly

---

[107] Douglas, *In the Wilderness*, p. 64.
[108] Cf. Exod. 34:11 which warns Israel about making a covenant and intermarrying with these same nations, excluding the Girgashites.

(קהל) is, of course, the covenant community of the sons of Israel and the use of assembly in Ezra in the context of inter-community conflict clearly echoes this Deuteronomic passage.[109] Regarding the Egyptians, Deut. 23:7 specifically exempts them (and the Edomites) from these exclusionary measures (described in terms of "not abhorring" them). That is to say, Ezra 9 represents a re-interpretation of Deuteronomy 7 and 23 which presupposes that these texts apply to the "current" inter-marriage problem.[110]

Though it is rather surprising that the contemporary "peoples of the lands" are identified with the Canaanite population of old, Williamson argues that the principle of these laws is nonetheless upheld; namely, that the surrounding peoples represented a religious (as indicated by the use of "abominations"), not racial or ethnic threat to the post-exilic community.[111] He does, however, acknowledge that the notion of the mixing of "holy seed" is essentially a racial definition of peoplehood. The phrase "holy seed" recalls Mal. 2:11ff where Israel is criticized for desecrating the holiness of Yahweh by marrying the daughter of a foreign god. In verse 15 the offspring of a proper marriage are called "godly seed." The genealogy of this concept may be traced back even further: Exod. 19:5–6, Deut. 7:6, and 14:1–2 speak of the corporate holiness of Israel in terms of it being a "holy nation" (גוי קדוש/עם קדוש). Ps. 106:35 speaks of Israel "mixing with the nations" that should have been destroyed when they entered the land. This constitutes an act of unfaithfulness (מעל) which, according to Ezra's prayer, has in the past led to them being "handed over to the kings of the lands, to the sword, to captivity, to plundering, and to utter shame, as is now the case" (Ezra 9:7). Those who, with Ezra are most deeply affected by this situation are described as "all who trembled at the words of the God of Israel."[112]

The matter is dealt with at a "very great assembly . . . out of Israel" (Ezra 10:1) and the people "make a covenant . . . to send away all these wives and their children, according to the counsel of my lord and of those who tremble at the commandment of our

---

[109] Lev. 18:23–30 condemns the Canaanites and their land because it impure (טמא) with abominations (תועבת) including incest (v. 19). Ammon and Moab were, of course, offspring of the incestuous relationship between Lot and his daughters [M. Fishbane, *Biblical Interpretation in Ancient Israel* (Oxford: Clarendon, 1985), p. 119].

[110] Fishbane, *Biblical Interpretation*, pp. 115–17.

[111] Williamson, *Ezra, Nehemiah*, p. 130.

[112] The context suggests that Ezra represented a group that observed the Torah according to a strict interpretation. See also Isa. 66.

God" (10:3). Those that do not show up for the mass divorce proceedings forfeit all their property (רכוש) and are "banned from the congregation of the exiles" (10:8).

The intermarriage crisis as described in Ezra 9–10, like the conflict between the returnees and their neighbours, is often interpreted in roughly the same terms as it is described in Ezra-Nehemiah; that it was really a question of their survival as an ethnically and/or religiously distinct community. Smith-Christopher, for example, understands Ezra's call for endogamy in terms of group boundary maintenance. When a group's identity is under stress it tends to fall back "on the primary ties of the kinship network."[113] Smith-Christopher wagers that lower status Jewish males were marrying up among higher status females outside their community.[114]

In a similar vein, Washington contends that intermarriage threatened the economic stability of the province by threatening its land base. Washington interprets the warnings about the strange woman in Prov. 1–9 in terms of the social context of Judah in the Persian period. The central text in Washington's argument is Prov. 2:21–22: "For the upright will abide in the land, and the innocent will remain in it; but the wicked will be cut off from the land and the treacherous will be rooted out of it." The "strange/foreign" (though not necessarily non-Israelite or even non-Judean) woman is an economic threat to the golah community because within the patrilineal land tenure system women were capable of inheriting and disposing of property.[115]

But Smith-Christopher and Washington's arguments are not entirely convincing. Is it possible for exogamy to be a widespread practice and still be understood as a threat to the survival of the community?

---

[113] D. L. Smith-Christopher, "The Mixed Marriage Crisis in Ezra 9–10 and Nehemiah 13: A Study of the Sociology of the Post-Exilic Judean Community," in T. Eskenazi and K. Richards (eds.), *Second Temple Studies*, vol. 2, *Temple and Community in the Persian Period* (JSOTS 175; Sheffield: JSOT Press, 1994), p. 252 [citing E. L. Cerroni-Long, "Marrying Out: Socio-Cultural and Psychological Implications of Intermarriage," *Journal of Comparative Family Studies* 15 (1984), p. 28].

[114] Smith-Christopher, "Mixed Marriage," p. 249.

[115] H. C. Washington, "The Strange Woman of Proverbs 1–9 and Post-Exilic Judean Society," in T. Eskenazi and K. Richards (eds.), *Second Temple Studies*, vol. 2, *Temple and Community in the Persian Period* (JSOTS 175; Sheffield: JSOT Press, 1994), pp. 217–42. Hoglund also cites the economic reason: "Loss of such [ethnic] distinction carried with it the possible diminution of collective privileges or property and subsequent impoverishment of the assembly" [K. Holgund, "The Achaemenid Context," in P. R. Davies (ed.), *Second Temple Studies*, vol. 1, *The Persian Period* (JSOTS 117; Sheffield: JSOT Press, 1991), p. 67].

Was not the practice of exogamy a reasonable balance between the need for ethnic "vertical" delineation and "lateral" interaction? Perhaps it was reasonable to some and not to others or was the community not completely in touch with the consequences of the actions of its members? Looking at it from another angle, what are we to make of Ezra's objections to intermarriage? One possible explanation is that immigrant communities, like the returnees, are initially willing to accept exogamy but that those who arrive later on, once the community is established, reject it.[116] In other words, economic necessity demands it early on but as time goes by it is no longer a compelling enough reason to override less pragmatic ethnic values. This line of reasoning requires that we seriously modify these economic explanations for exogamy or abandon them altogether.

What we are left with are the internal contradictions or dynamic tensions between different aspects of ethnic identity. Ezra's (or the author's) concern for ethnic purity can not be explained in terms of some unambiguous rationale. He may well have thought that he was acting in an unambiguous way—that he was protecting the unique identity of the post-exilic community—but that does not mean that his actions had these consequences. Nor can we assume that the "foreign" wives of Ezra 9 and 10 were really foreign. Smith-Christopher, though adopting a "boundary definition" approach, recognizes that these social boundaries were not firmly drawn and uncontroversial. The issue was as much the definition of a "mixed" marriage as the reality of mixed marriages. According to Smith-Christopher, Ezra's point of view is representative of those who limit "Jews" to the returnees while the "outsiders" are *Jewish* remainees; in other words, the issue was about the definition of Jewishness. He cites two types of evidence: the use of pejorative anachronistic terms to describe the "outsiders"[117] and other texts which show a more inclusive attitude to foreigners (e.g. Isa. 60:1–6, Ruth, Jonah).[118]

---

[116] Smith-Christopher, "Mixed Marriage," pp. 252–3.

[117] Smith-Christopher, "Mixed Marriage," pp. 255–8. According to Blenkinsopp, the conflict between Ezra and those less rigorous in their interpretation of the law is related to a rise in sectarianism [J. Blenkinsopp, "Interpretation and the Tendency to Sectarianism: An Aspect of Second Temple History," in E. P. Sanders (ed.), *Jewish and Christian Self-Definition*. Vol. 2, *Aspects of Judaism in the Graeco-Roman World* (Philadelphia: Fortress, 1981), pp. 1–26; and idem, "A Jewish Sect of the Persian Period," *CBQ* 52 (1990), pp. 5–20].

[118] Mary Douglas adds Numbers to the list of less esclusivist texts such as Isaiah 60, Jonah and Ruth [Douglas, *In the Wilderness*].

This interpretation is explored more fully by Eskenazi and Judd, who interpret the crisis as a conflict between orthodox and non-orthodox Jews, especially as it pertains to the interpretation of the Torah. They compare this situation to the issue of marriage in modern Israel and the Haredim (a group that takes its name from the biblical text in question, namely Ezra 9:4 and 10:3). New rules as to who constituted a Jew in 1970 excluded people who always considered themselves to be Jews. The Haredi call non-Haredi Jews "gentiles" and a marriage involving such a person is considered a mixed marriage. The Chief Rabbinate and the Haredi rabbis will not recognize these marriages because of their restricted definitions of who is a Jew. Those who don't observe the Torah as understood by the Haredi are said to have committed abominations. One should not, therefore, take Ezra's condemnation at face value as referring to non-Jewish practice but rather as referring to less strict Jewish practice or different Jewish practice.[119]

The ideology of identity expressed in Ezra 9–10 is thus more problematic than it may appear at first glance. Whilst it is clearly vertical in orientation, we cannot assume that the "authors" of this ideology were representing the interests of the community at large or that they were aware of the negative consequences such an ideology might have. The fact that we have texts such as Chronicles from roughly the same period that present a different ideology of identity highlights again the need for a dynamic definition of ethnicity.

Nehemiah 13

Neh. 13:1 refers once again to the Ammonites and Moabites though this time the law, as found in Deuteronomy 23, is applied to entry into "the assembly of God." This interpretation of the passage is based on the extension of priestly notions of sanctity and purity to encompass the city of Jerusalem and the community of returnees who "separated from Israel all those of foreign descent" (13:3). Just what sort of separation is meant is not known but the language and ideology is comparable to that found in Ezra 9–10.

Neh. 13:23–27 also refers to the Ammonites and Moabites along with the Ashdodites but this time with reference to another marker

---

[119] T. C. Eskenazi and E. P. Judd, "Marriage to a Stranger in Ezra 1–9," in T. Eskenazi and K. Richards (eds.), *Second Temple Studies*, vol. 2, *Temple and Community in the Persian Period* (JSOTS 175; Sheffield: JSOT Press, 1994), pp. 266–85.

of ethnicity, namely language. The children of those who have inter-married with these nations have lost their ability to speak "the language of Judah." The action taken by Nehemiah is not based on any specific injunction but rather represents a cobbling together of various ideas from the Torah to the story of Solomon in the form of a rigorous exclusivist marriage policy. Foreign women in general are dangerous, and Ashdotite, Ammonite and Moabite women in particular because they undermine the linguistic unity of the community. Those who have intermarried have done a "great evil" and have "acted treacherously" (13:27).[120]

Tagged onto this is the brief account in 13:28 of how Nehemiah "chased away" Jehoida, son of the high priest Eliashib, because he had married the daughter of Sanballat the Horonite (who features prominently among those who opposed Nehemiah's rebuilding project). The marriage involving these two prominent families from Jerusalem and Samaria and Nehemiah's response seems to imply a political clash between Nehemiah and leading elements both within the Jewish community and beyond it. In other words, intermarriage was of political, and not just religious and ethnic, significance. It also highlights that fact that Nehemiah's policies were not accepted by others within the community of returnees.

Hoglund explores the political dimension of these "exclusivist" policies in light of Persian imperial policy in the mid to late fifth century BCE arguing that both Nehemiah and Ezra's missions represent a departure in Persian-Judean relations. He bases this conclusion in part on the description of the building of the walls in Nehemiah 1–4. The use of the term בירה,[121] which in its Aramaic cognate refers to citadels for the garrisoning of imperial troops, together with the general contextual problem of trouble in Egypt suggest that Jerusalem was being more closely integrated into the administrative system and perhaps even the military strategy of the Persians vis-à-vis Judah. Jerusalem was not, of course, on the front line but the building of the walls (and there were many unwalled cities at the time) meant that Jerusalem was intended as a taxation and distribution centre with the garrison there to control the city and the province.[122]

---

[120] For a discussion of the inner biblical intrepretative moves in this text see Fishbane, *Biblical Interpretation*, pp. 125–8.

[121] Neh. 1:1, 2; 7:2.

[122] Hoglund, *Achaemenid*, pp. 207–26.

The security issue can be connected, Hoglund argues, to the inter-marriage problem. As we noted earlier, the Persians used pre-existing ethnic groups for special purposes within the imperial system. During the period of crisis at the beginning of Artaxerxes's reign it was important from the Persian perspective to enhance their control over these distinct communities, particularly those close to trouble spots such as Egypt. To do so would require that the distinctiveness of the community be maintained or enhanced.

The main problem with this explanation is that the missions of Ezra and Nehemiah caused, if anything, more internal dissert rather than less. On a more general level, Hoglund's approach aims at discovering a clear socio-political rationale to explain largely irreduceable ideological tensions that were part of the very fabric of the community.

Chronicles: A Lateral Ethnic Ideology

The ideology of identity in Chronicles represents, in my view, a lateral ethnicity versus a vertical one. The model the Chronicler uses for his community, the united monarchy of David and Solomon, represents the golden age of a greater Israel and contrasts sharply with the picture presented in Ezra-Nehemiah of a small community within a large and all-powerful empire. The contrast between the two ideologies of identity can be illustrated by the following simple two-dimensional diagram:

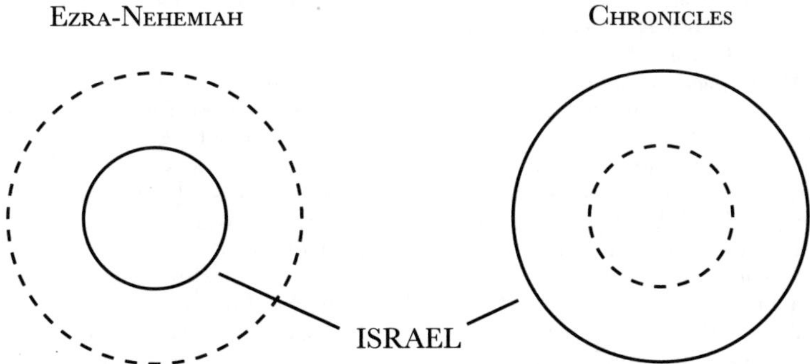

The outer boundaries of "Israel" are similarly defined in both texts. Israel is clearly distinguished from her immediate neighbours such as the Arabs, the Ammonites, the Ashdodites, and the Edomites (Neh. 4:7; 2 Chron. 20). The Chronicler's sense of Israel among the nations is also presented systematically by way of a genealogy in the first chapter of the book. The frame of reference narrows in concentric circles from a view to the whole world beginning with the generations from Adam to Noah (1 Chron. 1–4) and moving counterclockwise from those nations furthest away from Israel (Japheth, vv. 5–7) to those nearer to Israel (Ham, vv. 8–16, and Shem, vv. 17–23).[123] Within the genealogies of Abraham and Isaac the Chronicler first deals with Israel's nearest rivals, Ishmael (vv. 28–33) and Esau (vv. 34–54), before arriving at the focal point of the Chronicler's interest, the descendants of Israel (the patriarch). Israel (the nation) is thus portrayed as a constituent member of an world order established by God at creation.[124]

The internal boundaries within Israel are, however, radically different. Whereas Ezra-Nehemiah makes a clear distinction between the "Israelite" community comprised of the returnees and those who have separated themselves from the people living in the land of Israel, the Chronicler maintains an "all Israel" perspective throughout the book.[125] Again, one can illustrate this with reference to the genealogies. In Ezra-Nehemiah genealogy is used to establish the *exilic* origins of the community. The focus is on that which most clearly distinguishes

---

[123] M. Kartveit, *Motive und Schichten der Landtheologie in I Chronik 1–9* (ConBOT 28; Stockholm: Almqvist & Wiksell, 1989), p. 116.

[124] Cf. 2 Chron. 20:5.

[125] Willi, *Juda, Jehud, Israel*, pp. 55–60, has recently argued that Ezra-Nehemiah also adopts an "all Israel" perspective. He cites as evidence for this view the following: (1) in Ezra 1:3 Cyrus addresses all the people of "Yahweh the God of Israel" to go up and build the temple; (2) the list of returnees ends in 2:70//Neh. 7:73 with the words "and all Israel [lived] in their towns"; (3) in Ezra 7:13 "any of the people of Israel or their priests or Levites in [Artaxerxes] kingdom" may return with Ezra to Jerusalem; (4) 8:25 speaks of the gifts "all Israel" gave to Ezra to take back with him to Jerusalem; (5) in 8:35 those who returned with Ezra offered burnt offerings to the "God of Israel, twelve bulls for all Israel"; and (6) in 10:5 Ezra makes "the leading priests, the Levites, and all Israel swear" that they will put away their foreign wives. None of this adds up to the kind of "all Israel" perspective of the Chronicler which includes residents outside Judah. In fact these texts move in the opposite direction in that "all Israel" is used with reference to returnees only. As for the decrees by the Persians, both are concerned with the going up to Jerusalem and though "all Israel" or "the people of the God of Israel" is addressed the exiles would have thought that only they were meant.

the community of returnees from all the other inhabitants of the land of Israel. The Chronicler, on the other hand, uses the genealogies to present the Israel of the twelve tribes,[126] including those tribes that had (from a post-exilic point of view) long since disappeared.[127] This is not to say that Judah and Jerusalem do not have a distinct place within "all Israel" (hence the inner circle in the diagram),[128] but in comparison to Ezra-Nehemiah the Chronicler is clearly seeking to articulate the idea of Israel as an "encompassing whole."[129]

The connection with pre-exilic Israel is important in both works (cf. Ezra 2:59//Neh. 7:61) but the Chronicler's genealogy links his community with *all Israel* not just Judah, Benjamin and Levi. This is vividly illustrated in the conclusion to the genealogies. Having enumerated (almost) all the tribes, the Chronicler concludes that "All Israel was enrolled by genealogies; and these are written in the Book of the Kings of Israel" (1 Chron. 9:1a). The Chronicler then continues, rather surprisingly, with the notice that ". . . Judah was taken into exile in Babylon because of their unfaithfulness [מעל]" (9:1b). And if that were not enough of a chronological jump he adds:

> Now the first to live again in their possessions in their towns were Israelites, priests, Levites, and temple servants. And some of the people of Judah, Benjamin, Ephraim and Manasseh lived in Jerusalem.

---

[126] There are some lacunae, notably Zebulun and Dan. Some see a fragment of the Danite genealogy in 7:12 [R. Braun, *1 Chronicles* (WBC; Waco, TX: Word, 1986), pp. 106–9]. Since all the tribes are named in 2:1–2, the absence of these two is not explained in terms of a conscious motive [contra Kartveit, *Motive und Schichten*, pp. 130–1; and M. Oeming, *Das wahre Israel: Die "genealogische Vorhalle" 1 Chronik 1–9* (BWANT; Stuttgart: Kohlhammer, 1990), p. 166]. See most recently T. Willi, *Chronik* (BK; Neukirchen-Vluyn: Neukirchener Verlag, 1991).

[127] Simeon's genealogy (1 Chron. 4:24–43) and those of the Transjordanian tribes of Reuben, Gad, and East Manasseh, who were carried away into exile by Tilgath-pilneser (1 Chron. 5).

[128] The hierarchical aspect of the Chronicler's ideology of identity will be discussed in chapter four.

[129] To use Mary Douglas's term for it [*In the Wilderness*, p. 64]. According to her, the idea of the encompassing whole is the hallmark of a culture of hierarchy. An example of this, though on another level entirely, is the way in which the Chronicler synthesizes all of Israel's major "canonical" traditions. Albertz identifies four syntheses accomplished by the Chronicler: (1) the synthesis of Torah and the Former Prophets; (2) the inclusion of prophecy, especially the "conditional" prophecies of judgment and salvation; (3) the incorporation of the psalm traditions, and (4) the incorporation of the tradition of personal piety as expressed in Israel's wisdom literature [R. Albertz, *A History of Israelite Religion in the Old Testament Period*, vol. 2, *From the Exile to the Maccabees* (trans. J. Bowden; London: SCM, 1994), pp. 544–56].

The interpretation and indeed translation[130] of these two verses is disputed (and I will discuss some of the problems interpreters face in the chapter four) but for now (and on the basis of the above translation) I want to draw attention to what this text says about the Chronicler's ideology of identity. Firstly, the Chronicler seems to establish, by the simple juxtapositioning of these three statements, that the post-exilic community stands in direct continuity with the "all Israel" of the remote pre-exilic period, the sons of Israel as meticulously recorded in the "Book of the Kings of Israel." The Israel of the twelve tribes (or at least tribes representative of all Israel) is alive and well *after the exile* (according to the syntax of these sentences) *and living in Jerusalem*. The pairing of Judah and Benjamin, Ephraim and Manasseh, can be understood as a rough approximation of "all Israel," the first two representing the South, the other two the North.[131] In Ezra-Nehemiah, the exile separates the returnees who call themselves "Israel" from the rest who are either identified as specifically non-Israelite or ambiguously as "the people of the land". Israel and Judah are exiled, but only Judah, which calls itself Israel, returns. While there are a number of texts in Chronicles which mention the exile of Judah,[132] only one text deals with the exile of any of the other "northern" tribes, specifically the Transjordanian tribes Reuben, Gad and East Manasseh (1 Chron. 5:26–27). This leaves the impression that the bulk of northern Israel was not taken into exile.

That a radically different notion of Israel is on offer in Chronicles is supported by the Chronicler's account of Hezekiah's reign. It was just before Hezekiah's reign, according to 2 Kings 17, that the Assyrians overthrew the northern kingdom and deported some of its people. The account in Kings presents this deportation as a more or less complete de-population of Israel followed by the resettlement of the land by foreigners (2 Kgs. 17:5–6, 24ff) and the author of Ezra 4:1–3 concurs with this view. The Chronicler on the other hand makes no mention of this exchange of peoples in Shalmaneser's days. Instead he tells how "Hezekiah sent word to all Israel and Judah, and wrote letters also to Ephraim and Manasseh, that they

---

[130] Japhet, *I & II Chronicles*, proposes an emendation which will be discussed in ch. 4.

[131] See 2 Chron. 31:1 and 34:9.

[132] 1 Chron. 6:15 and the allusion to the exile in 3:17.

should come to the house of the LORD at Jerusalem, to keep the Passover to the LORD the God of Israel" (2 Chron. 30:1). Though the majority send their regrets (vv. 10–11) the celebration was still a success and "the whole assembly of Judah, the priests and the Levites, and the whole assembly that came out of Israel, and the resident aliens who came out of the land of Israel, and the resident aliens who lived in Judah, rejoiced" (v. 25).

For the Chronicler, then, the exile and return does not leave Judah as the sole remnant of Israel on the basis of which it can then claim to be the sole inheritor of the name Israel. *It does not establish an inside/outside distinction.* The exile is simply not remembered in the same way as it is in Ezra-Nehemiah. For the Chronicler, the exile is a gap that is overcome, as it is in 2 Chronicles 36, and the bridging of the gap between "pre-exilic" and "post-exilic" has the effect of making the middle term "exile" all but disappear. This blurring of the "then" and the "now" creates a degree of tension in the work which is, I would argue, rooted in a post-exilic struggle to fashion a new ideology of identity: an identity wherein the exile is *both* remembered and overcome. In these texts it is overcome.[133]

As in 2 Chronicles 36, the loss of land is no longer a living memory that marks out a new "leaner meaner" configuration of Israel as in Ezra-Nehemiah. The exile as a separation of people and land clashes with the sense we get from the geographical notices scattered throughout the genealogies of a people permanently connected to the land (and permanently centred on Jerusalem). These notices mark out the stage upon which the story of Israel is played out, from the time of David and (by implication) to the Chronicler's day. Every part of it is named and identified and connected with the people whose land it is: people and land, land and people are inseparable.

Japhet has shown the degree to which this differs from the account of Israel's origins found in the "Primary History." She points to the fact that no mention is made of the exodus or conquest and, more than that, to texts which appear to deliberately skip over the exodus-conquest tradition.[134] A startling example is 1 Chron. 7:20–29 which

---

[133] When it is remembered it is transformed into a cipher for the ultimate consequences of disobedience. I elaborate further on this tension in chapter six and in connection with the so-called doctrine of retribution.

[134] Japhet, "Conquest." Another indicator, according to Japhet, is the use of "settlements" in 1 Chron. 4:33, 6:54, and 7:28 instead of "inheritance" as found in Joshua

describes Ephraim's grief at the death of his sons at the hands of
the inhabitants of Gath.

> After their father Ephraim had mourned many days . . . Ephraim went
> in to his wife and she conceived and bore a son; and he named him
> Beriah, because disaster had befallen his house. His [Ephraim's or
> Beriah's?] daughter was Sheerah, who built Lower and Upper Beth-
> horon, and Uzzen-sheerah (7:22–23).

This text implies that Ephraim, his son and granddaughter were in
the land of Israel from the very beginning.[135] That Ephraim was
born in Egypt hundreds of years prior to the Exodus (according to
the chronology of Genesis and Exodus) simply does not fit the
Chronicler's portrayal of things. Thus, the genealogical picture of
Israel is just that, a *picture* of Israel—"a portrait of the people of
God in its ideal extent," though the extent to which it is "a symbol of both the particularity of his election and the breadth of his
grace"[136] needs to be examined more closely. The genealogies describe
Israel as it always was, its inner structure and geographical place.[137]
It treats of space not time. There is no contingency, no development, no promise to Abraham, no Moses, no exodus, no Sinai, no
conquest,[138] no point at which Israel came into being. Israel emerged
gradually and naturally from Adam, Abraham and Israel. Israel
emerged autochthonously in the land of Israel. This is God's order.
Israel among the nations. Israel as always in the land.

Why the difference in approach? What possible motives lie behind
this re-definition of Israel? One could, of course, speculate that the
different approach stems from a different era when the community
felt more at ease with itself and could afford to be more inclusive.
One could also hypothesize that the Chronicler was addressing the
contradictions inherent within a vertical *ethnie,* and was seeking to
take into account the need for interaction with communities outside

---

which is the *Vorlage* for the list of place names. Israel did not conquer or receive
an inheritance; it was always there.

[135] Japhet, *I & II Chronicles*, p. 181. This interpretation is disputed by Williamson
who argues that the text is too fragmentary to go as far as Japhet goes with it in
terms of the no-conquest hypothesis [H. G. M. Williamson, *1 and 2 Chronicles* (NCB;
London: Marshall, Morgan & Scott, 1982), p. 81].

[136] Williamson, *1 and 2 Chronicles*, p. 39.

[137] The genealogies abound with place names indicating the *where* of Israel: see
Kartveit, *Motive und Schichten*, pp. 166–7.

[138] Japhet, "Conquest."

of Judah. We do not, however, have access to information which could confirm or disprove these attempts to specify the Chronicler's motives. My hunch is that these two hypothetical observations are moving in the right direction for if one looks at the long-term trend the Jewish community centred in Judah and Jerusalem did eventually become the dominant ethnic group in Palestine under the Hasmoneans. This did not come about merely through the accident of history but, to my mind, would also have required an "all Israel" ideology of the kind that we find in Chronicles.[139]

One can, however, make more general sociological observations about how the Chronicler transforms key elements of the vertical ideology of identity into a lateral federalist ideology. One can, for example, compare this federalist vision to the federalist system of the Persians. The Persian empire of the Achaemenids was a federalist empire that grew out of the federalist kingdom of the Persians and Medes. The Persian kingdom is an example of large scale lateral *ethnie*.[140] The federalism at the kingdom level was, of course, an unequal federalism whereby the ruling families dominated the lesser communities and maintained a top-down ethnic and political identity. This same approach was used in the running of the empire; in other words, lesser communities such as kingdoms, city-states, tribes and ethnic groups of various kinds were integrated into the empire in the form of an unequal federalism.

The effectiveness of Persian ideology and administrative practice

---

[139] Given the geographical area within in which Jonathan and Simon are active, the references to "the land" in the eulogy of Simon (1 Macc. 14:4–15), a text which is replete with biblical allusions, imply a greater Israel. Albertz makes the point that the Maccabean restoration could be seen "as being a remote political effect of Chronicles" [R. Albertz, *A History of Israelite Religion in the Old Testament Period*, vol. 2, *From the Exile to the Maccabees* (trans. J. Bowden; London: SCM, 1994), p. 555]. Douglas remarks that the success of the Maccabeans and the end of colonial status meant that a culture of hierarchy was a viable option [M. Douglas, *In the Wilderness: The Doctrine of Defilement in the Book of Numbers* (JSOTS 158; Sheffield: JSOT Press, 1993), p. 51]. The idea that Chronicles was used in this way is supported by Eupolemus's use of Chronicles in his *On the Kings in Judea* (as preserved in Eusebius) in the mid-second century BCE (a Eupolemus is mentioned in 1 Macc. 8:17f and 2 Macc. 4:11 as Judas's ambassador to Rome). Eupolemus tells the story of the kings of Judea down to the exile, aggrandizing David and Solomon with reference to the temple project (as does the Chronicler). Anachronistic references to Galilee and Samaria as areas controlled by Solomon (Eusebius, *PrEv*, 9.33) as well as to "the twelve tribes of the *Jews*" (9.34.2) and a woman "from Judea and the tribe of Dan" (9.34.1) may reflect contemporary claims to territory outside of Judea but within a greater Israel.

[140] Smith, "Politics," pp. 713–4.

is illustrated by the remarkably positive attitude toward the Persian rulers found in the Old Testament, including Chronicles and Ezra-Nehemiah. The author of Ezra-Nehemiah seems to accept the community's status as a small enclave within the empire and Persian imperial policy allowed for local autonomy within a larger imperial order. From the Persian perspective, the empire was the centre and the local authorities were the periphery and the writer of Ezra-Nehemiah was reconciled to the Persian understanding.[141]

The Chronicler also accepts the basic premise that the Persian empire was legitimate and that it played a divine role in re-establishing Israel after the exile (2 Chron. 36:22–23), but the Chronicler "recasts" Israel's place within the divine economy in terms of a united federal nation in its own right, asserting cultic sovereignty over the land of Israel. Instead of defining Israel as an enclave within a large federalist empire, he applies the federalist model to Israel itself, thereby shifting attention away from the question of boundaries and toward the issue of Israel's internal differentiation.

Conclusion

In the foregoing chapter, I have sought to characterize the Chronicler's ideology of identity with reference to the place the exile has within it and in comparison to Ezra-Nehemiah. It is not difficult to reach the conclusion that the Chronicler defines Israel in terms of an "all Israel" theocracy in the fullest sense of that terms: all the tribes of Israel (or very nearly) in all the land of Israel. The perspective from which the Chronicler wrote was clearly *post*-exilic but by presenting the exile as but a brief interruption in the history of "all Israel" the Chronicler intended to demonstrate that a broader understanding of Israel (in comparison to Ezra-Nehemiah) was possible in his own day. I went on to explore the contextual functions of this ideology by reconstructing the Chronicler's overall situation—the Persian context and the citizen-temple community—and concluded that the Chronicler's approach to identity represents a different ethnic strat-

---

[141] And even if the author of Ezra-Nehemiah felt that the community had no choice but to accept Persian rule and work within these parameters (note in this regard the sentiments expressed in Nehemiah 9) this would still have had the unintended consequence of stabilizing Persian rule.

egy to that put forward in Ezra-Nehemiah. To use Smith's terms, it is a lateral ethnicity versus a vertical one, one which stresses territorial extension over against social depth. In order to explore the contextual functions of the Chronicler's ideology of identity further we will need to ask how it relates to the issue of power.

CHAPTER FOUR

LEGITIMACY AND HEGEMONY

An Unequal Federalism

In chapter three, I spoke of federalism in conjunction with Smith's definition of a lateral *ethnie* without emphasizing its important qualifier "unequal." The interpretation of the Chronicler's ideology of identity as a "federalist ideology" in which Judah is portrayed as the representative centre for all Israel is incomplete. Yes, one can find differences between Ezra-Nehemiah and Chronicles which point in the direction of a more inclusivist attitude to the inhabitants in all the land of Israel, but what are the contours and dynamics of this inclusivism. What sort of claim is this? Who is making it and why? Why should Judah be at the centre? Why is it that the history of the northern kingdom is to be considered solely in relationship to Judah's? Yes, there are positive inclusivist notices but they occur within *Judah's* story. It would seem, therefore, that the qualifier "unequal" is put on the agenda as much by a close reading of Chronicles as it is from adopting a particular theory of ideology and ethnicity.

The thesis to be put forward in this chapter is that *the ideology of identity in Chronicles is at the same time an ideology which legitimates Jerusalem's role as the sole legitimate centre of Israel in the Chronicler's day*. In other words, identity and legitimacy go hand in hand.[1] In this second reading of Chronicles I will be going over some of the same ground as in the last chapter but with a view to discerning the ideological force of the text as it relates to legitimation. As in the last chapter, this is still a question of asking about what the text says, the Chronicler's intentions and motives, and the contextual functions of what is said. That is, I am again working in the area of intersection where text, author and context meet, though broadening this in the direction of motive and contextual function.

---

[1] See the discussion of Ricoeur and Geertz on this issue in chapter two.

Status in the Genealogies

The genealogies of 1 Chronicles 1–9 which graphically illustrate the Chronicler's "all Israel" federalism need to be looked at again in relationship to the question of legitimacy. In the genealogies the issue is not only the identity of all Israel but also the centrality and legitimacy of Judah, Benjamin and Levi. In the following section I will examine the way in which the Chronicler has structured the genealogies in order to ascertain the way in which he has pictured "all Israel" and the way in which this *picture* connects up with his *story* of Israel, that is, the story of David and his descendants.

The genealogies deal with roughly three periods of time: (1) the period from Adam to Israel (ch. 1); (2) the pre-exilic period (2:3–8:40); and (3) the post-exilic period (ch. 9). Apart from this rough chronological structure the internal principle by which these chapters are organized has to do with status.

From Adam to Israel (1 Chronicles 1)

As we saw in the last chapter, 1 Chronicles 1 begins with the generations from Adam to Israel moving in concentric fashion as it positions Israel among the nations of the world, those furthest away from Israel (the sons of Japheth, vv. 5–7) to those nearest to Israel (the sons of Ham, vv. 8–16 followed by the sons of Shem, vv. 17–23).[2] Having sketched Israel's place in the wider world the Chronicler continues the list of direct descendants from Adam to Abraham begun in verse 4:

> Adam, Seth, Enosh, Noah, Shem . . . (v. 4) . . . Shem, Arpachshad, Shelah, Eber, Peleg, Reu, Serug, Nahor, Terah, Abram, that is Abraham (vv. 24–27).

Within the descendants of Abraham the Chronicler again treats Israel's closest rivals Ishmael (the other son of Abraham: vv. 28–33) and Esau (the other son of Isaac: vv. 34–54) before moving on to the real focus of this genealogy, the descendants of Abraham, Isaac

---

[2] Chapter one is a condensed version of the genealogies found in Genesis 5, 11, 25, 35 and 36. It omits Gen. 4:17–22 (the sons of Cain); 22:20–24 (the sons of Nahor); and 19:37–38 (the offspring of Lot's daughters, namely Ammon and Moab). See S. Japhet, *I & II Chronicles* (OTL; Louisville, KY: Westminster/John Knox, 1993), pp. 52–3, for a detailed analysis of the source material.

and Israel. Included in the Edomite genealogy is a list of Edomite kings and chiefs (vv. 43–53) who "reigned in the land of Edom before any king reigned over Israel" (v. 43).[3] This phrase registers the overall purpose of the genealogies which is to set the stage for the narrative that begins in chapter ten, the story of Israel's monarchy.[4] The genealogy is thus segmentary, indicating who the other nations were at the point of Israel's emergence as a nation, and linear, tracing a direct line from Adam to Abraham to Israel.[5]

The Tribes of Israel

The list of Israel's sons[6] in 1 Chron. 2:1–2 is based on Gen. 35:23–26[7] in which the sons are listed according to their mothers, but the order of the genealogies in chapters two to eight does not correspond with this list. The ordering principle is not a "natural" order, according to mother or according to birthright, but an order based on status; namely, the priority of Judah and the centrality of Levi. A complementary ordering principle in these chapters is geography, and here too the prominence of Judah and Jerusalem is underlined.[8] The genealogy begins at the centre with Judah and its close relation Simeon to the south, moves east into the Trans-Jordan to Reuben, northwards to Gad, and East Manasseh, across the Jordan again to Issacher, [Dan], Naphtali, before making its way south through

---

[3] This phrase indicates that "there are two phases in the political history of Edom": the period prior to David in which Edom was ruled by kings and the period after David in which Edom was ruled by chiefs; Japhet, *I & II Chronicles*, pp. 63–65.

[4] Japhet, *I & II Chronicles*, p. 123; see also 4:31b: "These were their (i.e. the Simeonites's) towns until David became king."

[5] According to M. Oeming, *Das wahre Israel: Die "genealogische Vorhalle" 1 Chronik 1–9* (BWANT; Stuttgart: Kohlhammer, 1990), pp. 89–91, this linear aspect of the genealogies stresses Israel's election out of all the nations of the world.

[6] The use of "Israel" versus "Jacob" is a consistent feature of the Chronicler's history and points to his concern for the identity of Israel, the nation made up of the sons of Israel. One could even point to the priority of Israel over Abraham in Chronicles indicated most clearly in the substitution of "the seed of Israel" for "the seed of Abraham" in 1 Chron. 16:13 (quoting Psalm 105:6). According to Rudolph, Abraham does not definitively establish Israel's identity because not all of Abraham's descendants were Israelites [W. Rudolph, *Chronikbücher* (HAT; Tübingen: Mohr, 1955), p. 120].

[7] Only Dan's position is changed.

[8] E. L. Curtis and A. A. Madsen, *The Books of Chronicles* (ICC; Edinburgh: T & T Clark, 1910); H. G. M. Williamson, *1 and 2 Chronicles* (NCB; London: Marshall, Morgan & Scott, 1982), pp. 46–7; M. Kartveit, *Motive und Schichten der Landtheologie in I Chronik 1–9*, ConBOT 28 (Stockholm: Almquist & Wiksell: 1989), pp. 166–7.

Ephraim and West Manasseh to the centre again, namely Benjamin. Another geographical feature of these texts are the geographical notices scattered throughout the genealogies. We are told not only *who* Israel is but also *where* Israel is, and this might just have programmatic significance in the Chronicler's day.[9]

Judah, whose genealogy is presented first (2:3–4:23), is prominent because of David. David's genealogy (ch. 3) is the central feature of the Judahite genealogy (sandwiched between genealogies of the rest of the tribe in chs. 2 and 4) and extends into the post-exilic period. The Chronicler recognizes that beginning with Judah contradicts the natural order of succession and explains this in the introduction to the genealogy of the tribe of Israel's firstborn, Reuben.

> He was the firstborn, but because he defiled his father's bed his birthright was given to the sons of Joseph son of Israel, so that he is not enrolled in the genealogy according to the birthright; though Judah became prominent among his brothers and a ruler came from him, yet the birthright belonged to Joseph (5:1–2).

The Chronicler recognizes three levels of priority: biological priority which Reuben lost as a punishment for sin, legal priority which benefited Joseph who received a double portion, and actual political priority which is Judah's.[10]

Levi occupies the central spot in the genealogical chapters and is the longest genealogy after Judah's. The genealogy is divided into two main parts. The first part (6:1–49) treats the three most significant groups of Levites (from the Chronicler's perspective): the high priests, the three main Levitical families and the Levitical singers. The list of high priests extends from Aaron to the exile and parallels the list of Davidic kings (3:10ff) though it does not extend beyond the exile as does the latter. The second part (6:50–81) is of particular interest because, in listing the Levitical cities according to the tribes in which they are located, the Chronicler has interwoven an "all Israel" inclusivism and an emphasis on the centrality of Levi. Temple (or temple personnel), people, and land are inseparable, held together by the tribe which does not have land like the others but which is

---

[9] Oeming, *Das wahre Israel*, p. 129; Kartveit, *Motive und Schichten*, pp. 166–7. Willi, on the other hand, believes that this is not part of the "original intention" of the Chronicler [T. Willi *Juda, Jehud, Israel: Studien zum Selbstverstandnis des Judentums in persischer Zeit* (Tübingen: J. C. B. Mohr (Paul Siebeck), 1995), p. 124].

[10] Japhet, *I & II Chronicles*, p. 133.

nevertheless "settled" (6:54) throughout the tribes in their cities with their pastures.

The last tribe enumerated is Benjamin whose genealogy is included in three places (7:6–12; 8; 9:35–44). Chapter eight is the main genealogy and verses 29–38 of this chapter are repeated in chapter 9 (presumably as an introduction to the story of Saul, the subject of chapter 10). The Benjamite genealogy is, perhaps, singled out for special attention as the *other* central tribe and as one of the three tribes involved in the return (Ezra 1:5).

From Israel to Jerusalem (1 Chronicles 9)

As we saw in the last chapter, the genealogical section ends with a list of the post-exilic inhabitants of Jerusalem asserting a continuity between the all Israel of the pre-exilic period and the "all Israel" of the post-exilic period (the all Israel of "Judah, Benjamin, Ephraim and Manasseh" in 9:3). This was presented as further evidence of an inclusivist tendency in Chronicles.

This interpretation is, however, incomplete and ultimately misleading. The "all Israel" of the genealogies (which presumably refer in the Chronicler's mind to the pre-exilic period, no matter how much he deflates the pre-exilic-post distinction) is, as we have just seen, led by Judah and centred on Levi. It also completes the spatial schema adopted in these first chapters which moves from the periphery to the centre, that is, from World→Israel→Jerusalem→Temple.[11] This is a Judahite-Levitical-Jerusalemite vision of Israel and the inclusion of Ephraim and Manasseh should not to be understood as an unambiguously inclusivist gesture on the part of the Chronicler to large sections of greater Israel living outside his own community.

There are, however, a number of difficulties with this interpretation arising from the translation of הראשׁנים in 9:2: "Now the *first* inhabitants to live again [the "again" being supplied with reference to the "return"] in their possessions in their towns were Israelites, priests, Levites, and temple servants." הראשׁנים can also mean "former" and Japhet argues that this is the correct translation in this sentence.[12] She notes that "[n]othing in the context in fact indicates

---

[11] Oeming, *Das wahre Israel*, p. 200.
[12] Japhet puts forward the case for translating *rishonim* as "former" on the basis of Zech. 1:4; 7:7; and Eccl. 7:10 [*I & II Chronicles*, pp. 206–8].

a 'return' or 'restoration'. . . ."[13] Japhet's reading of the context does not, however, include verse 1b ("and Judah was taken into exile in Babylon") arguing that it is possible that the reference to Judah's exile "is in fact a gloss, intended to restore to the text a reality which the Chronicler had tried to avoid."[14] With this text critical proviso, Japhet can state that since "one of the main interests of 1 Chron. 2–9 is the "dwellings" or territories of the tribes" it is only natural that the inhabitants of Jerusalem, associated if anything with the time of David, should be included here.[15] In her reckoning, the Chronicler wanted to continue his genealogies with a list of the inhabitants of Jerusalem. He had a list of post-exilic inhabitants to hand and simply appended it to the genealogies changing the ascription to Judah, Benjamin *and Ephraim and Manasseh* and deleting other indications of the "original" provenance of his source.[16]

Japhet's solution is attractive in that it reduces an otherwise irreducible tension in the text stemming from the rough juxtapositioning of the "all Israel" (9:1a), "exile of Judah" (9:1b), "Israelites, priests, Levites, and temple servants" (9:2), and "Judah, Benjamin, Ephraim and Manasseh in Jerusalem" (9:3). But I would argue that the tension this creates, far from being something we should seek to resolve via text critical surgery, are the very things which point to the Chronicler's struggle for a new definition of Israel. These tensions are, of course, the result of the combination of different sources with different agendas. The reference to the exile of Judah is clearly drawn from the account in Kings, as discussed in chapter three. In Kings, Judah refers to the kingdom of Judah (which includes Judah, Benjamin and Levi)[17] and is always distinguished from the kingdom of Israel. Those who return from Israel take the name Israel, at times with reference to the whole community and at times with reference to laity.[18] This is Ezra-Nehemiah's presentation of the relationship between the kingdom of Judah and the assembly of returnees and it is from here that the Chronicler takes his list of the inhabitants of Jerusalem, including the phrase "Israelites, priests, Levites, and temple servants"

---

[13] Japhet, *I & II Chronicles*, p. 208.

[14] Japhet, *I & II Chronicles*, p. 206.

[15] Japhet, *I & II Chronicles*, p. 208.

[16] Specifically, "the cities of Judah" of Neh. 11:3.

[17] 1 Kgs. 11:31 speaks of "ten tribes" for Jeroboam versus the "one tribe" for Rehoboam (cf. 11:13) but the "one tribe" appears to include Benjamin (12:21).

[18] E.g. Ezra 2:59 and 2:2, respectively.

(9:2). The ideological import of this identification of returnees with Israel is exposed in the very next verse of Nehemiah 11 which reads: "And in Jerusalem lived some of the sons Judah and Benjamin" (Neh. 11:4). This was an unacceptable narrowing of the definition Israel so the Chronicler transforms this via the addition of "Ephraim and Manasseh." In doing so the Chronicler may have wanted to present an inclusivist vision of Israel but it is one thing to collate all the available material on the tribes of old, quite another to present Jerusalem as the undisputed centre whether that is with reference to the pre-exilic period (as Japhet would have it) or to the post-exilic period (as I would have it). What we have before us, I would argue, is a picture of Israel "in its ideal extent,"[19] a people permanently connected to the land, a nation differentiated by tribes, *but also* a people unified by virtue of a hierarchical structure in a land permanently centred on Jerusalem.

This picture of Israel painted with words and names, lists of peoples and places finds an analogy in the city of Persepolis. Persepolis defied imperial administrative and economic logic in that it was built away from major trade routes, out on the high open plateau in the Persian heartland. The main administrative centres were Susa and Babylon. Persepolis is thus somewhat problematic in terms of its function.[20] Some scholars have hypothesized that Persepolis was essentially a large religious shrine built specifically for a New Year festival the central feature of which was, allegedly, a procession of representatives from every nation in the empire.[21] These representatives are the subject of the reliefs which decorate the stairs and sides of the platform of the massive audience hall known as the Apadana. They are distinguishable according to their modes of dress and the gifts being brought to the Persian king. They are arranged according to an hierarchical schema with the most important nations such as Media and Elam at the top of the stairs. According to Muscarella, who is critical of the New Year festival hypothesis, "the Apadana relief was intended to represent (albeit in concrete terms)

---

[19] Williamson, *1 and 2 Chronicles*, p. 39. According to Oeming this is an implicit claim to these lands. Cf. Neh. 11:25–35 which is also an idealistic portrayal [*Das wahre Israel*, pp. 209–10]. Stern speaks of a "utopian ideal" [E. Stern, *The Material Culture of the Land of the Bible in the Persian Period (538–322 BCE* (Warminster: Aris & Philips, 1982), p. 85].

[20] E. Yamauchi, *Persia and the Bible* (Grand Rapids, MI: Baker, 1990), pp. 339–42.

[21] Notably G. Walser, *Die Völkerschaften auf den Reliefs von Persepolis* (Berlin: Gebrüder Mann, 1966).

a certain abstract vision of the empire and of imperial harmony."[22] The analogy I see here with the genealogies is not only the principle of differentiation—the "new federalism" as described in the last chapter[23]—but also and more importantly the hierarchical ordering of the nations, an order imposed by the centre. The Persepolis reliefs are not so much an expression of the kind of federalism we know but rather of the ideology of a world-ordering universal empire. I am suggesting that this claim to hegemony is not unlike the claims being made on behalf of Jerusalem by the Chronicler.

David, Solomon and the Kingdom of Yahweh

The *story* of Israel, as opposed to the preceding *portrait* of Israel, really begins with the story of David and Solomon, the account of Saul's death on Mt. Gilboa (1 Chronicles 10) being a prelude to it.[24] The story of David and Solomon is about two things: temple and dynasty. These two themes are, however, so closely intertwined in the narrative that they constitute one story about the establishment and legitimacy of the theocratic kingdom, "the kingdom of the LORD in the hands of the sons of David" (2 Chron. 13:5; cf. 28:5 and 29:11). And what is more, the issue of the legitimacy of dynasty and temple does not stand on its own but is integrated with the story of Israel's establishment as the people of God in the land of Israel. Ruling dynasty, central institution, people, and land, are so thoroughly intertwined in the Chronicler's presentation that, while they are dealt with "in turn" (and this is simply a matter of expediency), we cannot assign from the outset their relative priority. My aim in the following is to demonstrate the extent to which the question of identity is subsumed within the quest for legitimacy.

David and the People

David's rise to power in Chronicles is not fraught with hardship nor is it the culmination of a long march; it is not subject to the whims

---

[22] I. Muscarella, "Review of G. Walser, *Die Völkerschaften*," in *JNES* 28 (1969), p. 278.

[23] With reference to the work of C. Nylander, "Achaemenid Imperial Art," in M. Trolle Larsen (ed.), *Power and Propaganda: A Symposium on Ancient Empires* (Mesopotamia 7; Copenhagen: Akademisk Forlag, 1979), pp. 345–59.

[24] I discuss the Saul chapter below.

of an opponent or the precariousness of circumstance; it is not a political struggle at all but rather an abrupt elevation to kingship via unanimous acclamation following Saul's death.

> Then all Israel gathered to David at Hebron (1 Chron. 11:1)

More important, however, than the dynamics of this story (if dynamics is the word) is the way the Chronicler passes over the division of Israel between north and south as this is represented in Samuel-Kings. The coming together of "all the tribes of Israel" in Samuel is the culmination of a gradual process of David winning their support. In Chronicles, on the other hand, the transition from the genealogical portrait of all Israel to the coming together of all Israel is virtually seamless. The account of Saul's death is but the "steady" between "ready" and "Go!."

David's first act as king is to capture Jerusalem, with the help of "all Israel" (1 Chron. 11:4). Jerusalem is to be Israel's capital not the private domain of "the king and his men" (2 Sam. 5:6). And as if unable to resist demonstrating that he really means all Israel, the Chronicler enumerates the allies of David, beginning with "the chiefs of David's warriors" (1 Chron. 11:10) and continues with those who came from *all* the tribes "to Hebron with full intention to make David king over all Israel; likewise all the rest of Israel were of single mind to make David king" (12:38). It is as if the purpose of the genealogies, the reason for the comprehensive recording of all the sons of Israel, has been fulfilled in the coming together of all Israel under David (as intimated here and there in the genealogies themselves). It is here in making David king that all Israel acts and speaks for the first time. This coming together of king and people is not only in accordance with "the word of the LORD by Samuel" (11:3; cf. 12:23) but is initiated from the side of the people. These are David's "helpers" (12:1, 22), his volunteers, his believers who come with "whole hearts" and who act with "one mind" . . . "a great army, like an army of God" (12:22). This symbiosis established, David can commence his main project which is to establish the temple and its service in Jerusalem.

David (and the People) and the Ark

De Wette first noted in detail the way in which David and Solomon's reigns have been transformed into the story of the founding of the cult. This tendency was of interest to de Wette in connection with the history of Israel's religion and the dating of the Pentateuchal sources and, thus, was not explored for its own sake. But his basic point still stands[25] and finds its classic expression in Wellhausen's *Prolegomena*:

> See what Chronicles has made out of David! The founder of the kingdom has become the founder of the temple and the public worship, the king and hero at the head of his companions in arms has become the singer and master of ceremonies at the head of a swarm of priests and Levites; his clearly cut figure has become a feeble holy picture, seen through a cloud of incense.[26]

Apart from the derogatory language used to describe this theme, Wellhausen's conclusion is broadly based on overwhelming textual evidence. A broad overview of the chapters dealing with David and Solomon makes this plain:

11–12   David's coronation, the capture of Jerusalem the *temple city*, David's allies

13   the *Ark* is brought from Kiriath Jearim to the house of Obed-edom

14   David's military successes, which follow the story of his concern for the *Ark* (a concern not shared by Saul)[27]

15–16   arrangements for the *temple service*

---

[25] See for example R. Braun, *1 Chronicles* (WBC; Waco, TX: Word, 1986), pp. xxxii–xxxv, and W. Riley, *King and Cultus in Chronicles: Worship and the Reinterpretation of History* (JSOTS 160; Sheffield: JSOT Press, 1993), pp. 57–8.

[26] J. Wellhausen, *Prolegomena to the History of Ancient Israel* (trans. W. Robertson Smith; 1885; Gloucestor, MA: Peter Smith, reprint edn., 1973), p. 182.

[27] Welten notes a more important connection between the capture of Jerusalem, these wars and the bringing of the ark to Jerusalem. Although David had captured Jerusalem, it was not yet "functional" as the resting place (מנוחה) for the Philistines still held territory between Kireath-Jearim and Jerusalem (the valley of Rephaim and Baal-perazim). In other words, they blocked the way of the ark on its journey to its final resting place. Following the victories over the Philistines, David gets straight back to the task of preparing Jerusalem for the ark. But even with the ark in Jerusalem (16:43) it is not at rest until it is placed in the temple. Thus, the narrative from here on in is dominated by temple preparations. But the ark isn't important for its own sake; "Die Lade markiert gewissermaßen den Weg Jahwes nach Jerusalem, in den Tempel" [P. Welten, "Lade-Temple-Jerusalem: Zur Theologie der Chronikbücher," in A. Gunneweg und O. Kaiser (eds.), *Textgemäss: Aufsätze und Beiträge zur Hermeneutik des Alten Testaments* (FS Würthwein; Göttingen: Vandenhoech und Ruprecht, 1979), pp. 182–3]. According to Welten, 1 Chron. 11–2 Chron. 9 have an "urgeschichtlicher Charakter" in comparison with the the rest of the book and in keeping with the fact that they constitute "der Gründungs- und Legitimationsgeschichte von Jerusalem, Tempel und Kult" [Welten, "Lade-Temple-Jerusalem," p. 183].

17	the dynastic promise which is focused on Solomon as the chosen *temple builder*
18–21	other military successes of David, which, among other things, provide materials for building the *temple* (18:8, 10–11)
22	David's *temple* preparations and charge to Solomon to complete the task
23–27	arrangements for *cultic* and "secular" administration
28–29	Solomon given *temple plans* and anointed king
1	Solomon at Gibeon, the wisdom dream'
2–4	Solomon builds the *temple*
5–7	dedication of the *temple* and the prayer of Solomon, which God answers in a vision
8	Solomon's control over the kingdom (military and administrative) is secured after the building of the *temple*
9	Solomon's accomplishments, particularly his *temple-building* accomplishments, are recognized by foreign rulers (like the Queen of Sheba)

1 Chron. 13:1–5

As soon as the coronation is over, David (or should we say the Chronicler) gets right down to the task at hand. His second act as king, following his unanimous acclamation as king at Hebron and the taking of Jerusalem, is to bring the ark of the covenant to the new capital. Again, all Israel is closely involved for David is careful to consult with "the commanders of the thousands and of the hundreds, with every leader" (13:1) but the initiative has shifted decisively in David's direction. The leaders agree to convene an assembly in order to bring the ark of God to the new capital.

> So David assembled all Israel from Shihor of Egypt to Lebo-Hamath, to bring the Ark of God from Kiriath-jearim (13:5).

This deference to the leaders and the people of Israel has been interpreted as a "democratizing" move which when taken together with other similar passages is construed as a significant tendency of the work.[28] The use of this term is unfortunate because it pre-determines the way in which we understand the inter-relationship between the ideologies of identity and legitimacy in Chronicles. In fact, it precludes

---

[28] Riley, *King and Cultus*, p. 92.

us from seeing the way in which these two ideologemes interact at all for it depends on a literalistic reading of the text showing no sensitivity to its rhetorical aspects.[29]

The dimensions given for the land of Israel, "from Shihor" (which most identify as the easternmost branch of the Nile) "to Lebo-Hamath" (between Damascus and the Euphrates) are unusual in that they correspond to the broadest picture of the land of Israel that is found in the Old Testament. In Joshua 13:3–5 (the only other time these two terms are used) these two places mark out the extent of the land that *has yet to be* conquered by the Israelites. This area, in turn, roughly corresponds to the land promised to Abraham (Gen. 15:18) namely the land between the Nile and the Euphrates. "The Chronicler takes this very picture [of the "promised land" at its greatest extent] . . . to depict the territory in which the people of Israel are actually settled; not at the end of David's rule and after his military campaigns, but at the very beginning of his reign."[30] The genealogies also pictured the land in its ideal extent and this picture, if connected historically to any particular historical period, refers to the time of David. The distinctive shape of the Chronicler's complex picture of Israel is beginning to emerge with some clarity at this point: an all inclusive people settled in the land promised to Abraham unified in purpose and intention in making David king and in establishing Jerusalem as the central sanctuary.

1 Chronicles 16

The journey of the ark to Jerusalem is a two-part journey from Kiriath-jearim to the threshing floor of Chidon (ch. 13) and from there to Jerusalem (15:3, 25–28 and 16:1–3). The break is occasioned by Uzzah's wrongful handling of the ark and this mishap, taken over from Samuel, gives the Chronicler opportunity to spell out the new role of the Levites in the post-tabernacle era. Prior to the establishment of a permanent resting place for the ark in Jerusalem, the Levites were the sole legitimate ark-bearers (see Deut. 10:8 and 18:5) and the Chronicler introduces this as the reason for the death of Uzzah (15:4–15). But after the ark's final journey David defines a new role for them as Levitical singers and gatekeepers (15:16–24).

---

[29] On rhetoric as an aspect of poetics and politics, see P. Ricoeur, *The Rule of Metaphor* (trans. R. Czerny, et al.; Toronto: University of Toronto Press, 1977), pp. 9–43.

[30] Japhet, *I & II Chronicles*, p. 278.

In the second stage in the journey, as in the first, "all Israel" (15:3, 28) and "the elders of Israel and the commanders of the thousands" (15:25) are involved, but the conclusion of this journey marks the end of the "consultative" phase for from this point on David (and Solomon after him) sets the agenda. This generates a degree of tension with regard to what sort of kingdom this is. Is it a Davidic kingdom or a theocratic kingdom? A kingdom for David or a kingdom for Israel or some combination of the above? What I discern in the Chronicler's construction of Israel's origins is, in the first instance, an attempt to embrace a wide range of ideas (diachronic and synchronic) about the constitution of Israel (regardless of whether or not these cohere with each other) and to give them an overall shape or directionality. At the heart of Israel's "national" identity is a disposition or orientation to worship the LORD their God *and* to worship him in the temple in Jerusalem. The disposition of worship involving heart and mind unites the people as one and is expressed in concrete action in their rallying behind David and their giving full support in establishing the temple. We thus observe a snowball effect whereby the intentions of the people are taken up and subsumed within David's intentions, carried forward by him and his successor and focused increasingly on the temple which becomes the concrete embodiment of that which makes Israel Israel. Again, this is the overall shape I discern in the Chronicler's construction of Israel and I do not want to imply hereby that he is entirely successful in this regard.

The psalm of thanksgiving (16:8–36) which celebrates the ark's homecoming illustrates the Chronicler's method of construction. The psalm is a synthesis of parts of Psalms 105, 95 and 106. The setting is, as we noted above, David's instructions to the Levites concerning their new responsibilities as singers and this psalm is, perhaps, the first hymn in their hymnal.

The exhortations to give thanks are repeated in language characteristic of the Chronicler: "those who seek the LORD rejoice" (16:10) and "seek the LORD and his strength, seek his presence continually" (16:11). Thanksgiving and seeking the LORD is also an act of remembrance whereby "the wonderful works he has done" (16:12) are recalled. The Chronicler addresses these exhortations to the "offspring of his servant Israel" (16:13)[31] and "the children of Jacob

---

[31] Contra Ps. 105:6 which has "Abraham," again emphasizing the all Israel point of view.

[as listed in full in the genealogies], his chosen ones." If Israel re-members (contra Ps. 105:8 in which God remembers) "his covenant forever" (16:15a), they will ensure the continuing validity of "the word that he commanded, for a thousand generations, the covenant that he made with Abraham, his sworn promise to Isaac, which he confirmed to Jacob as a statute, *to Israel as an everlasting covenant*" (16:15b–17). Fisch speaks of a covenantal discourse in the Psalms whereby the covenantal community is constituted in the very act of verbally affirming it via the language of the Psalms. The "I" of the Psalms is every "I" that finds "its" salvation in communal affirmation of God's mighty acts on their behalf.[32] The people are thus consti-tuted via worship and in this they are to rejoice.

Thus, the theme of rejoicing echoes and re-echoes in the ark nar-rative as told by the Chronicler. In 15:16 David appoints the Levites "to raise loud sounds of joy" and they bring up the ark with "loud music" (15:28) and one can all but here their refrain "O give thanks to the LORD, for he is good; for his steadfast love endures forever" (16:34; cf. 16:41; 2 Chron. 5:13; 7:3, 6; and 20:21).[33]

The impression that the genealogies give of all Israel ever-centred on the temple and indeed ever-present in the land is reinforced and given depth in the Chronicler's psalm. Psalm 105 is a call to thanks-giving for the mighty acts of God on behalf of his people. The Psalter then recalls these mighty acts concentrating on the exodus from Egypt which fulfils the promise of God to give the "land of Canaan as [Israel's] portion for an inheritance" (Ps. 105:11 // 1 Chron. 15:18). The Chronicler, however, skips directly from the promise to the patriarchs and their sojourning "in the land" (16:19), their "wan-dering from nation to nation" (15:20), to the fulfilment of the promise: "Sing to the LORD, all the earth; tell of his salvation from day to day" (16:23). Japhet interprets this text in conjunction with those texts we looked at earlier that seem to side-step the conquest entirely and which, in her view, make people and land inseparable. I fol-lowed this interpretation to a certain extent in the previous chapter on the exile which, in the Chronicler's treatment, does not repre-sent a fundamental realignment of God's promise to Abraham concern-

---

[32] H. Fisch, *Poetry with a Purpose: Biblical Poetics and Interpretation* (Bloomington: Indiana University Press, 1988), p. 118.

[33] 1 Chron. 16:34 is a quote from Ps. 106:1 and is found elsewhere in the Psalter (Pss. 107:1; 118:1, 2, 3, 4, and 29; 136:1–26) and in Ezra 3:11. All these citations illustrate the degree to which liturgy of the Second Temple was stabilizing.

ing the land "from the river of Egypt to the great river, the river Euphrates." Again, one notes that the description in 1 Chronicles 13:5 of the land from which all Israel is assembled (and, presumably, to which they return; 16:43), from Shihor of Egypt to Lebo-Hamath, roughly corresponds to this maximalist expression of the land in Genesis. In light of what God has done for *this* people in *this* land "let them say among the nations, 'The LORD is king'" (16:31).

David, the Kingdom and the Temple

The Davidic Covenant (1 Chronicles 17)

This chapter is an agenda-setting chapter in relation to the Davidic dynasty-temple nexus. Up to this point the Chronicler has implied that there is an intimate connection between the two. The previous chapters established a synthesis of people, king and cult without explicitly articulating the relationship between them. The mechanics of the Chronicler's rhetoric is, perhaps, analogous to a snowball whereby the notions of nationhood, kingship, and cult are gradually rolled into one large (and not easily differentiated) object. Another analogy might be the vortex which draws far-flung objects into the centre in an ever faster, tighter spin. The all Israel entity is drawn into the story of David so that the story of one becomes inseparable from that of the other. I discern in the combination of these two themes a centripetal force with David as the focal point. Chapter seventeen takes us one stage further by expanding this synthesis to include the temple which is the crucial element binding the two house, one people theocracy together.[34]

The way in which this synthesis is achieved is not unrelated to the way in which it is interpreted, ideologically-critically speaking. The difficulty one has in separating concerns for the identity of Israel from those concerning the legitimacy of David's rule and the temple built by him and his son is not the accidental by-product of too blunt an exegetical scalpel. The question as to the direct communicative

---

[34] According to Kelly "the Davidic covenant has constituted Israel as the earthly expression of Yahweh's kingdom . . ."; thus the kingdom of David and Solomon is "the concretized form of Yahweh's kingship, the theocracy in its fullest sense" [B. Kelly, *Retribution and Eschatology in Chronicles* (JSOTS 211; Sheffield: Sheffield Academic Press, 1996), p. 156].

intentions of the Chronicler—Is David's story simply the best way of presenting a new inclusivist view of Israel or is this new inclusivism simply part of a different agenda for which the centrality of David, Jerusalem and the temple is all important?—cannot be solved on the level of direct intention and conscious motive alone and without reference to the ideological import of what is being said. While it is true that the text "says" things about the identity of Israel and the legitimacy of the Davidic dynasty, the things said are also things done, contextually-speaking. These particular words are not arbitrary to what gets done, thus reading Chronicles from an ideological critical perspective means keeping one eye on what is being said and the other trained on what that which is said might have been doing. I am not "imagining" the close relationship between the identity and legitimacy themes but I am "imagining" their ideological implications while paying attention to the way in which the Chronicler takes up these themes, combines them and moves them on.

The close connection between dynasty and cult made in chapter seventeen is not a Chronistic invention for the dual election of David and Zion is the central feature of Judean royal ideology.[35] What the Chronicler does in his references to the so-called Davidic covenant (here and in subsequent texts) is to re-position the temple vis-à-vis the dynasty giving greater prominence to the latter in comparison to 2 Samuel 7.

The Chronicler's treatment of this text hinges on the flexibility of the word בית. The word can refer to a palace, a temple, a dynasty or a kinship group. In 1 Chronicles 14 David builds himself a palace (בית) with the help of King Hiram of Tyre (14:1). His successes so far confirm to him that "the LORD had established him as king over Israel" and what is more that "his kingdom was highly exalted for the sake of his people Israel." The ambiguity of the possessive pronouns raises, even if only momentarily,[36] the basic question as to whose kingdom this is. The Chronicler returns to this issue in chapter seventeen, as does David "when [he had] settled in his house" (17:1). David is struck by the contrast between his palace and the

---

[35] See Pss. 89 and 132. Nor is the king-cult nexus an Israelite thing, as Riley's study has demonstrated [Riley, *King and Cultus*].

[36] Note the parallelism which indicates whose kingdom and whose people it is: for/for, as king/his kingdom, over Israel/over his people (1 Chron. 14:20).

LORD's tabernacle and resolves to remedy it by building a temple for the LORD. The LORD, however, has a different plan or at least a different timetable and it is the LORD who (speaking for the first time in Chronicles at any length)[37] takes the initiative and personally articulates the relationship between dynasty and temple.

He begins negatively: "You will not build for me the house to live in." The ironic question of 2 Samuel "Will you build a house for me to live in?," which works in conjunction with the following verses on Yahweh's lengthy sojourn in the tabernacle (about which he had no complaints), is transformed into a straight forward "You will not . . ." destroying in the process the point that Yahweh might not want to have a temple in the first place. The other change in which house is made definite "the house," anticipates the main point that the Chronicler wants to make in this chapter namely that Solomon (not "You" David) will build *the* temple. The idea of a temple itself is not in doubt as it is in 2 Samuel. The following verses about the tabernacle are nevertheless retained but don't work well in conjunction with these changes.

The key factor in the LORD's timetable for the temple construction project has to do with the notion of "rest." According to Deuteronomy 12 the central sanctuary is to be built once Israel is at rest in the land. The narrative setting of Deuteronomy is, of course, pre-conquest and the promise to Abraham of the land has not yet been fulfilled. The Chronicler retains the idea that the establishment of a central sanctuary marks the fulfilment of all that the LORD promised Abraham[38] and must therefore wait until Israel is established in the land vis-à-vis the other nations (cf. 17:9). But the conquest, though alluded to here and there,[39] is replaced by David's military successes and they are more a matter of consolidation than of conquest. In other words, the Abrahamic covenant is fulfilled in the time of David and Solomon.[40] Though David himself achieves the conditions necessary for building the temple, the full enjoyment

---

[37] The LORD speaks prior to this only briefly in 1 Chron. 14:10, 14–15. The next and last time the LORD speaks at length is at another pivotal point in his answer to Solomon's prayer at the dedication of the temple (2 Chron. 7:12–22).

[38] References to the patriarchal promise: 2 Chron. 6:25, 31; 7:20; 33:8 [cited in Kelly, *Retribution*, p. 181].

[39] 1 Chron. 17:5, 21; 2 Chron. 5:10; 6:25; 7:22 [cited in Kelly, *Retribution*, p. 181].

[40] Note in this regard the close association of Abraham and the central sanctuary and Solomon's dedicatory prayer in 2 Chron. 20:7–9.

of this "rest" is associated with Solomon (cf. 1 Chron. 22:8 and 28:3 where this is explained on the basis of his name as well as the overall political security that existed from the start of his reign) not with David. Hence the removal of the word "rest" from 17:1 and 17:10. Thus, even though the Chronicler heightens David's role in the building of the temple, the full realization of this project lies beyond David's reign. The positive outcome of this (assuming that David was disappointed with the LORD's prohibition) is that the temple straddles the dynasty and is thus inexorably linked with the dynasty as such and not just to David.

The interlocking of dynasty and temple is copper-fastened in the concluding section of the LORD's speech to David. Picking up where he left off in 1 Chron. 17:4, "You will not build me a house (temple) . . .," the LORD states (more positively this time) that ". . . the LORD will build you a house (dynasty)."

We now come to the tricky bit, namely, for how long will this kingdom be established? The answer given in 2 Samuel 7 suggests that even "when he commits iniquity . . . I will not take away my steadfast love (חסד) from him" (2 Sam. 7:15). The Chronicler does not include this clause thereby reducing, ironically, the unconditionality of the promise to David while retaining the clause "I will not take my steadfast love from him . . ." (17:13b). Yahweh's promise is clarified negatively with reference to Saul (though he is not named as in 2 Samuel): ". . . as I took it away from him who was before you" (17:13c). But this doubly negative way of defining forever is mildly unsettling for it allows conditionality in by the back door even as it is tosses the idea out of the front door. Since the future of this promise to David and the nature of the conditions attached to it becomes the dominant sub-text of the rest of the narrative a closer look at the story of Saul's death is warranted.

The Death of Saul (1 Chronicles 10)

Up to this point we have observed the way in which the Chronicler has depicted the reign of David as the culmination of the promises of nationhood, land, central sanctuary embodying the kingdom of Yahweh on earth. At the heart of this theocracy is the steadfast love of Yahweh—his eternal commitment to Israel. Israel's commitment to Yahweh, on the other hand, is in the very nature of things not eternal; it has to be renewed by each generation. This instability or conditionality at the heart of the theocracy, this negative possibility, is anticipated in the account of Saul's death at the hands of the Philistines.

The Chronicler has adapted the story of Saul's death as found in 1 Samuel 29 so that it speaks more directly to the origin and status of the Davidic dynasty. For example, whereas 1 Sam. 31:6 reads:

> So Saul and his three sons *and his armor-bearer and all his men* died together on the same day.

The Chronicler states:

> Thus, Saul died; he and his three sons *and all his house* died together (1 Chron. 10:6).

Saul's dynasty is wiped out with no bothersome remainder such as Ishbaal (2 Sam. 2:8) and Mephibosheth (2 Sam. 4:4). The closing verses of 1 Chronicles 10, which have no parallel in Samuel, make the point more directly:

> So Saul died for his unfaithfulness [מעל]; he was unfaithful [מעל] to the LORD in that he did not keep the command of the LORD; moreover, he had consulted a medium, seeking guidance [דרש], and did not seek guidance [דרש] from the LORD. Therefore the LORD put him to death and turned the kingdom over to David son of Jesse (1 Chron. 10:13–14).

This text alludes to Saul's encounter with Samuel via the medium at Endor (1 Sam. 28). In this encounter Saul asks Samuel for advice before the battle with the Philistines. Samuel answers: "Why then do you ask me, since the LORD has turned from you and become your enemy? The LORD has done to you just as he spoke by me; for the LORD has torn the kingdom out of your hand, and given it to your neighbour, David" (1 Sam. 28:16–17).

The use of "unfaithfulness" (מעל) and "seek" (דרש) to describe the end of Saul and his dynasty indicates the significance of this passage for understanding Chronicles as a whole. "Unfaithfulness" is a key word in Chronicles and is used to refer to unfaithfulness to the cult.[41] "Seeking Yahweh" is a matter of showing concern for the legitimate cult.[42] The ultimate punishment for unfaithfulness is removal

---

[41] As discussed in chapter three with reference to the exile (1 Chron. 9:1 and 2 Chron. 36:14). See also chapter six.

[42] There are two words used for seeking Yahweh in Chronicles: דרש (seventeen times; plus one time of Baal) and בקש (six times). The two words are synonymous as seen in the quote from Ps. 105:4 found in 1 Chron. 16:11: "Seek [דרש] the

from the land, a fate first experienced by the east Jordan tribes (1 Chron. 5:25–26) and in the end by the kingdom of Judah as well (1 Chron. 9:1 and 2 Chron. 36:14ff).[43] This link between unfaithfulness and the land is reminiscent of Leviticus 26:40–43:

> But if they confess their iniquity and the iniquity of their ancestors, in that they committed treachery [מעל] against me and, moreover, that they continued hostile to me—so that I, in turn, continued hostile to them and brought then into the land of their enemies; if then their uncircumcised heart is humbled and they make amends for their iniquity, then I will remember my covenant with Jacob; I will remember also my covenant with Isaac and also my covenant with Abraham, and I will remember the land. For the land shall be deserted by them, and enjoy its Sabbath years by lying desolate without them, while they make amends for their iniquity, because they dared to spurn my ordinances, and they abhorred my statutes.

The connection between this text and Chronicles is made even clearer in that the Chronicler also adopts the idea of the land enjoying its Sabbaths (2 Chron. 36:21).

The implication of this for the narrative of Saul's death is that, in the Chronicler's view, Saul's failure was a failure with reference to the cult. 1 Chronicles 13:3 makes this more explicit: "Then let us bring again the Ark of our God to us; for we did not turn to it in the days of Saul." Recent commentators have, therefore, followed Mosis[44] in ascribing a paradigmatic value to the death of Saul narrative.[45] The paradigm could be summarized as follows:

מעל	דרש
unfaithfulness to the cult	faithfulness to the cult
exile	rest and restoration
dynasty lost	dynasty gained

LORD and his strength, seek [בקש] his presence continually." The former is more important to the Chronicler and is only used once in Samuel-Kings. Oddly enough the one time it is used is in the story of Saul and the medium of Endor (2 Sam. 28:7). The Deuteronomistic formulation of this idea maybe the basis for the Chronicler's use of it. "But you shall seek the place that the LORD your God will choose out of all your tribes to put his name there. You shall go there . . ." (Deut. 12:5).

[43] W. Johnstone, "Guilt and Atonement: The Theme of 1 and 2 Chronicles," in J. D. Martin and P. R. Davies (eds.), *A Word in Season: Essays in Honour of William McKane* (JSOTS 42; Sheffield: JSOT Press, 1986), pp. 113–38.

[44] R. Mosis, *Untersuchungen zur Theologie des chronistischen Geschichtswerkes* (Freiburger theologische Studien 92; Freiburg: Herder, 1973), pp. 17–43.

[45] Williamson, *1 and 2 Chronicles*, p. 96; Braun, *1 Chronicles*, p. 149.

The promise of a dynasty is thus conditional *in general terms* on loyalty to the cult. Could the same fate apply to the Davidides? Is this what we are supposed to understand given the fact that the book closes with the end of this dynasty (and no mention is made of its restoration in the final hopeful verses)? I will address these questions in greater detail in chapter six, but so as not to leave the impression that the Chronicler is both deeply concerned and fatalistic about the future of the Davidic dynasty it is worth noting again that the theocracy, though embodied in the Davidic dynasty, is also the kingdom of Yahweh. Yahweh turns "*the* kingdom over to David" (10:14); in other words, the kingdom pre-dates David and transcends the dynastic transition.

The establishment of the Davidic dynasty is, however, also conditional *in specific terms*, namely, that Solomon build the temple. This condition is hardly problematic and is promptly fulfilled by Solomon, but it explains both the abiding significance of the Davidic covenant and the way in which Yahweh's kingship is realized in all subsequent generations. In other words, the Chronicler is not so much concerned with the establishment of the Davidic dynasty as such but with the establishment of the theocratic kingdom which finds concrete expression in its two houses: the one giving it political weight, the other making it a theocracy. With reference to this entity the promise is absolute:

> I will confirm him in *my house* and in *my kingdom* and his throne[46] will be established forever (1 Chron. 17:14).[47]

The Temple Site (1 Chronicles 21)

In the "time" between the Davidic covenant and David's handing over of the kingdom to Solomon, David consolidates the kingdom externally (1 Chronicles 18–20) thereby establishing the "rest" required for Solomon and the temple-building.[48] What remains however is the temple site itself. The Chronicler adapts the story of David's census into the story of the divine sanctioning of the future site of the temple.

The story of the census and subsequent plague are not of interest

---

[46] Elsewhere it is described as Yahweh's throne: 1 Chron. 28:5 and 2 Chron. 9:8 (both unique to the Chronicler).

[47] 2 Sam. 7:16 reads "your house" and "your kingdom" refering to David.

[48] These wars also provide treasures for the temple vessels (1 Chron. 18:8).

in and of themselves save that they highlight one of the tensions at the heart of the Chronicler's theocracy, namely the degree to which the people are not involved in determining their fate (despite the Chronicler's so-called "democratizing" *Tendenz*). Joab speaks the truth in more ways than one when he says to David: "Are they not my lord [and the ambiguity of kingship as to who is king, this "lord" or "the LORD," is better expressed in the English] the king all of them my lord's servants?" (1 Chron. 21:3). They are indeed his servants and as his servants are made to pay the price for David's sin to the tune of seventy thousand (21:14). Jerusalem, however, is spared at the last moment and this moment of salvation also marks the place of salvation. With the angel hovering over Jerusalem at the very spot at which Abraham himself hovered over Isaac,[49] David "built an altar to the LORD and presented burnt offerings and offerings of well-being" (21:26a). Yahweh's response in 21:26b is unique to Chronicles:

> He called upon the LORD, and he answered him with fire from heaven on the altar of burnt offering (1 Chron. 21:26).

The consecration of the new site for the central sanctuary with fire from heaven recalls pre-Davidic traditions relating to the altar. In the first instance one notes that Aaron's sacrifice on the altar before the tabernacle (which was still the sole legitimate place of sacrifice) was consumed in like manner (Lev. 9:24). This act of God confirms the legitimacy of this new altar and places David's achievements with reference to the temple on par with Moses's achievements. All of which leads David to declare: "Here shall be the house of the LORD God and here the altar of burnt offering for Israel" (1 Chron. 22:1). Further on in Chronicles, the temple is also linked with the tabernacle in terms of its design. David gives Solomon the temple plans (תבנית: 28:11–19) in the same way as God gave the tabernacle plan to Moses (Exod. 25:9, 40).[50] The temple site is named Mt. Moriah (2 Chron. 3:1) which was of course the site of the sacrifice of Isaac.

---

[49] Again, unique to the Chronicler.

[50] Riley, *King and Cultus*, pp. 62–3. Williamson also adds (1) Huramabi the temple builder has the same skills as Bezalel the tabernacle builder (2 Chron. 2:13–14 and Exod. 35:35); and (2) the reference to the veil in the temple which is the only such reference in the Old Testament (2 Chron. 3:14; cf. Exod. 26:31ff and 36:35 for the tabernacle veil) [H. G. M. Williamson, "The Temple in the Books of Chronicles." in W. Horbury (ed.) *Templum Amicitae: Essays on the Second Temple Presented to Ernst Bammel* (JSNTS 48; Sheffield; JSOT Press, 1991), pp. 15–31].

And finally in Solomon's reign, once the ark was in its final resting place and at the dedication of the temple "fire came down from heaven and consumed the burnt offering and sacrifices; and the glory of the LORD filled the temple" (2 Chron. 7:1).[51]

Final Preparations and Orders

Immediately after the consecration of the altar marking the future site of the temple, David prepares to transfer the kingdom over to Solomon. The material from here to the end of 1 Chronicles is virtually without parallel in Samuel-Kings and, apart from describing David making elaborate preparations for the building of the temple and the organization of its service, contains a number of important speeches by David which articulate again the fundamentals of the theocratic kingdom.

In his first speech and addressing Solomon, David specifies more fully the connections between the dynastic promise and the building of the Temple, and explains his disqualification with regard to the latter:

> My son, I had planned to build a house to the name of the LORD my God. But the word of the LORD came to me saying, "You have shed much blood and have waged great wars: you shall not build a house to my name, because you have shed so much blood in my sight on the earth. See, a son shall be born to you; he shall be a man of rest [מנוחה]. I will give peace and quiet to Israel in his days. He shall build a house for my name. He shall be a son to me, and I will be a father to him, and I will establish his royal throne in Israel forever" (1 Chron. 22:7–10).

David's unacceptability as temple-builder as "a man of war and bloodshed" is here understood in comparison to Solomon's acceptability as a man of peace (a play on his name) who enjoys, from the beginning of his reign, the "rest" necessary for establishing the temple. As discussed above, the concept of rest according to Deuteronomy

---

[51] Williamson also notes connections between the temple site and other premonarchic cultic sites: (1) 1 Chron. 21:20 compares well with the story of Gideon's encounter with an angel at a threshing floor that included supernatural fire (from which Gideon hid-turned-saw) and resulted in the establishment of a permanent holy place (Judg. 6); (2) David's purchase compares with Abraham's purchase (Gen. 23:9), including the use of בכסף מלא "at its full price" and נתן with the meaning "to buy." Both owners, Ornan and Ephron want to give the site away (1 Chron. 21:22–25); and (3) the temple site is referred to as Mt. Moriah (Genesis 22) which has definite cultic associations (2 Chron. 3:1) [Williamson, "Temple"].

12 establishes the timetable for the building of the temple. The complete conquest of the land would bring about the rest required for the setting up of the central sanctuary.

> When you cross over the Jordan and live in the land that the LORD your God is allotting to you, and when he gives you rest from your enemies all around so that you live in safety, then you shall bring everything that I command you to the place that the LORD your God will choose as a dwelling for his name . . . (Deut. 12:10–11).

The Chronicler does not, as noted earlier, retain the exodus and conquest as definitive moments in the establishment of Israel but he does retain the dynamics of conquest as associated with the word ירש ("to possess" or "to dispossess"). Israel's "possession" of the land comes about through the "dispossession" of the Canaanites which is conditional on their faithfulness to Yahweh. David too reminds Solomon of the *general* terms of the covenant:

> Only, may the LORD grant you discretion and understanding, so that when he gives charge over Israel you may keep the law of the LORD your God. Then you will prosper if you are careful to observe the statutes and the ordinances that the LORD commanded Moses for Israel. Be strong and of good courage [חזק ואמץ]. Do not be afraid or dismayed (1 Chron. 22:13).

David's words echo the words of Moses to Joshua prior to the conquest of the land:

> Be strong and courageous [חזק ואמץ]; for you shall put this people in possession of the land that I swore to their ancestors to give them. Only be strong and courageous, being careful to act in accordance with all the law that my servant Moses commanded you; do not turn from it to the right hand or to the left, so that you may be successful wherever you go (Josh. 1:6–7).

According to the Chronicler, David had completed the conquest and had brought about a situation of rest for Solomon so that he could build the Temple. Addressing the leaders of Israel (and carrying forward the synthesis of dynasty and people) David says:

> Is not the LORD your God with you? Has he not given you peace on every side? For he has delivered the inhabitants of the land into my hand; and the land is subdued before the LORD and his people. Now set your mind and heart to seek the LORD your God. Go build the sanctuary of the LORD God so that the Ark of the covenant of the LORD and the holy vessels of God may be brought into a house built for the name of the LORD (22:18–19).

The full realization of Israel as the kingdom of Yahweh in the land of Israel is affected (exclusively) via the establishment of these two houses, or more accurately the establishment of the house of Yahweh by the house of David. This latter point in reiterated in David's speech to the leaders of Israel (1 Chron. 28) where he again explains that he was disqualified from building the temple. This does not, however, diminish David's role as the one chosen "to be king over Israel forever" (28:4) and his son Solomon who, as the one chosen "to sit upon the throne of the kingdom of the LORD over Israel" (28:5), will "build my house and my courts, for I have chosen him to be a son to me, and I will be a father to him. I will establish his kingdom forever . . ." (28:6–7a). But so as not to be misunderstood, "forever" is conditional (and in general terms again) on "keeping my commandments and my ordinances" (28:7b) and if both Solomon and the leaders of Israel continue to do just that they will indeed "possess this good land, and leave it for an inheritance to your children after you forever" (28:8).

Turning once again to Solomon, David charges him to "Be strong and of good courage, and act. Do not be afraid or dismayed; for the LORD God, my God, is with you. He will not fail you or forsake you, until all the work for the service of the house is finished" (28:20). The last clause makes it quite clear that the *immediate and specific condition* of the dynastic promise is the building of the Temple. Whatever the future implications of the promise, the building of the Temple is the lasting achievement of this covenant. The temple is the "forever" of the covenant and though conditional on Solomon completing the project this "forever" is never in doubt. The temple did continue to be the eternal focal point of the kingdom of Yahweh long after the dynasty was removed. Whatever the future expectations for the other house of the theocracy Yahweh's kingship over this people in this land was assured . . . assured that is as long as the people and their Davidic king (or failing that simply "his people": 2 Chron. 36:23) seek the LORD and keep his commandments.

David's final charge, this time to "the whole assembly" (1 Chron. 29:1), is that they support Solomon in building the temple. The "leaders of the ancestral houses" (29:6) respond with freewill offerings (setting a fine example for their post-exilic counterparts (cf. Ezra 2:69 // Neh. 7:70) and "the people rejoiced" (29:9) as they rejoiced after the first phase of the establishment of the central sanctuary (15:25). David then blesses the LORD with a psalm of praise (29:10–11;

cf. 16:8–36) and instructs "the whole assembly, 'Bless the LORD your God'." Worship is the focusing lens of this theocracy, establishing its synthesis, its continuity *and its hierarchy* as is made abundantly clear in the people's response: "for all the assembly (not only) blessed the LORD (but also) . . . prostrated themselves before the LORD *and before the king*" (29:20).

Theocracy and Hegemony in 2 Chronicles

Before discussing the ideological implications of this picture of the theocracy, and in particular the nature of its hierarchies, I will examine the way in which the Chronicler handles the transition from the full realization of the ideal theocratic state to its dissolution under Solomon's successor.

Solomon

Having completed the temple project which his father began,[52] Solomon (or the Chronicler) turns his attention to the on-going significance of a theocracy so constituted, seeking clarification of the terms of the covenant between Yahweh and David especially as they relate to the notion of "steadfast love" (חסד). The steadfast love of Yahweh stands for his commitment to the theocracy and is used with reference

---

[52] The unity between the Davidic-Solomonic "period" is evident in such phrases as "they walked . . . in the way of David and Solomon" (2 Chron. 11:17), "God said to David and to his son Solomon" (33:7), and "the written directions of King David of Israel and the written directions of his son Solomon" (35:4). Riley summarizes the other continuities as follows: ". . . during his night vision at Gibeon, Solomon recalls Yahweh's חסד to David and asks that the divine word to David be fulfilled (1:8–9); Solomon's announcement of his intention to build continues the trade relationship with Tyre which was begun by David (2:3); Solomon's request for workers is intended to supplement the skilled workers already provided by David (2:6–7); the Chronistic account of the actual construction begins by identifying the site with the place David had prepared, and ends with those things that David had dedicated being brought into the finished construction (3:1; 5:1); the dedication of the Temple contains many references to the promise made to David and the deeds done by him, both in the words of Solomon and in the account of the liturgical action (6:4–10, 15–17, 42); the account of the assembly of the people and the bringing of the Ark into the Temple echoes explicitly the Ark liturgy of the Chronistic David (5:11b–13), just as the manifestation of Yahweh's presence in Solomon's Temple is reminiscent of the manifestation in the story of David at Ornan's threshing-floor (7:1–3); Yahweh's blessing of Solomon and promise to him makes a double reference to David's deeds and covenant" [Riley, *King and Cultus*, pp. 85–6].

to both its houses. I noted earlier the refrain "For the LORD is good, his steadfast love endures forever" which is introduced in 1 Chronicles 16 and is as it were the clarion call of temple worship (as conducted by the Levites). It is also used as an expression of Yahweh's commitment to David (1 Chron. 17:13). Solomon turns to the question of the "steadfastness" of Yahweh at the beginning of his dedicatory prayer (cf. 1 Kings 8:23ff):

> O LORD, God of Israel, there is no God like you, in heaven or on earth, keeping covenant in steadfast love [חסד] with your servants who walk before you with all their heart. . . . Therefore, O LORD, God of Israel, keep for your servant, my father David, that which you promised him, saying, "There shall never fail you a successor before me to sit on the throne of Israel, if only your children keep to their way, to walk in my law as you have walked before me." Therefore, O LORD, God of Israel, let your word be confirmed, which you promised to your servant David (2 Chron. 6:14–17).

And at the end of his prayer (which is unique to Chronicles):

> Now, O my God, let your eyes be open and your ears attentive to the prayer from this place. Now rise up, O LORD God, and go to your resting place, you and the Ark of your might. Let your priests, O LORD God, be clothed with salvation, and let your faithful rejoice in your goodness. O LORD God, do not reject your anointed one. Remember your steadfast love for your servant David (6:40–42).[53]

Yahweh answers Solomon in dramatic (though not direct) fashion with fire from heaven consuming the burnt offering and sacrifices, whereupon "the glory of the LORD filled the temple" (7:1). The theocracy is now fully established and "all the people of Israel. . . .

> . . . bowed down on the pavement with their faces to the ground and worshipped and gave thanks to the LORD, saying, "For he is good, for his steadfast love endures forever" (7:3).

This is the climax of the story of the establishment of the theocracy. Every constituent element has been accounted for in the process— all the tribes, leaders of the people, priests, Levites, all Israel in the land of Israel. Each element has been incorporated in turn into this

---

[53] This interpretation translates the חסדי דויד as an objective genitive. See *TDOT*, vol. 5, pp. 44–64. Some, notably A. Caquot, "Les 'grâces de David.' A propos de'Isaie 55/3b," *Semitica* 15 (1965), pp. 45–59, argue that it is a subjective genitive, i.e. David's steadfast love, which in his view makes it less future oriented. See Kelly, *Retribution*, p. 137, for a summary of his argument.

complex entity in vortex-like fashion via the activities of one "house" for the sake of another "house." The direction of integration, however, has never been in doubt; it is always inwards and always upwards, culminating in this moment of dedication. But all along the view has been to the future and specifically the future of the Chronicler's present. This self-conscious doubling back upon itself of the story of Israel whereby the Chronicler attempts to read the past structurally and historically at the same time may undermine *our* sense of story but it powerfully reinforces the idea that this is *someone's* story, someone's problem, someone's solution, someone's theology, someone's politics, someone's ideology.

Had I been the storyteller I might have ended right here with this the cultic anthem of the post-exilic community (cf. Ezra 3:11) praising God for the fulfilment of his promises to the patriarchs and his promise to David. Has not Solomon fulfilled the specific condition of the Davidic covenant? Indeed, he has but Solomon anticipates (as David did before him) Israel's failure to live up to the challenge of theocracy. The bulk of his dedicatory prayer deals with these potential failures (from the human side) of theocratic rule culminating with this petition:

> If they sin against you—for there is no one who does not sin—and you are angry with them and give them to an enemy, so that they are carried away captive to a land far or near; then if they come to their senses in the land to which they have been taken captive, and repent, and plead with you in the land of their captivity, saying, "We have sinned, and have done wrong; we have acted wickedly"; if they repent with all their heart and soul in the land of their captivity, to which they were taken captive, and pray toward their land, which you gave to their ancestors, the city that you have chosen, and the house that I have built for your name, then hear from heaven your dwelling place their prayer and their pleas, maintain their cause and forgive your people who have sinned against you (2 Chron. 6:36–39).

The petition presupposes, on the one hand, that the promise is still conditional in that if Israel sins they will be punished, the final punishment being exile. But the promise is also unconditional in that Yahweh is called upon to forgive his people (and bring them back to the land) even if they sin. It foresees the exile as the dissolution of the theocracy, symbolized by the loss of land, and (from the point of view of the book as a whole) as the ultimate affirmation of the theocracy; for inspite of Israel's unfaithfulness Yahweh has brought them back to the land. I noted in the last chapter how the exile is treated as something to be overcome in contrast to something remembered (in Ezra-Nehemiah). Solomon's request and Yahweh's response to it (to be discussed below) indicate that the exile is also remembered in Chronicles, if "remembered" is the correct word. But the purpose for which it is recalled is not the same as in Ezra-Nehemiah. There it marked out boundaries whereas here the dissolution of the theocracy stands as a cipher for the negative side of the internal dynamic of theocracy; the potential dark night before the inevitable new dawn of Yahweh's theocratic kingdom.

This is how I would interpret God's answer to Solomon (and in particular the Chronistic section in italics) which holds the conditional and the eternal in tension:

> I have heard your prayer, and *have chosen this place for myself as a house of sacrifice. When I shut up the heavens so that there is no rain, or command the locust to devour the land, or send pestilence among my people, if my people who are called by my name humble themselves, pray, seek* [בקש] *my face, and turn from their wicked ways, then I will hear from heaven, and will forgive their sin and heal the land. Now my eyes will be open and my ears attentive to the prayer that is made in this place. For now I have chosen* and consecrated this house so that my name may be there forever; my eyes and my heart will be there for all time (7:12–16).

Solomon had sought clarification vis-à-vis the covenant with regard to both the dynasty itself and with regard to the fate of the people as a whole (though, as we have seen, these two facets are not always clearly distinguished in the Chronicler's treatment of the Davidic covenant). Yahweh's answer addresses both the question of the future of the people (7:12–16 cited above) and the future of the dynasty itself (7:17–18). This "additional" focus on "my people" is significant in that the central statement of the theocratic principle (from the mouth of God and the Chronicler's pen) should concern the people and not the dynasty. Though he goes on to address the dynastic question, "As for you (Solomon)..." (7:17ff), the book as a whole leaves the question as to the future of the dynasty open. In the meantime (and this includes the Chronicler's own time)[54] what is required of the people is an unambiguous commitment of loyalty to Yahweh as expressed in loyalty to his temple.

---

[54] As noted by Kelly, "the expression 'I will heal their land' also implies the return of the exiles" [*Retribution*, p. 61]. Cf. Jer. 30:17–18 and 33:6–37.

After Solomon

This theocratic principle, which is also described as the Chronicler's "doctrine of immediate retribution,"[55] is the fundamental criteria by which Solomon's successors are judged. The punishments incurred by subsequent Davidides for unfaithfulness to the cult are merely lesser versions of Judah's ultimate calamity. It is impossible to review all the relevant textual data here nor would this be necessary, for whatever one might say about the Chronicler *modus operandi* one cannot accuse him of inconsistency in this regard. A brief look at the reigns of Ahaz and Hezekiah, as negative and positive examples respectively, of this principle will suffice.

Ahaz did evil in the eyes of the LORD by worshipping Baal and engaging in other "abominable practices of the nations whom the LORD drove out before the people of Israel" (2 Chron. 28:4). He, therefore, suffers the consequence of a partial "exile" at the hand of Aram (and Israel; v. 8) who "took a great number of people captive" (v. 5).[56]

Ahaz's son Hezekiah, by contrast, "did what was right in the sight of the LORD, just as his ancestor David had done" (29:2) by cleansing the temple (29:3–19) and restoring proper worship there (29:20–36). This restoration of the temple paves the way for a reconciliation and re-unification of Israel and the theocracy as it was in the days of David and Solomon.[57] A further precondition for the restoration of theocratic kingdom, in the Chronicler's scheme of things, is the absence of the rebellious dynasty. The Chronicler omits direct reference to the destruction of the northern kingdom by Shalmaneser,[58] which is co-terminus with Ahaz's reign, and in doing so omits the reference to the foreign nations brought in by the Assyrians to take the place of the Israelites. As argued in chapter three, the reason the Chronicler omitted this narrative is most likely connected with his desire to advance a broader notion of Israel.

The occasion for reconciliation is a great Passover celebration in Jerusalem begins with an invitation to the North to join in. Note at

---

[55] On the merits of this notion, see chapter six.

[56] There is even a "good Samarians" tale in 2 Chron. 28:8–15. See R. Braun, "The Message of Chronicles: Rally "Round the Temple." *CTM* 42 (1971), p. 510.

[57] H. G. M. Williamson, *Israel in the Books of Chronicles* (Cambridge: Cambridge University Press, 1977), pp. 111–13, 125–30.

[58] It is obliquely refered to in 2 Chron. 30:6, quoted below.

this point the degree to which "ecumenical"[59] worship is "transformed" into a demonstration of loyalty to the theocracy, or (more
specifically) to the sanctuary at the heart of the theocracy.

> O people of Israel, return to the LORD, the God of Abraham, Isaac,
> and Israel, so that he may turn again to the remnant of you who have
> escaped from the hand of the kings of Assyria. Do not be like your
> ancestors and your kindred, who were faithless [מעל] to the LORD
> God of their ancestors, so that he made them a desolation, as you
> see. Do not now be stiff-necked as your ancestors were, but yield your-
> selves to the LORD and come to his sanctuary, which he has sanctified
> forever, and serve the LORD your God, so that his fierce anger may
> turn away from you. For as you return to the LORD, your kindred
> and your children will find compassion with their captors, and return
> to this land. For the LORD your God is gracious and merciful, and
> will not turn away his face from you, if you return to him (2 Chron.
> 30:6–9).[60]

But the story of Hezekiah as the prototype restoration, raises again
the issue of the identity of people Israel so restored. Though this
story is perhaps the clearest example of a more inclusive definition
of Israel (and was cited as such in chapter three) it also (and more
importantly) exposes the hierarchical dynamics of the theocratic kingdom and in such a way as to make their ideological implication for
the post-exilic period clear. Hezekiah's restoration (as noted in chapter three) is the occasion of his seemingly generous and inclusive
offer to the residents from the North. The letter of invitation, addressed
to "the people of Israel" (30:6), advises them not to be like their
ancestors who were "stiff-necked" but to "submit themselves before
the LORD and come to his sanctuary" (v. 8). To be a part of the
theocratic kingdom simply requires one to recognize his sanctuary
in Jerusalem; and yes, this offer is open to all those in the land of
Israel and is as such rooted in an inclusivist vision of Israel in comparison to Ezra-Nehemiah. But this broader vision of all Israel under
God, is (without putting too fine a point on it) Judah's and Jerusalem's
concept of Israel. All the texts cited in support of the inclusivist interpretation are, like this text, *also* about the legitimacy of the kingdom
of God as centred on Jerusalem and its two houses (or at least the
one surviving house thereof). The "positive" references to the North

---

[59] The word is Williamson's not mine [Williamson, "Temple"].

[60] Notice again how the issue of returning to the LORD and his Temple; loyalty to the Davidic dynasty is not mentioned.

(2 Chron. 11:13–17; 15:9; and 28:8–15) refer to residents in the North who have a loyal and submissive attitude towards Judah and Jerusalem. These residents from the North are included in the "all Israel in Judah and Benjamin" *but they are included on Judah's terms.* Other kings of Judah besides Hezekiah also continue to show an interest in the political and religious life of the North.[61] The ideological force of these texts (as distinct from the direct intentions of the Chronicler) amounts to a claim to hegemony on the part of the theocratic "kingdom" of the Chronicler's era over *all* the people in the *entire* land of Israel.[62]

This conclusion is confirmed when we broaden the scope of our inquiry and look at the way in which the Chronicler uses the term "Israel" in 2 Chronicles 10–36. Up until the end of Solomon's reign, the Chronicler's view of Israel was fairly consistent with the traditional view of Israel as composed of the twelve tribes (give or take a few). Even though he clearly states that Judah was the leading tribe, he is consistent in picturing Israel as united. I have already discussed the "all Israel" emphasis found in the genealogies and in the story of David and Solomon. The Chronicler's communicative intention is unmistakable: Israel is made up of all tribes united under David and around the Jerusalem Temple. This viewpoint may be tendentious in relation to historical reality and their may be a hierarchical ordering within this "broad church" but neither of these considerations is problematic in terms of the internal logic of the narrative. The Chronicler can make great claims about "all Israel" and the legitimacy of Judah and David without making sacrifices either way. The Chronicler's "all Israel under David" ideal is, however, both an opportunity and a trap as von Rad rightly points out.[63] During David's reign he can best present the dogmatic view that Israel = Israel + Judah, but the same "all Israel under David" stance also forces him to reject the northern kingdom. The Chronicler has to make adjustments to his ideal picture of Israel in its *Urzeit*; he has to work out a new balance between identity and legitimacy.

---

[61] 2 Chron. 15:8 (Asa); 19:4 (Jehoshophat); and 34:6, 9 (Josiah).

[62] Ruffing believes that the two are mutually exclusive. Its not a question legitimation but of showing that the temple can (still) be a "Symbol nationaler Hoffnung" [A. Ruffing, *Jahwekrieg als Weltmetapher: Studien zu Jahwekriegtexten des chronistischen Sondergutes* (Stuttgart: Katholisches Bibelwerk, 1992), p. 327].

[63] Von Rad, *Das Geschichtsbild des Chronistischen Werkes* (BWANT 54; Stuttgart, Kohlhammer, 1930), pp. 34–6.

As noted in chapter one, von Rad identifies three viewpoints on the identity of Israel in the latter part of Chronicles: (1) Israel = the southern kingdom of Judah and Benjamin; (2) Israel = Israel of the twelve tribes; and (3) Israel = the northern kingdom.[64] The first view which asserts a continuity between the united monarchy and the Judean monarchy is manifested, first of all, in the lack of interest in the history of northern Israel after the division of the kingdom. The Chronicler also makes direct comment about this kingdom which reveals a less than favourable disposition towards it. Jehoshaphat, for example, is reprimanded for allying himself with "the wicked and those who hate the LORD" (2 Chron. 19:2), and again for entering into a trading partnership with Israel; a partnership that ends (literally) in shipwreck (20:35–37). Another example comes from the reign of Amaziah. Amaziah is told not to hire mercenaries from Israel for "the LORD is not with Israel—all the sons of Ephraim" (2 Chron. 25:7).

More significant for our purposes, however, are the fourteen texts which use "Israel" with reference to the kingdom of Judah alone.[65] An important example (2 Chron. 11:3) is found in the context of the breakup of the kingdom under Rehoboam, the son of Solomon.

> When Rehoboam came to Jerusalem, he assembled one hundred eighty thousand chosen troops of the house of Judah and Benjamin to fight against Israel, to restore the kingdom to Rehoboam. But the word of the LORD came to Shemaiah the man of God: Say to King Rehoboam of Judah, son of Solomon, and to *all Israel in Judah and Benjamin, . . .* (11:1–3).

It is clear from this text that the Chronicler was consciously using "Israel" in two different ways: the third view (Israel = the northern kingdom) in verse one and the first view (Israel = the southern kingdom) in verse three. The Deuteronomist did not feel the need to equivocate on the word Israel; he applies it to the northern kingdom alone. These two definitions of Israel are also found together in the verses preceding 11:1–3:

> When all Israel [i.e. the Northerners] saw that the king would not listen to them, the people answered the king, "What share do we have in David? We have no inheritance in the son of Jesse. Each of you to

---

[64] Von Rad, *Geschichtsbild*, pp. 18ff.

[65] 2 Chron. 11:13; 12:1, 6; 15:17; 19:8; 20:29; 21:2, 4; 24:5, 16; 28:19, 23, 27; and 29:24.

> your tents, O Israel! Look now to your own house, O David." So all
> Israel departed to their tents. But Rehoboam reigned over the people
> of Israel who were living in the cities of Judah. . . . So Israel has been
> in rebellion against the house of David to this day (10:16–19).

Both these texts recall that intriguing reference to Judah and Benjamin,
Ephraim and Manasseh in Jerusalem (1 Chron. 9:3). The "all Israel
in Judah and Benjamin" (2 Chron. 11:3) and "the people of Israel
who were living in the cities of Judah" (10:17) expresses a comparable
idea, namely, that the southern kingdom (as opposed to simply Jerusalem in 1 Chron. 9:3) comprising the tribes of Judah and Benjamin
is nevertheless still representative of Israel as a whole. Japhet explains
this as signifying that the Chronicler defined both the southern and
northern kingdom as geographical entities regardless of the make-up
of the population.[66] I would argue, however, that this interpretation
does not account for the idea (expressed in this context and elsewhere) of the legitimacy of the southern kingdom which was still
centred on the two houses of the theocracy.

The most important "Israel = the southern kingdom" text is found
in Abijah's speech to the northerners before a battle in which they
and their rebel king Jeroboam are defeated (2 Chron. 13).

> Listen to me, Jeroboam and all Israel! Do you not know that the
> LORD God of Israel gave the kingship over Israel forever to David
> and his sons by a covenant of salt? Yet Jeroboam son of Nebat, a
> servant of Solomon son of David, rose up and rebelled against his
> lord; . . . And now you think that you can withstand *the kingdom of the
> LORD in the hand of the sons of David,* . . . O Israelites, do not battle
> against the LORD, the God of your ancestors; for you cannot suc-
> ceed (2 Chron. 13:4b, 5–6, 8, 12b).

It is quite clear in this passage that the kingdom of God was still
operative and still in the hands of the descendants of David, even
if the North was in a state of rebellion.[67] God's relationship with
"Israel" continues and he will even help the legitimate part of Israel
in their fight against the rebels. On the other hand, it has been
noted that Abijah avoids blaming the people themselves for they are
still children of Israel and Yahweh is still the "LORD, the God of

---

[66] S. Japhet, *The Ideology of the Book of Chronicles and its Place in Biblical Thought*
(BEATAJ 9; trans. A. Barber; Frankfurt: Peter Lang, 1989), pp. 308–24.

[67] Ruffing argues that this text is not so much a judgment on the North as a
statement concerning the continuing validity of the Davidic promise, that despite
historical setbacks such as this the promise to David and his descendants is still
valid [Ruffing, *Jahwekrieg*, p. 70].

your ancestors" (2 Chron. 13:12).[68] The possibility for reconciliation is, thus, left open and the Chronicler's continued interest in a united Israel (though united around Judah) is confirmed in the subsequent narrative and most notably in the narrative of Hezekiah's reign as discussed above.

Conclusion

This brings us back to the model I used in chapter three to compare the way in which Chronicles and Ezra-Nehemiah define Israel:

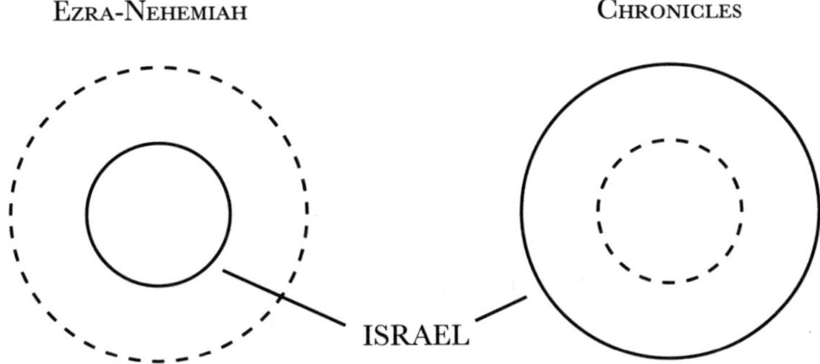

This two-dimensional model now needs to be modified into a three-dimensional model in order to represent the hierarchical nature of the ethnicity propounded in Chronicles.

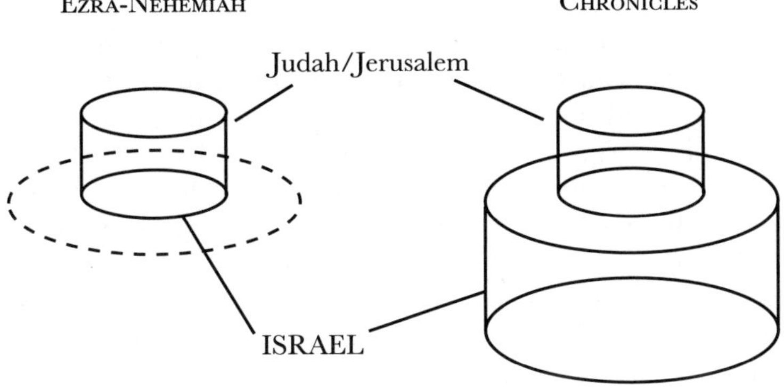

---

[68] Japhet, *Ideology*, pp. 323–4; Japhet, *I & II Chronicles* (OTL; Louisville, KY: Westminster/John Knox, 1993), pp. 685–700; Williamson, *Israel*, pp. 112–14.

This diagram illustrates how the distinction between the post-exilic community and the "people of the land" is in fact retained in Chronicles though in the form of an internal hierarchy. The Chronicler's immediate community is still the community of returnees and thus he shares with the writer of Ezra-Nehemiah the "exile-(re)conquest" tradition of origin. The focus of Israel's identity on the centre is a transformation of the Ezra-Nehemiah ideology, not an abandonment of it. I would go on to argue that this had more than a nostalgic (von Rad, Japhet) or benignly ecumenical (Williamson) meaning in the Chronicler's day. *This amounts to Jerusalem's claim to hegemony over all the land of Israel.* Whereas the author of Ezra-Nehemiah merely asserts the continuity between his community and pre-exilic Israel, the Chronicler works this idea out in all its historical detail, amplifying the significance of this claim in the process.

But who making this claim and to whom? How do we identify the Chronicler and his audience? I would argue that the Chronicler was addressing, in the first instance, the ruling and priestly classes in Jerusalem of which he was a part and that Chronicles is thereby representative of the self-understanding of these ruling classes. His ideology is a part of, sustained, and perhaps even transformed an ideological discourse at the heart of the theocratic establishment. The Chronicler is asking his audience to imagine Jerusalem as the centre of a nation, territorially-defined, and not simply the cultic centre of a small citizen-temple community within an empire. Whereas the author of Ezra-Nehemiah exhibits a defensive posture, the Chronicler articulates a more confident understanding of Jerusalem's role as the centre of Israel—people and land. In comparison to Ezra-Nehemiah, the Chronicler recognises an opportunity for his community to expand its horizons, to claim its rightful place over Israel thereby restoring the theocratic kingdom to its full extent.

This is not to suggest, however, that the Chronicler was only addressing this immediate audience or that his ideology of identity is merely an expression of their limited interests. This is to misunderstand the nature of ideologies of identity and legitimacy. My conclusion regarding the ideology of identity in Chronicles—that it was also an ideology of legitimacy—does not mean that it could not have functioned in a truly integrative way for the inhabitants of "all Israel." If the Chronicler's motive was to generate belief in his vision of a greater federalist Israel among the people in general, and if his intention was to do this in terms of a grand narrative concerning the foundation of its central institution, we cannot assume that it did not in fact have this effect. That is to say, the "manifest content" of the Chronicler's ideology—and indeed the motives and intentions behind it—may have cohered with its "functional properties" but we must not assume that it did. There is a danger in taking ideologies of identity at face value without taking into consideration that ideologies of identity are the point at which the beliefs of the people are taken hold of for the purpose of power. One is asked to believe but can' one disbelieve? What are the consequences of belief?

This question can be approached in two ways, both of which begin by considering the social context in which Chronicles was written. One way has already been tried. Noth argued, as we saw in chapter one, that the motive of the Chronicler was to legitimate the Jerusalem temple on the one hand and attack the legitimacy of the sanctuary on Mt. Gerizim on the other. His intention was to demonstrate the continuing validity of the temple in Jerusalem as the sole legitimate sanctuary for Israel by re-telling the history of the temple from its foundation to the post-exilic restoration. This particular reconstruction of the historical and ideological context of Chronicles is no longer tenable given that recent archeological work on Mt. Gerizim has uncovered no sign of a temple or settlement from the Ptolemaic period. The sanctuary recently unearthed was built in the Seleucid period, probably during the reign of Antiochus III.[69] And even if there was a continuing cultic tradition on Gerizim it is hard to believe that Jerusalem would have felt threatened by it. Its a bit like saying that expressions of American national pride (such as are no doubt found in recent histories of the American revolution) are anti-British. The assumption involved in the anti-Samaritan hypothesis is that apologetic language must be directed at outside rivals. That is not to say that the Chronicler and his set did not entertain imperialistic thoughts, it is just that these should perhaps be classified as forward looking and optimistic concerning Jerusalem's potential rather than as straight-forward polemic. By questioning this assumption I am not saying that an "external" factor is ruled out. There is, no doubt, room to speculate on the possible occasion for Chronicles.

---

[69] I. Magen, "Gerizim, Mt.," in E. Stern (ed.), *The New Encyclopedia of Archaeological Excavations in the Holy Land* (Jerusalem: Israel Exploration Society/New York: Simon & Schuster), vol. 2, pp. 484–7.

Was he writing at a time of greater community self-confidence? Did the (immanent or actual) demise of the Persians and the rise of the Macedonians present itself as an opportunity to think big? One only has to think of the story in Josephus about Alexander meeting the high priest. Was the Chronicler one of the high priest's entourage? I don't mean this literally, of course, but the self-understanding of this story seems to represent just the sort of thing that empires seem to provoke in smaller nations that are nonetheless keen to show that they have a divinely ordained place in the world.

Another avenue of inquiry, however, and one which has not yet been explored is to ask about the internal dimension of the Chronicler's ideology. In the next chapter, I will begin to explore this idea by reconstructing the internal social context of the theocratic ideology of the Chronicler.

CHAPTER FIVE

HIERARCHY WITHIN

Introduction

The purpose of the next two chapters is to explore the "internal consequences" of the Chronicler's ideology, beginning with a reconstruction of the internal social context of Chronicles. I use the word "consequences" not in the sense of actual sequential consequences (as if we can discern what the actual effects of Chronicles were) but with reference to Giddens's unintended consequences and the social conventions and institutions which they sustain. As applied to Chronicles, "consequences" is shorthand for the view that Chronicles was embedded in and is an expression of a particular discourse which in turn was connected with the hierarchical structure of the theocratic community with the Second Temple at its apex.

In the last two chapters, I examined the role of ideology in the shaping identity and establishing the legitimacy of the post-exilic theocratic community. I concluded with a hypothesis concerning the identity of the Chronicler and his circle namely that he belonged to the ruling classes in Jerusalem. I did not at that point specify what I meant by ruling classes nor did I elaborate on what the interests of these classes might be over against the interests of the majority of the population. My concern was to demonstrate that the broader definition of Israel on offer in Chronicles, a broader ideology of identity as compared to that presented in Ezra-Nehemiah, was at the same time part of and indeed an essential ingredient in an ideology which legitimated Jerusalem's claim to hegemony over all Israel. So why identify this ideology with the ruling classes at all? Is it not simply a Judean-Jerusalemite versus a non-Judean-Jerusalemite point of view? To leave it at that would be, I believe, to misconstrue the way in which ideology works, for whom it works and to whom it is addressed. The Chronicler was addressing in the first instance his immediate clerical peers in Jerusalem who, along with leading lay members of the community, had a vested interest in the prestige of the Second Temple. It is unlikely that they needed any convincing as to the importance of the temple.

So why did he go to the effort of rewriting the history of Israel? One of the possible reasons has already been discussed, namely, that the Chronicler is trying to broaden the political horizons of this immediate community by picturing Jerusalem at the centre of a greater Israel: the Chronicler as political visionary. It is here that the comparison with Ezra-Nehemiah is useful in identify the contours of an inner-Judean-Jerusalemite debate about identity. The overt terms of this debate involved the question of just who is included in this theocracy. The Chronicler's claim to the legitimacy of the temple as the cultic centre for all Israel is in effect a claim to hegemony over regions and people who would not necessarily welcome such hegemony. But, as I will argue in this chapter, this vision of a greater Israel and the all-encompassing legitimacy of Jerusalem and its temple also addresses the question of the legitimacy of this temple as the dominant institution *within* the post-exilic community. We cannot assume that this claim was uncontroversial[1] or that the interests of those who controlled the temple were the interests of the majority. Even if it had no rivals (and Mt. Gerizim was no rival) a leading institution such as the temple would have had to actively maintain its position in its discourses and through its practices. It is my view that Chronicles is a cross-section of this discourse.

In order to demonstrate the plausibility of this thesis, I need to demonstrate that there was a hierarchy within. In this chapter I will argue that there was a system of hierarchies within the post-exilic community reaching all the way down to the basic social unit of the community, the "house of the fathers" or בית אבות. These hierarchical structures were not overtly parasitic on the community structures (like the imperial administration) but were native to it and constructed from the inside.

Hierarchy and Exploitation

The Socio-Economic Situation in General

In the first part of this chapter, I examine the hierarchical structures of Judean society in the Persian period. Far from being a unified

---

[1] Though just what sort of controversies raged is hard to say. Trito-Isaiah and Malachi, though critical of current (current when?) cultic practice simply confirm the dominance of the temple as the symbolic centre for Judaism at the time.

and relatively classless society I find evidence for hierarchical structures within the very building blocks of the community, the בתי אבות or "houses of the fathers." Intimately connected with these hierarchies is the question of economics and the production and distribution of goods within society. That is not to say, however, that the economic dimension is the fundamental cause or explanandum vis-à-vis all other aspects of social life. The case to be made here is that ideology, politics and economics are so thoroughly intertwined as to preclude giving any one dimension causal priority. Nor do we have anything like the sort of data with which to say concretely and in detail what the economic situation was. What we do have is some textual evidence which is at once less satisfying, empirically-speaking, and richer, sociologically-speaking. We have to make educated guesses about the former—the broad brush or rough outline must suffice—but with regard to the latter we have in the ideology of the text the very thing of which social realities were constructed.

Before turning to examine the evidence for hierarchies within Judean society and the potential for economic exploitation that existed within it, I will look at two previous studies of the socio-economic context within which (broadly speaking) Chronicles was written. Both studies use Marx's concept of "mode of production" as a way of modelling the often opaque relationship between politics, ideology, hierarchy and economics. Whilst I am not particularly committed to this model and do not accept the historical materialist baggage with which it is encumbered, I do feel that there is some mileage left in the Marxist formulation of the "Asiatic" and "ancient" modes of production. Marx's formulation of the Asiatic mode of production in particular is a significant attempt to unravel the structures of and indeed the genesis of power within what are ostensibly "community" structures. I begin therefore with a general discussion of what is meant by mode of production and a brief examination of Marx's definition of the two relevant modes of production.

Excursus: The Concept of Mode of Production
The concept of mode of production as put forward by Marx refers to the relationship between the forces or *means of production* and the social *relations of production*. The means of production denotes that to which labour is applied (such as land) and the tools and technologies used in the production of goods. In the ancient world, the means of production changed very little over time for societies were primarily

agrarian and technological advance was slow. The relations of production, however, did vary significantly over time and from place to place in the ancient world, especially in relationship to the ownership of land. Thus, what distinguishes the modes of production in the ancient world are the relations of production and, within that, chiefly the question of who owned the land.

The mode of production also refers to the stages of progression in the evolution of economic systems and societies. Thus, according to Marx, the ancient or classical world came to be dominated by one mode of production called (appropriately enough) the "ancient" mode of production. This mode of production is said to have given way to the feudal mode of production which in turn gave way to the capitalist mode of production. This is, as we shall soon see, one of the more controversial aspects of the "mode of production"-type analysis.

The Asiatic Mode of Production[2] or AMP designates agrarian societies in which the land is "owned" by the community as organized into villages which in turn support a central government. Productive activity is organized and carried out primarily at the village level and within the village there is very little division of labour. Manufacturing and trade are not significant aspects of the economy as whole. The central government or state is almost exclusively dependent upon the surplus production of the villages and is, therefore, essentially a bureaucratic apparatus that collects these surpluses in the form of taxes. The relationship between the villages and the centre is one-sided in that the central state apparatus exists by means of its capacity to exploit the village communities. But a degree of reciprocity does exist insofar as the state serves the (real or perceived) needs of the community such as the building and maintenance of irrigation canals and/or temples. The centre is also the institution which holds all the villages together as a distinct social entity in an otherwise de-centralised economic system. The "cohesion-enforcing centre"[3] of the AMP is thus both exploitative and functionally necessary at the same time; simultaneously classless and despotic, absolutist and arbitrary.[4]

---

[2] It is called "Asiatic" because the societies so designated by Marx were in China and India.

[3] E. Gellner, "Foreword," in J. O'Leary, *The Asiatic Mode of Production* (Oxford: Blackwell, 1989), p. viii.

[4] The AMP is an anomolous and controversial element within the historical mate-

The central issue in the AMP is the question of power. The AMP describes, in a worst case scenario, a situation in which the exercise of power is both absolute and irreducible: absolute in not being contained via a system of checks and balances and irreducible in the sense of being the sole ordering principle of the society as a distinct society. Power and social order are conjoined and embedded in one another. Apart from sheer coercive force or the threat of force, the AMP sustains itself in the face of exploitation via an illusory ideology which plays on the ambiguity of the "community-higher community" relationship. The higher community—the central authority or state—represents (itself as) the "real" community at a higher level and acts on behalf of the community. As O'Leary puts it: "The direct producers make a fetish of the despot, or higher unity, vesting the despot rather than themselves with the power and capacity which their works have demonstrated."[5] The presence of a despot is not a necessary element in the community-higher community ideology for, as Aristotle himself argued, democratic government when unconstrained by law "aims at absolute power and becomes like a despot" and is "the exact counterpart of tyranny among monarchies."[6] The AMP is thus a classic example of the ideology problematic (as identified by Ricoeur) in which an ideological system identifies, legitimates and distorts all at the same time.

The definitive feature of the AMP as it relates to economic matters was the absence of (or the weakness of) private property. According to Marx, community ownership of the land presupposes in the first instance the kinship group or "clan community"[7] which settles on the land *as a community*. In the central passage dealing with the AMP, Marx describes this form of landownership as follows:

---

rialist scheme of things since it contradicts the orthodox Marxist account of the state. According to orthodox Marxism, the state is the instrument of propertied classes and hence post-dates the development of these classes. In the AMP the ruling classes do not have "special, socially localized rights over resources" [Gellner, "Foreword," p. x]; the class-exploitation that does exist in the AMP is of a different kind and is co-terminus with the state and class conflict does not determine its further development. The absense of propertied classes "leads not to freedom and harmony but on the contrary, to despotism" [Gellner, "Foreword," p. x].

[5] J. O'Leary, *The Asiatic Mode of Production* (Oxford: Blackwell), p. 98.

[6] Aristotle, cited in O'Leary, *Asiatic Mode*, p. 43. Other political philosophers, such as Occam, distinguish between despotism and tyranny whereby the despot is said to rule with the consent of the ruled while in the latter is not [O'Leary, *Asiatic Mode*, p. 47].

[7] German "Stamm"; i.e. any extended kinship grouping.

> The earth is the great workshop, the arsenal which furnishes both means and materials of labour, as well as the seat, the *base* of the community. They relate *naïvely* to it as the *property of the community*, and of the community producing and reproducing itself in living labour. Each individual conducts himself only as a link, as a member of this community as proprietor or possessor. The *real appropriation* through the labour process happens under these *presuppositions*, which are not themselves the product of labour, but appear as its natural or *divine* presuppositions.[8]

In the earliest "landed" (i.e. settled) communities the relationship between the community and the land, wherein the land is thought of as "the property of the community," *appears* to be a natural, or even divinely ordained, not a socially constructed, relationship. In other words, there is a lack of differentiation between the community and the means of production at its disposal. There is also a lack of differentiation within the community in terms of the relations of production. Power differentials emerge but only within the community and via the manipulation of its ideology of identity. Thus,

> ...it is not the least in contradiction to it [i.e. the "primitive" community-land relationship] that, as in most of the *Asiatic* landforms, the *comprehensive unity* standing above all these little communities appears as the higher *proprietor* or as the *sole proprietor*; and the real communities hence only as hereditary occupiers. Because the *unity* is the real proprietor, and the real presupposition of communal property, it follows that this unity can appear as a *particular* entity above the many real, particular communities, where the individual is then in fact property-less, or, property ... appears mediated for him through a cession by the total unity—a unity realized in the form of the despot, the father of many communities—to the individual, through the mediation of the particular commune. The surplus product ... thereby automatically belongs to this highest unity.[9]

This rather opaque paragraph is, unfortunately, also the pivotal text with regard to the AMP and on these two counts must be looked at carefully. The contradiction at the heart of the AMP (though not, he believes, at the heart of his thesis) turns on the fact that the AMP community is a "comprehensive unity" which transcends the level of the pre-given or naturally-occurring kinship ("primitive") community. The degree to which the lifeworld of the "real" village community,

---

⁸ K. Marx, *Grundrisse der Kritik der politischen Ökonomie* (Frankfurt: Europäische Verlagsanstalt), p. 472. All italics are in the original.

⁹ Marx, *Grundrisse*, pp. 472–3.

the activities it carries out in the on-going production and reproduction of social life in the land, are "taken up" and co-ordinated
with those of other villages and become part of a larger lifeworld is
the degree to which this new lifeworld, this new "comprehensive
unity" transcends, and is *perceived to* transcend, the horizon of any
one of these smaller communities. The lifeworld of these "real" communities is *perceived as* dependent on, or a part of, a larger lifeworld
and on that basis obligated to it. The systemic interconnection of
action consequences still occurs, by and large, within the horizon of
the lifeworld of individual village or kinship communities for the
movement of surplus goods to the centre is the only point at which
action consequences transcend the horizon of village life. The actions
taken at the centre, on the other hand, are of consequence or systemic significance for the mode of production as a whole insofar as
they directly affect the means of production (irrigation canals are a
paradigmatic example of this). The AMP is thus not a rational economic system geared to the efficient co-ordination of action vis-à-vis
the material reproduction of the community. The decisive characteristics of the AMP are social, political and ideological.

The ideology of the AMP is defined in terms of appearance versus reality. For Marx, the "appearance" of one thing is juxtaposed
to the "reality" of something else, as in the "the unity" appearing
as the "sole proprietor" over and above the real "primitive" communities. But this "appearing" is at once an illusion and a reality
of a different sort. On the one hand, Marx identifies illusions on the
basis of a materialistic understanding of reality—the reality of living
labour, or real communities working on community land—but on
the other hand that which is but an appearance is a reality of a
different sort, namely, the reality of the comprehensive unity; the
sense that the community has a shared identity which transcends the
kinship group and/or village boundaries. This sense of community
or collective self-consciousness is as much an inextricable part of
human life as is the real living work carried out in the field. If this
is to be described as an illusion it is a real and necessary one, functionally speaking, and whilst one may want to accept this distinction
between reality and appearance for heuristic reasons one should also
be aware of the limits of this distinction and take note of the point
at which it breaks down. More important perhaps is the degree to
which Marx also recognises the limitations of the materialist understanding of reality as embodied in the base-superstructure model.

The higher community within the AMP (part of the superstructure) did not emerge as a result of pre-existing economic factors. He describes it as having emerged seamlessly from the primitive community with the expansion of the limits of the community and the emergence of the higher community within it.

This community-higher community ideology, this only partial distinction between community and power, is the heart of the AMP. We can all spot the blatant abuse of power but can we determine or isolate the genesis of power in the life of a community? Is power and order the same thing? What Marx starts with is unequivocal exploitation on the one hand and "real" living communities on the other. He then attempts to articulate how the one can exist within the other without being anchored in "special, socially localized rights over resources."[10] The key to unlocking this secret is the so-called "primitive community," the kinship group, the extended family, and the patriarchal family in particular. The unity of the latter group and its power structure is focused on one individual, the patriarch. Thus, "it follows that this unity [now speaking about the AMP] can appear as a *particular* entity above the many real, particular communities, where the individual is then in fact propertyless, or, property . . . appears mediated for him through a cession by the total unity—a unity realized in the form of the despot, the father of many community's. . . ." The despot is a patriarch writ large: his interests are the community's interests; his power is the expression of the power of the community; his destiny, the community's.[11] Any attempt to discern a fundamental distinction between community and higher community can only come from the outside; the community-higher community ideology can only be critiqued from the point of view of a different understanding of power, and with that a different understanding of community.[12]

---

[10] Gellner, "Foreword," p. x.

[11] Before moving on to consider the so-called "ancient mode of production," it is important to note that there is a good deal of variety among the historical societies which Marx described as AMP's. At the one end of the continuum the "comprehensive unity" hovers above many independent village communities in which the individual families work independently on their allotments. At the other end of the continuum the unity of the community extends to the "communality of labour itself" as applied for example to the building of irrigation canals. These works then "appear as" the work of the higher community. The higher community in an AMP may be represented by one person—the despot—or as a unity of patriarchs [Marx, *Grundrisse*, p. 473].

[12] Marx was speaking not only as a materialist but also as a European and for

According to Marx, the ancient mode of production (also known as the classical mode of production or slave-based mode of production) . . .

> . . . also assumes the *community* as its first presupposition, but not, as in the first case, as the substance of which the individuals are mere accidents, or of which they form purely natural component parts— it presupposes as its base not the countryside, but the town as the already created seat (centre) of the rural population (owners of land). The cultivated field appears as a *territorium* belonging to the town; not the village as mere assessory to the land.[13]

Within the territorium of the town or city, the land is further divided into the *ager publicus* and private properties owned by individuals. The idea of private property can only arise, Marx maintains, when the taken-for-grantedness of the community-land relationship is shattered by the presence of "other communes, which have either already occupied the land and soil, or which disturb the commune in its own occupation. War is, therefore, the all-embracing task, the great communal labour which is required either for the occupation of the objective conditions for being alive, or for the protection and perpetuation of this occupation."[14] The struggle for survival is not with the land itself but with other city-centred communities.

> The commune—as state—is, on one side, the relation of these free and equal private proprietors to one another, their bond against the outside, and is at the same time their safeguard.[15]

The differentiation of community and land also transforms relations of production as they relate to the individual.

> It is not cooperation in wealth-producing labour by means of which the commune member reproduces himself, but rather cooperation in labour for the communal interests (imaginary or real), for the upholding of the association inwardly and outwardly.[16]

Unlike the AMP, the ancient mode of production is "at its base" different than the primitive community from which it evolved. The

---

him the different understanding of power and community from which he critiqued the AMP was the understanding that emerged out of evolution of western society, from the ancient mode of production through to the emerging socialist mode of production.

[13] Marx, *Grundrisse*, p. 474.
[14] Marx, *Grundrisse*, p. 402.
[15] Marx, *Grundrisse*, p. 475.
[16] Marx, *Grundrisse*, p. 476.

ancient mode of production presupposes, first of all, the city and the citizens of the city as the higher community. The city is a centre of trade and manufacture and stands apart from the agricultural sector. Full citizenship is based on landownership and unlike kinship, it can be lost. The ultimate loss is slavery at the hands of alien conquerors. Thus, the taken-for-grantedness of individual-community-land relationship as it obtained in the "primitive community" is shattered with the result that the citizens are self-conscious of the conditions of their existence and the reproduction of their city-community in its territory.

In the *Grundrisse*, these two modes of production, the Asiatic and the ancient, are not linked up as successive stages in the evolution of society. But in *A Contribution to the Critique of Political Economy* (itself a distillation of *Grundrisse*), Marx does give occasion to those who would link up the modes of production in unilinear fashion when he states that "[i]n broad outline, the Asiatic, ancient, feudal and modern bourgeois modes of production may be designated as epochs marking progress in the development of society."[17] The *Grundrisse* was not published until the middle of this century and so the view of social evolution that came to dominate orthodox Marxist scholarship in the Soviet Union was heavily influenced by Marx's later writings and the writings of Engels. In these later writings the AMP is either only mentioned in passing or not at all. In Engels's *The Origin of the Family*, for example, only the "ancient" path of development is discussed leaving the impression that there is only one form of the dissolution of the primitive community.[18] According to the unilinear interpretation of orthodox Marxism, all societies had passed (or would pass) through the same stages of evolution from primitive communism to slave-holding to feudalism to capitalism to socialism. Among ancient historians the "orthodox" viewpoint was defended by Struve whose position is known as the "pan-slavery" interpretation of ancient history. All of antiquity, he argued, could be explained in terms of slavery, and although some ancient communities retained strong traces of the primitive community, this was no more than a patriarchal form of slave-holding.[19]

---

[17] K. Marx, *Karl Marx – Frederick Engels: Collected Works*, vol. 29, *Karl Marx: 1857–61* (London: Lawrence and Wishart), p. 263.

[18] Y. Garlan, *Slavery in Ancient Greece* (trans. J. Lloyd; Ithaca, NY: Cornell University Press, 1988), p. 7.

[19] V. V. Struve, "The Problem of the Genesis, Development, and Disintegration

Those who, on the other hand, take a multilinear approach such as Godelier[20] dispute the unilinear inevitability in the transition of one world-historical epoch to the next and that each stage is characterized by only one distinct mode of production. Each historical society has, in fact, consisted in the overlay and structural co-existence of several modes of production. Revolution is not the sudden transition from one mode of production to another but the coming to surface of dynamics of conflict present over long periods and the goal in the study of historical societies is not to identify the mode of production but the conflict of modes of production.[21] The

---

of the Slave Societies in the Ancient Orient," in I. M. Diakonoff (ed.), *Ancient Mesopotamia. Socio-Economic History: A Collection of Studies by Soviet Scholars* (Moscow: Nauka, 1969), pp. 17–69.

[20] M. Godelier, "The Asiatic Mode of Production," in A. M. Bailey and J. R. Llobera (eds.), *The Asiatic Mode of Production: Science and Politics* (London: Routledge and Kegan Paul, 1981), p. 264. The value of the multilinear approach is confirmed, indirectly, by the work of a number of ancient historians in the Soviet Union. Diakonoff, for example, found substantial regional variations in pre-capitalist modes of production. In his essay, he responds directly to Struve's pan-slavery interpretation. According to Diakonoff, the major producers in the third and second millenium BC were what he calls "free citizens" who worked on their own portion of the community land and had a share in political life via the assembly. The local community of full-enfranchised citizens did, however, lose ground with the rise of the despotic state in the Akkadian, Neo-Sumerian and Old Babylonian periods and became increasingly subject to debt-bondage etc. There was indeed a growing disparity between classes, but class conflicts were not a straight-forward "free man and slave" affair [I. M. Diakonoff, "The Rise of the Despotic State in Ancient Mesopotamia" in I. M. Diakonoff (ed.), *Ancient Mesopotamia: Socio-Economic History. A Collection of Studies by Soviet Scholars* (Moscow: Nauka), pp. 173–203].

Dandamaev reached similar conclusions about slavery in Babylonia in the Neo-Babylonian and Persian periods. The role of slaves in production, whether in agriculture or handicrafts, was much less important than that of free labour. Babylonia of the first millenium BC was not a slave-based society [M. A. Dandamaev, *Slavery in Babylonia from Nabopolassar to Alexander the Great (626–331 BC)* (trans. V. A. Powell, ed. M. A. Powell and D. B. Weisberg; DeKalb, IL: Northern Illinois University Press, rev. edn., 1986)].

[21] Whilst these conflicting social evolutionary theories are not immediately relevant to this study, the reading of Marx presented above has much in common with the "multilinearists." The internal contradiction between community and higher community finds a parallel in the relationship between the central and local administration. The centralized system of the AMP can only work well and process power relations which lie along the centre-periphery axis. The centre produces ideology and political forms and consumes material goods; the periphery produces material goods and consumes ideology and political forms. But the AMP also needs local representation and these local representatives tend to strive for independence at the first sign of weakness at the centre. Furthermore, the motor of growth in the AMP is the increasing density of exchange relations between its local communities and, externally, among equals, as in the ancient mode of production. In a well-working AMP, the money-lenders and merchants can be seen as state-functionaries alongside

approach taken here is much more like the multilinear approach in that my reading of Marx is more in tune with the sense of contradiction within social formations, economic or ideological.

Kreissig

Turning now to the question of the socio-economic situation in Judah, Heinz Kreissig presents what I would call a simple co-existence hypothesis—the co-existence of the ancient mode of production and the AMP in Judah in the Persian period. He defines the AMP as "der auf Hörigkeit des Produzenten und Eigentum einer privilegierten Schicht an den Produktionsmitteln basierenden Produktionsweise." Though the ancient mode of production was subordinate to the AMP,

> ... doch behielt sie mit der Einführung des Münzgeldes und der Festigung der städtischen Wirtschaft dann eine gewisse Stärke, die ihre Existenz zumindest in den Gebieten mit intensivem Exportanbau (Jordantal) und mit Viehzucht (Hebron) sicherte.... Ich glaube nicht, daß man die judäische Wirtschaft dieser als eine Mischproduktionsweise ansprechen kann. Die beiden vorkapitalistischen Produktionsweisen bestanden vielmehr selbst im Bereich eines Eigentümers nebeneinander.[22]

Like Marx, he defines the two modes of production on the basis of the relationship between the labourer and the land: in the AMP the labourer is in possession of land but is not the landowner whereas in the ancient mode of production the labourer either owns the land or works the land as wage-labourer or slave. This distinction between "owner" and "possessor" is reminiscent of Marx's discussion of the higher community as "sole proprietor" and the real community as "hereditary occupiers." Kreissig, however, is not talking about the higher community as landowner but about a class of *individual* landowners.[23] Thus, in Kreissig's definition, the AMP is reduced to the

---

the local representatives, but all these groups can exploit their distance from the central administration and start to control wealth in land and trade on the periphery of the AMP and beyond the reach of central administration. Thus, according to Krader, the non-axial relationships are both the engine of growth and the motor for the demise of the AMP [L. Krader, *The Asiatic Mode of Production: Sources, Development and Critique in the Writings of Karl Marx* (Assen: Van Gorcum, 1975), pp. 286ff. Krader's discussion is summarized in D. Jobling, "Deconstruction and the Political Analysis of Texts: A Jamsonian Reading of Psalm 72," in D. Jobling (ed.), *Ideological Criticism of Biblical Texts* (Semeia 59; Atlanta: Scholars, 1992), pp.114–16].

[22] H. Kreissig, *Die sozialökonomische Situation in Juda zur Achämenidenzeit* (Schriften zur Geschichte und Kultur des alten Orients 7; Berlin: Akademie, 1973), p. 115.

[23] For the pre-exilic period Kreissig includes the king among this class of landowners.

question of whether or not the individual labourer is owner or possessor, not (as in Marx) whether the community as a whole has a weak or strong sense of private property. The AMP, according to Kreissig's definition, describes the situation in which the labourer is somehow bound to the land because he is indebted to a large individual landowner and must pay a percentage of his harvest to this landowner. He is not bound to the land via some notion of community ownership[24] which does not fully differentiate between the individual and the community and between the community and the land nor is his surplus payable to the higher community which "represents" itself as the embodiment of the comprehensive unity at a higher level.[25] The relations of production in the AMP as Kreissig defines it are not that different to those which are said to obtain in the ancient mode of production. In both modes one finds a class of large landowners who either have direct control over production (labour in the form of wage-labour or slavery is fully mobilized and detached from the means of production) or indirect control (the labourer is bound to the land via debt and has diminished control over production but there are restrictions on the free sale of the land and hence the removal of the labourer from the land). In other words, the latter is not much better off than the former and, according to Kreissig, has the same class interests which stand juxtaposed to the interests of the large landowners.

> Die Geschichte Judäas zur Achämenidenzeit ist angefüllt mit dem Klassenkampf der Bauern gegen die großen Grundeigetümer, die bestreben waren, die Kleineigentümer in abhängige Besitzer zu verwandeln oder die Landbesitzer zu enteignen, um so billige Lohnarbeiter oder Schuldsklaven für ihre Wirtschaften zu erhalten. Das rief in der Mitte des 5. Jahrhunderts v. u. Z. einen Bauernaufstand hervor, der Nehemia zu Reformen veranlaßte, die nur zeitweiligen und vorübergehenden

---

[24] Kreissig finds no evidence for community landownership though his key argument in this regard is rather far off the mark. In Ezra 10:8, Ezra threatens to excommunicate those who don't show up at the meeting concerning foreign wives and confiscate their property (רכוש). Kreissig assumes, erroneously, that רכוש includes landed property and deduces that if the land belonged to the community it would have been unnecessary to confiscate it; one would simply have to ban the violaters from the community [Kreissig, *Sozialökonomische*, p. 84]. Kreissig fails to address the question of what right Ezra had to confiscate property.

[25] H. Kreissig, "'Antike' Produktionsformen im hellenistischen Asien, 'Orientalische' Produktionsformen in der klassischen Ägäis," *Acta Conventus XI* (Warsaw: 1971), pp. 42–5.

> Erfolg hatten; denn der beginnende Aufschwung der ökonomie in den
> Gebieten intensiver Landwirtschaft vertiefte die soziale und ökonomische
> Differenzierung, verstärkte. den "Trend zur antiken Productionsweise."[26]

Kreissig's account of the AMP thus only partially resembles Marx's. The fact that he uses the same name is regrettable for the differences amount to a serious curtailment of what this mode of production encompasses. The chief characteristic of the AMP as Kreissig sees it is the presence of debt-bondage which presupposes some sort of irreducible tie between the producer and the land allowing him to continue as "hereditary possessor." Nowhere does Kreissig discuss these ties that bind the individual and the community to the land. These ties to the land manifest themselves in the terms of the inalienability of land; but what exactly underlies this restriction on the sale of land? Why is the concept of private landownership weak for some and strong for others? Unlike Marx's version of the AMP in which community ownership of land is systemic, Kreissig envisions a situation in which private property is in fact the norm and where small, medium and large landowners exist side by side. So why call this the Asiatic mode of production? I believe that it is misleading to do so but even if he had coined another term his account of the relations of production leaves a good deal of questions unanswered.

A narrow definition of modes of production is, of course, a characteristic feature of orthodox Marxist historiography which regards politics and ideology as epiphenomenal. But as the above reading of Marx showed, another approach to the mode of production-type

---

[26] Kreissig, *Sozialökonomische*, p. 241. With regard to the origins of the AMP in Judah in the pre-exilic period, Kreissig cites texts which imply a strong sense of private ownership, including the king as private landowner (Omri's purchase of the Samaria in 1 Kgs. 16:24; Ahab and Nabaoth's vineyard in 1 Kgs. 21; and Uzziah's estates in 2 Chron. 26:10) [Kreissig, *Sozialökonomische*, pp. 25–6].

Kreissig reconstructs the origins of the post-exilic situation in terms of the exile. When the land owning class was removed by the Babylonians, what remained were the producers or "possessors" (still the majority of the population), the wage labourers and the priests and Levites without temple functions (Lam. 1:4). Jer. 39:10 concerns the change in ownership from the Judean elite to the Babylonian emperor and/or those loyal to him. The possessors remained the same. Kreissig's most important point, though still only an educated guess, is that there was a tendency for the possessors of the land to try and become owners in areas where the owners were exiled and where Babylonian control was weak (Ezek. 33:24). Thus, by the Persian period there was a considerable group of small landowners whose interests conflicted with the large landowners (Persian kings, governors, administrators, heads of rich families). The land of these large land owners was worked by possessors or by wage labourers and slaves [Kreissig, *Sozialökonomische*, pp. 23–7].

analysis and to the AMP is open. On this reading the ideology of the AMP is as decisive for the whole as are the actual relations of production "on the ground." Whilst it is important that we remain attuned to the actual conditions under which people worked, it is equally important to ask about the larger political and ideological context, about the circumstances which allow class structures to emerge in the first place and on what basis the principle of inalienability was sustained.

Kippenberg

Kippenberg's *Religion und Klassenbildung im antiken Judäa*[27] is a more thorough-going treatment of the socio-economic situation in comparison to Kreissig's and specifically deals with some of the questions Kreissig left unanswered. Kippenberg's aim is to examine the emergence of class divisions in Judah in the Second Temple period and the political and religious responses to these developments. His account is developmentalist in orientation in that he attempts to place the Persian period in the larger framework of the Second Temple period as a whole. The events narrated in Nehemiah 5, for example, are but the thin edge of a wedge which sees the rise of an aristocratic class of landowners whose economic interests conflict with and eventually override the traditional kinship structures and egalitarian ethos of Judean society. Kippenberg's account is also broadly comparative in that he places these social and economic transformation within the context of the transformation of ancient society as a whole—Nehemiah's actions on behalf of the poor are comparable to Solon's attempts to restrict the exploitation of the small farmer.

Like Kreissig, Kippenberg uses Marx's concept of the ancient mode of production in his typology of these developments, but he reformulates it in a number of important ways. Whereas Marx classifies the ancient mode of production on the basis of the presence of private property and slavery (which arise as a result of external relationships such as trade, warfare, and conquest), Kippenberg's study focuses on the process of dispossession within the community and the resultant class conflict. That is to say, his study examines

---

[27] H. Kippenberg, *Religion und Klassenbildung im antiken Judäa: Eine religions-soziologische Studie zum Verhältnis von Tradition und gesellschaftlichen Entwicklung* (SUNT 14; Göttingen: Vandenhoeck & Ruprecht, 2nd edn., 1982).

the way in which principles of egalitarianism and solidarity that are associated with the inalienability of land are eroded from within and replaced by the private landownership of the few. In Marx's terms this concerns the transition from the "primitive" community to the "ancient" community. His definition of the ancient mode of production reflects this change in emphasis:

> "Antike" soll im folgenden gesellschaftliche Verhältnisse kennzeichnen, in denen ein nennenswerter Anteil der Bauernschaft die Kontrolle über die zur Produktion notwendigen Faktoren wie Saatgut, Vieh und Geräte, Land, eventuell Wasser verloren hat und eine am Handel interessierte Aristokratie den Anbau neuer Kulturen erzwingt.[28]

According to Kippenberg the driving force behind this transformation of the relations of production in Judah was, on the one hand, the expansion of trade and manufacturing in the empire and, on the other, the interests of the large landowners in profiting from this trade. According to this theory, the intensification of trade from the eighth century BCE onwards encouraged the transformation of the economy away from traditional subsistence crops (such as barley) to those from which one could make a decent profit (such as wine and olive oil). Because the large landowners were (according to Kippenberg's calculations)[29] in a better position to make this transition and reap the benefits, the push towards the mobilization of surpluses would have come from them and not from "below."[30] Whilst Kippenberg recognizes that class divisions existed prior to the emergence of the ancient mode of production,[31] the rise of the ancient mode of production brought with it "einem Wachsen der Ungleichheit in den

---

[28] Kippenberg, *Religion*, p. 13. One of the distinguishing features of the ancient mode of production is the mechanism by which the small farmer loses control over the means of production and enters into varying degrees of servitude. Kippenberg observes a transition from personal liability for loans, whereby the debtor remains on his land but enters into debt-bondage, to property liability, whereby the debtor can lose ownership of the land. Unlike the prior "tradition" form of debt-bondage in which land is inalienable outside the family or clan, land in the ancient mode of production is transformed *internally* into private property to be bought and sold without restriction. For an extended theoretical-comparative treatment of the ancient mode of production see H. Kippenberg, ed. *Seminar: Die Enstehung der antiken Klassengesellschaften* (Frankfurt: Suhrkamp, 1977), pp. 9–61.

[29] He calculates things such as the time between planting a vineyard or an olive grove and reaping the first harvest, which is anywhere from five to ten years. Hence only those with sufficient reserves and an inclination to make a profit, would attempt the switch from barley to wine.

[30] Kippenberg, *Seminar*, pp. 19–20.

[31] Kippenberg, *Religion*, p. 13.

traditionellen sozialen Verhältnissen."[32] In other words, the ancient mode of production witnessed the emergence of a class conflict which pitted the aristocracy, in whose interests it was to undermine the traditional social order and gain control of production, against the dispossessed and their political and religious allies.[33] The ancient mode of production was not, however, simply an economic conflict but was also and at the same time a social, political, and religious conflict.

> Der Begriff "antik" kann aber nicht ausschließlich an diesem Phänomen der Rentabilität orientiert werden. . . . Der politische Widerstand gegen die Aristokratie, der revolutionäre Bruch mit diesen Formen der Abhängigkeit gehört daher zur Typik der antiken Entwicklung dazu. Beide Merkmale zusammen, eine Ausrichtung der ökonomie auf Surplus-Produktion und ein egalitärer Bruch mit aristokratisch genutzten traditionalen Institutionen der Abhängigkeit, erst machen die antike Gesellschaft aus.[34]

Notably absent in all this is the AMP (unless "traditionalen Institutionen der Abhängigkeit" is to be understood in this light). According to Kippenberg, the process of class formation of the "ancient" variety began in the eighth century BCE, but class divisions of a different kind already existed, "diese bildeten sich jedoch primär durch die Aneignung von häuslichem und dörflichem Surplus."[35] This seems to agree with Kreissig's definition of the AMP and suffers likewise from being too narrow in focus and hence not addressing the larger political and ideological aspects of this mode of production (something which Kippenberg does do in relationship to the ancient and kinship modes of production).[36] In contrast to Kreissig co-existence hypothesis, Kippenberg places the ancient and the kinship modes of production on a continuum.

It is clear from this comparison that Kippenberg's study is more comprehensive than Kreissig's as it relates to the relations of production and the conflict between modes of production. In both cases the additional element is the kinship mode of production which he uses to explain the class conflict that arose as a result of the emergence of the ancient mode of production. He conceives of class conflict not only in terms of a conflict of economic systems but also as a

---

[32] Kippenberg, *Religion*, pp. 32–3.
[33] Kippenberg, *Religion*, pp. 32–3.
[34] Kippenberg, *Religion*, pp. 32–3.
[35] Kippenberg, *Religion*, p. 13.
[36] Kippenberg himself does not use the term kinship mode of production.

conflict of ideologies; solidarity and egalitarianism clashing with greed.

While I don't doubt that there were conflicts of this sort in Judah in the Persian period or later I do not think that these conflicts can be reconstructed in terms of two relatively coherent modes of production and from the ground up (i.e. in terms of kinship groups clashing with large landowners). By side-stepping the AMP and the question of what role central institutions play in the emergence of class divisions he has side-stepped the problem of ideological distortion within the community and even within its kinship structures. This is particularly important when it comes to using texts such as Ezra-Nehemiah in reconstructing social realities because the texts as a whole may represent a distorted picture of the community. References to the בתי אבות cannot be taken at face value as referring directly to the basic kinship structures of the community. The really important question is how the author is constructing his community in telling its story in this way. What does its mode of narration tell us about the structure of the post-exilic community?

The Mode of Production in the Persian Empire

Before turning to address some of the substantive issues raised by Kippenberg and Kreissig, I want to deal briefly with the broader question of the mode of production in the Persian empire as a whole with a view to placing the socio-economic situation of Judah (as far as that can be discerned) in context.

The debate about the mode of production in the Persian empire (or the ancient near eastern empires in general) is framed very much in the terms used by Kreissig and Kippenberg, namely, the status of the producers. Most economic historians would argue that the dominant mode of production was the AMP insofar as the majority of producers were free peasants (as opposed to slaves) yet bound to the land in one way or another.[37] Looking at the Persian empire from the top down one would have to say that here too one observes an AMP-like system in that, like all empires, its primary interest was the exploitation of the surplus production of the regions under its rule. Thus, at the top and at the bottom of these empires, one finds

---

[37] L. L. Grabbe, *Judaism from Cyrus to Hadrian* (Minneapolis: Fortress, 1992), p. 21. Dandamaev and Lukonin argue that debt-slavery, in the sense of pledging ones person as security for a loan, was no longer widespread in the Persian period [M. Dandamaev and V. G. Lukonin, *The Culture and Social Institutions of Ancient Iran* (Cambridge: Cambridge University Press, 1989), p. 155].

features of the AMP as described by Marx. The problematic part is
the middle, or the relationship between the imperial administration
and the relations of production at the level of individual producer
and his or her community. In an empire the community-higher community ideology which binds the villages and the centre together
into one "comprehensive unity" is a non-starter as the empire is by
definition a multi-national/multi-ethnic entity in which one community or nation has a claim to the surplus production of other
communities; the higher community is a different community altogether. There is no pre-existing sense of identity which is manipu-
lated or distorted in hierarchical terms. The imperial ideology which
I discussed briefly in chapter three is thus not a community-higher
community ideology.

Nor did the empire own the land in any practical sense[38] and
whilst traditional forms of landownership (free peasants variously
bound to the land) continued to be the most common form of production, community ownership of land was not systemic in terms of
the empire as a whole. There was no over-arching economic policy
and whilst one could argue that the economy was underdeveloped
as a whole,[39] the presence of large private estates, slave labour, and
burgeoning trade in the eastern Mediterranean region precludes us
from saying that it was indeed an example of the AMP. The Persian
imperial system of administration led, if anything, to the expansion
of the ancient mode of production in the gaps between the many
AMP-like formations. The mode of production in the Persian empire
could be described as a mixed mode of production or a mixture of
modes of production.

An important feature of relations of production in the Persian
empire were the large private estates located primarily in the highly
productive areas of Mesopotamia and Egypt. These large estates were
predominantly owned by large temple communities or by those connected with the imperial administration.[40] The Achaemenids were

---

[38] Dandamaev and Lukonin, *Ancient Iran*, p. 133. Practical ownership refers to
the fact that land sold freely and even in Egypt, which had a long-standing tradition of state control in the economy, private sales were agreed without the permission of the king. It is debated whether or not the king was regarded as the
theoretical owner of the land.

[39] Grabbe, *Judaism*, p. 23.

[40] M. Dandamaev, "Politische und Wirtschaftliche Geschichte," in G. Walser (ed.),
Beiträge zur Achämenidengeschichte (Historia Einzelschriften 18; Wiesbaden: Harrassowitz,
1972), pp. 19–24; and C. Tulpin, "The Administration of the Achaemenid Empire,"

themselves major landowners and indeed greatly expanded the "royal sector" of the economy. After conquering a country, the best land (usually the estates of the former rulers) went to the king who either kept it as his own private property or gave it (tax free) to other members of the royal family, friends and high officials.[41] Rulers who submitted to the Persians without a fight were generally allowed to keep their private estates or were rewarded by being given additional lands.[42] The land on these large estates was, generally speaking, leased to tenant farmers who were required to pay a portion of what they produced in terms of rent. Wage labourers were also used widely on these large estates alongside the tenant farmers, but slave labour was much less common in the agrarian sector of the economy. The slaves owned by the large landowners (and the temples of Mesopotamia in particular) were generally employed in the manufacturing and service activities of the cities and temples.[43]

---

in I. Carradice (ed.) *Coinage and Administration in the Athenian and Persian Empires* (BAR Int'l Series 343; Oxford: B.A.R., 1987), pp. 113–33.

[41] Dandamaev and Lukonin, *Ancient Iran*, p. 133.

[42] There is also evidence of whole cities, towns and even provinces belonging to members of the royal family. For eg. Echmun'azer, king of Sidon, was given Dor and Jaffa in the Plain of Sharon for his "great deeds" (Dandamaev and Lukonin, *Ancient Iran*, 136–9).

[43] Weinberg formulates his citizen-temple community hypothesis in terms of these relations of production. The citizen-temple community was, supposedly, a particular social formation that arose within the unique social and economic circumstances created by the Persian empire. Foremost in Weinberg's mind is the growth of production and the development of a commodity-money economy. The two main sectors of the economy were the royal sector and the private-communal sector. Within the latter, the temple communities were semi-autonomous, self-governing organizations.

In these temples, conditions permitted many possibilities for the development of private activities in land deals, manufacturing and trade. In the sixth to fourth centuries BCE the tendency for the development of private activities and initiative was encouraged by the growth of production and encompassed not only the elite of the so-called "royal people," but all those who could deal with an expansion of their activities, mainly in a commodity economy. There were many who were interested in separating from the royal sector, particularly in conquered areas where this sector dominated and dependence on them was marked.

Under these circumstances of the sixth to fourth centuries BCE, the separation from the royal sector was best carried out by a unification with the temple. Through this unification of a city community and a temple, an essentially new structure was built—the citizen-temple community, which was a unified organization of community members and the priesthood of the temple. This citizen-temple community gave its members an organizational unity and collective self-government, and provided for internal political, social and economic welfare [J. Weinberg, *The Citizen-Temple Community* (JSOTS 151; trans. D. L. Smith-Christopher; Sheffield: JSOT Press, 1992), p. 26].

Alongside those working on the large estates we find small land-owners who work the land themselves and who occasionally bringing in labourers or slaves to help with the harvest. Small land grants were also given to soldiers and low-level civil servants in the form of the bow-fief. The possessor of a bow-fief would owe either military service or pay taxes (in kind and in lieu of military service) in return for this grant. This land could not be sold by the possessor but the bow-fief could be handed on as an inheritance. As a result of this the military colonist or his descendants would never lose the land outright when in financial difficulties but they could and in fact did become dependent via debt-bondage to usurers.[44]

An important (though short-lived) economic entity connected to the large estate sector of the economy were the houses of Egibi and Murashu. The house of Egibi was a trading house and banking establishment that existed before the Persians came to power and continued to operate in the Persian period. Some of the members of the House were simultaneously in the administrative service of the emperor. The House of Murasu was not a trading house but an agricultural credit institution that carved out a lucrative business between the empire and the small farmer. Land (and irrigation canals) owned by the emperor, members of the royal household, or officials of the administration was leased to the Murasu firm and re-leased to farmers. The Murasu would also pay the taxes on behalf of small landowners and require a percentage of the harvest in return. The firm was not a formal agency of the empire but depended on imperial sanction and patronage. This it received insofar as it served the interest of the empire in increasing tax revenues. The Murasu firm did this by enlarging the dependent population and in general by commercialising agricultural production. As Stolper puts it, it "served as an instrument of intensification and development."[45] In the long

---

The basic weakness of his theory is its developmental perspective which explains the emergence of the temple sector on the basis of movement of people from the royal to the temple sectors. He cites no evidence to support the claim that people had this sort of freedom. Nor does his theory take into account that fact that the Persians placed a heavier tax burden on the temples and in fact inhibited their growth as compared to the Neo-Babylonian empire [see M. W. Stolper, *Entrepreneurs and Empire: The Murashu Firm and Persian Rule in Babylonia* (Istanbul: Nederlands Historisch-Archaeologisch Instituut Istanbul), p. 154] and that the economy was only partially a money economy (see below).

[44] Dandamaev and Lukonin, *Ancient Iran*, pp. 147–9.

[45] Stolper, p. 151. See also Dandamaev, "Politische," p. 52.

term, however, this system eroded the traditional constraints on the relations of production between large landowners and dependent labourer by exploiting the dependent population to an ever greater degree. Or to put it another way, the Murashu firm, operating according principles of efficiency and profitability, ultimately clashed with a more traditional economically under-developed (AMP-like) mode of production, a mode of production oriented toward subsistence and social stability.

Another aspect of the economic situation in the empire was the expansion of trade and manufacturing. This took place largely in the eastern Mediterranean area and involved Greek cities located both within the empire and outside it. The chief products of trade were olive oil, wine and ceramics and whilst the cities along the coast were most heavily involved in this trade, more remote regions such as Judah were also affected by it (see below).[46] Like the house of Murashu, the criteria of this form of economic activity was efficiency and profitability, though the means by which these were achieved varied considerably. The expansion of trade was also encouraged by the development of a partial money economy.[47]

This broad spectrum of relations of production gave rise to three social groups within the empire. The first group were the citizens of cities with full rights. Full citizens were members of popular assemblies associated with a particular temple. They participated in the temple cult and had a right to a share of temple income as derived from its estates. This group of free persons with equal rights included state and temple civil servants, priests, scribes, merchants, free craftsmen and farmers. They owned land in the vicinity of the temple and this land as well as their status as citizens was hereditary. Secondly, there was a group of freemen who were deprived of civil

---

[46] Dandamaev and Lukonin, *Ancient Iran*, pp. 207–14.

[47] The use of money in everyday trade relations was very uneven within the empire. It was highly developed along the Aegean coasts and the Levant, but less so in a region such as Judah. Heltzer argues that the commercial relations were weak in Judah on account of the small size of the coins found there and the absense of weight stones among the archeological finds [M. Heltzer, "The Provincial Taxation in the Achaemenian Empire and 'Forty Shekels of Silver' [Neh. 5:15]," *Michmanim* 6 (1992), pp. 18, 20–1]. Nor was the role of the empire entirely conducive to the full-exploitation of money; heavy taxation levels impeded production as did the removal of silver out of circulation for long periods of time (i.e. the storage of silver revenues in treasuries). Nor were taxes only paid in silver; taxes continued to be paid in kind, particularly at the local level [Dandamaev, "Politische," pp. 43ff].

rights. These included royal military colonists, and foreigners including foreign civil servants. They were "deprived" of civil rights because they did not own land in the "community reserve fund" and were not therefore members of the popular assembly.[48] The third segment of the population were the semi-free and slaves. This group consisted of farmers deprived of their land who worked on the estates of the king, the temple or private individuals. They lived in the countryside and one could say that in general there were no "free" people in the countryside.[49]

Archaeological evidence supports the thesis of an expansion of trade in Judah. Stern notes, for example, an increase in Greek ceramic ware in Judah in the last half of the Persian period.[50] Textual references to trade are to be found in Ezekiel 27 and Neh. 13:15–18 though one has to question whether or not one can read this as evidence for a trend and whether or not this played into the hands of the aristocracy, as Kippenberg argues. Kippenberg's theory of the emergence of "ancient" class structures in Judah suggests that the large landowners had an interest in transforming the economy from one geared to subsistence (and subsistence crops) to one geared toward trade, and specifically trade in oil and wine. In support of this viewpoint he cites a number of textual references[51] which suggest (to him) that there was an expansion of cash crop production in Judah in the Second Temple period.[52] This is, of course, a possibility given that the lime-based soil in the Judean hills was more suited to the production of wine and olive oil than of cereals, but it is still only a possibility and the texts cited in support of this thesis are hardly an adequate basis for a large-scale theory of socio-economic development. The most we can say at this point about the affects of the general economic situation on Judah is that it would have favoured those with production surpluses at there disposal rather than the small subsistent farmer. Whether or not the hierarchies that existed in Judah and the economic exploitation that went along with it are

---

[48] As we saw in chapter three, foreign groups sometimes had their own organisations of self-government.

[49] Dandamaev and Lukonin, *Ancient Iran*, p. 152.

[50] See E. Stern, *The Material Culture of the Land of the Bible in the Persian Period (538–322 BCE)* (Warminster: Aris and Philips, 1982).

[51] Comparing Hag. 1:11, Neh. 5:11 and 13:15 with Letter of Aristeas 112. In the earlier texts cereals are listed first whereas in the later text cash crops come first.

[52] Kippenberg, *Religion*, p. 45.

to be explained in terms of the ancient mode of production is another matter for, as the Murashu texts demonstrate, the exploitative potential of a socio-economic formation can have as much to do with political, cultural and ideological factors as with "pure" economic factors such as the expansion of trade and the development of a money economy.

The Hierarchical Structure of Judean Society

The "House of the Fathers" (בית אבות)

The בית אבות appears to be the basic social unit within the post-exilic community (if the frequency with which it is referred to in Ezra-Nehemiah is anything to go by).[53] There is some dispute over the nature of this social unit. Following Meyer,[54] Kippenberg asserts that it was a "clan" (*Geschlecht*) comparable to the pre-exilic term משפחה. Because the משפחה is, in Kippenberg's view, a classic kinship group, the structure, function and ethos of *post-exilic* Judean society can be illuminated with reference to pre-exilic texts concerning the משפחה *and* the anthropological study of kinship.[55] The overriding assumption here is that there is an essential continuity at the level of kinship groups between the pre-exilic and post-exilic periods: in other words, the "tribe—clan (משפחה)—extended family (בית אב)" sequence (as operative in Josh 7) is essentially intact, only that the tribe is no longer all that significant and the name for the middle term has changed. Thus, the בית אב continues to be a sub-division of the "clan" in the post-exilic period which goes by the name בית אבות.[56]

Another approach, first put forward by Weinberg in conjunction with the citizen-temple community hypothesis,[57] is to see the בית אבות as a new exilic structure and not simply the continuation of

---

[53] Weinberg cites the following lexical statistics: the terms בית אבות and אבות (a shortened form of בית אבות) occur six times in Joshua to 2 Kings and fourty six times in Chronicles and and nineteen times in Ezra-Nehemiah. בית אב, on the other hand, occurs thirty five times in Joshua to 2 Kings and ten times in Chronicles and once in Ezra-Nehemiah [Weinberg, *Citizen-Temple*, p. 49].

[54] E. Meyer, *Die Entstehung des Judentums: Eine Historische Untersuchung* (Halle: Niemeyer, 1896), pp. 134–5.

[55] According to Kippenberg's typology the משפחה had the following characteristics: patrilineal descent; corporate ownership of the land; militia unit; common residence; right of possession passed on as inheritance; sub-divided into בית אב; mutual support; endogamous marriage; maintains religious customs and the collective memory; a unit of the tribe [Kippenberg, *Religion*, pp. 25–8].

[56] Kippenberg, *Religion*, pp. 23–41.

[57] Weinberg, *Citizen-Temple*, pp. 49–62.

the משפחה under another name or the rising to prominence in the exile of the smaller בית אב following the demise of the משפחה. The size of the בית אבות, reaching in some cases into the thousands (Ezra 2:6), suggests a radical departure from the pre-exilic בית אב and cannot be attributed simply to natural growth within a kinship group. In line with this, Smith would argue that the most likely scenario is that the בית אבות is a conglomerate of a number of בתי אב under the fiction of a common ancestor.[58] It resembles the משפחה in size, the בית אב in name, but its origin and function have more to do with structural adaptation in exile than with the tribal-kinship system of pre-exilic Israel.[59]

The textual evidence outside of Ezra-Nehemiah which supports this argument is found in Numbers (P) and Chronicles where the term בית אב is confused with larger social units.[60] In Num. 1:4 and 17:2, for example, the בית אב is used as a synonym of מטה "tribe." This confusion may stem from the failure of the writer to differentiate between the smaller pre-exilic בית אב and the larger post-exilic בית אבות. This "mistake" on the part of the post-exilic writer, however, may be more than just a question of confusing nomenclature, to be sorted out with reference to less-confused/confusing social realities; it may in fact be indicative of more substantial social ambiguities. It is true, of course, that the difference between kinship terms used before and after the exile raises the question of what happened in the exile, but it may be that the post-exilic realities, within which this nomenclature was used, are more relevant to our inquiries, especially in view of the fact that the most important texts concerning the בית אבות are post-exilic.

Ezra 2//Nehemiah 7 and the בית אבות

The "list of returnees" in Ezra 2//Nehemiah 7 is the single most important text with which we have to contend. In chapter three I examined this list as it related to the ideology of identity in Ezra-Nehemiah and the role of the exile within it. I observed that the connection with the exile, forged in a very tangible way by this list,

---

[58] D. L. Smith, *The Religion of the Landless: The Social Context of the Babylonian Exile* (Bloomington, IN: Meyer Stone, 1989), p. 102.

[59] See Smith, *Religion*, pp. 101–2.

[60] In 1 Chron. 15:12 the leaders (סרים) of the secondary sub-divisions within the tribe of Levi are called the ראשי אבות or "heads of the fathers (houses)" of Levi, whereas in 1 Chron. 6:4 the secondary subdivisions are called משפחות while the tertiary units are אבות (cf. 1 Chron. 23:7–11).

was a central feature of the self-identity of the community as portrayed in Ezra-Nehemiah. I now want to consider the way in which
these genealogical connections were used to establish not only the
"exilic" identity of the community—who we are—but also its internal hierarchies—who rules.

This "list of returnees" is not as straightforward a list as the heading might imply:

> These are the sons of the province who came up from the captives
> of the exile, whom Nebuchadnezzar king of Babylon carried into exiled
> to Babylon. And they returned to Jerusalem and Judah, each man to
> his city (Ezra 2:1).

The Ezra 2 version of this list follows hard on the heals of the edict
of Cyrus and the favourable response of the exiles who, with the
support of their neighbours, prepare to go up to Jerusalem. The only
difficulty with the sequence of these two chapters is the fact that
whereas Sheshbazzar is the leader of the community in chapter one,
Zerubbabel is the one named in the list of chapter two. Zerubbabel
is, of course, known elsewhere as the governor of Judah in the reign
of Darius (Haggai and Zechariah). One of the suggestions, therefore,
for the setting of this list is that it names those who returned from
the time of Cyrus to the rebuilding of the temple under Zerubbabel
in the time of Darius.[61]

The other main alternative is suggested by the association of this
list with Nehemiah. In Nehemiah 7 this list is found as a result of
Nehemiah's request to have a new census taken, and the phrase "all
the congregation" (Ezra 2:64//Neh. 7:66) may reflect such a census.[62]
The unevenness of the list—the fluctuation between personal and
place names—as well as the large numbers are also suggestive of a
later date, though the heading is explicitly "the book of the genealogy of those who were the first to come up" (Neh. 7:5).[63] The literary

---

[61] W. Rudolph, *Ezra und Nehemia* (HAT; Tübingen: Mohr, 1947), pp. 16–20; with
the proviso that an original list was added to later as indicated by the switch from
"sons of" to "men of" in Ezra 2:22. His main argument has to do with (1) the
lack of the title of high priest for Jeshua, which points to a time before the temple
is complete, and (2) the priestly status of the sons of Hazzok who are banned from
priestly activity in this text (2:61) but whose son Meremoth does not seem in any
way disadvantaged in the days of Ezra (Ezra 8:33) and Nehemiah (Neh. 3:4). See
also H. G. M. Williamson, *Ezra, Nehemiah* (WBC; Waco, Tx: Word, 1985), pp. 30–32.
[62] J. Blenkinsopp, *Ezra-Nehemiah* (OTL; Philadelphia: Westminster, 1988), p. 83.
[63] Batten's arguments for a late date are still telling [L. W. Batten, *Ezra and*

relationship between these two versions of the list is equally problematic. Many scholars like Williamson take the Ezra 2 version to be a revision of the Nehemiah 7 version, whilst Blenkinsopp considers Ezra 2 to be the older version.[64] The crucial thing with regard to this list is, however, neither the specific historical setting nor its literary history but rather the sort of picture it presents as to the internal differentiation of the community. At the very least this picture tells us something about the social context of the author.[65] What really interests me is the internal differentiation of this list and what this might tell us about the internal differentiation of post-exilic society.

The list is divided into the following sections:

Ezra 2:2–35   "the men of the people of Israel [אנשי עם ישראל]" (31 groups, 25,406 men)

:36–39   "the priests" (4 groups, 4289 men)

:40   "the Levites" (1 group, 74 men)

:41   "the singers" (1 group, 148 men)

:42   "the gatekeepers" (6 groups, 138 men)

:43–54   "the temple slaves [נתינים]" (35 groups)

:55–58   "the sons of Solomon's servants" (10 groups; a combined total of 392 men is given for this and the previous group)

:59–63   those who "could not prove their ancestral house [בית אבותם] or their descent [זרעם], whether they belonged to Israel"

Within this final group of "second-class Israelites" are three lay groups (v. 62: of 652 men) and three priestly groups (v. 63: no number given). The consequences of this lack of Israelite pedigree (and I will discuss what this might mean below) is only spelled out with reference to the priests. Because they are unclean, "the governor [תרשתא] told them that they were not to partake of the most holy food

---

Nehemiah (ICC; Edinburgh: T&T Clark, 1913), pp. 71–3]. Mowinckel also argued for a late date on the basis of the grounds that the groups involved are fictionalized lineages in the vein of the "guilds" of Neh. 3 [S. Mowinckel, *Studien zu dem Buche Ezra-Nehemiah* (Oslo: Universitetsforlaget, 1964), p. 75].

[64] Williamson, *Ezra, Nehemiah*, p. 29; Blenkinsopp, *Ezra-Nehemiah*, pp. 43–5, 83.

[65] An early date and a literal reading of the superscription would rule the interpretation which asks whether the list includes remainees and goes on to ask how this is possible.

[קֹדֶשׁ הַקֳּדָשִׁים], until a priest with Urim and Thummim should come"
(v. 65). The relationship between descent (fictional or otherwise) and
cultic purity is not spelled out though one finds an echo of this in
the intermarriage "crisis" of Ezra 9 which also concerns the "seed"
(זרע הקדש no less; 9:2) and cultic concerns as indicated by the use
of בדל and תועבות (9:1). According to Smith, the priestly concerns
for pure categories reflects the concerns of a minority community
which is seeking to maintain its distinct identity, ethnic and religious,
via ritual and social practices which emphasize separation (בדל).[66]

The so-called "Israelites" are sub-divided into those groups designated as "sons of [eponym]" and those designated "men of [local-
ity]." It would appear from Ezra 2:59, however, that all these groups
are known as בתי אבות, or (to put it otherwise) the list appears to
be a composite list of a number of group types which somehow
come under the rubric בתי אבות and which together make up "the
assembly" (2:64). But the text also registers some subtle and some
not so subtle distinctions which need to be examined more closely.

As noted earlier, the "typical" בית אבות (i.e. the ones named after
an eponym) compares in size more to the pre-exilic משפחה than to
the בית אב. According to Rogerson, the משפחה was "probably a maximal lineage—that is, a descent group which established ties of kinship between families through a common ancestor who was no longer
living."[67] The actual distance between the living descendants of this
common ancestor varies and hence the size of the group varies.
Thus, the term משפחה is used variously to designate a group within
an Israelite tribe (e.g. Num. 27:1–11; 36:1–9), a tribe (e.g. Judah in
Judg. 17:7) and even Israel (Amos 3:1). בית אב, on the other hand,
is used to designate (among other things) an ordinary lineage or res-
idential group consisting of a living head (i.e. the grandfather or
father) and his sons together with wives and children (Gen. 50:8).
The משפחה could thus contain a number of smaller, ordinary lineages
or בתי אב. Assuming that the בית אבות is a kinship group on this
model, this difference between ordinary and maximal lineages might
account for the large size of many of the בתי אבות. On this reading,
a small group like the "sons of Ater" (v. 16) is a smaller lineage
within the larger בית אבות of Hezekiah, making the full name of the

---

[66] Smith, *Religion*, pp. 145–8.
[67] J. W. Rogerson and P. R. Davies, *The Old Testament World* (Cambridge: Cambridge
University Press, 1989), p. 57.

group "the sons of Ater, namely of Hezekiah (בני אטר ליחזקיה)."[68] On the other hand, the lack of a category name for these smaller groups and the fact that only one such group is mentioned suggests, a weak kinship structure in the post-exilic community. I say "weak" because the "strength" of a kinship-based society rests in its being based upon the pre-given family unit. Smaller groups obviously existed at the time but they didn't have a well-defined status. This would mean that the בית אבות is some sort of hybrid quasi-kinship social unit and not an "ordinary" maximal lineage. Thus, in line with Smith, the comparison between the משפחה and the בית אבות only takes us so far.

It would appear also that the בית אבות was not as flexible as the משפחה. The eponym of the בית אבות is used like a surname, much like the Scottish clan names. Though members of a Scottish clan claim descent from the founder of the group, they are not necessarily able (or required) to demonstrate the genealogical link to this ancestor (except, of course, the head clansman). Indeed the clan system whereby people identified themselves in this way is an eighteenth century development. The important element is the surname itself which marks out one clan from the next for "contemporary" social and political purposes. There are only as many Scottish clans as there are clan names: the MacGregors, the MacDonalds, and Macleods, etc., and since "names" cannot be divided these clans cannot split up to form new clans. Hence, the clans simply grow in size over time.[69] The משפחה, on the other hand, takes its name from the *given* name of the ancestor. The משפחה, unlike the clan, was thus an inherently flexible kinship grouping in that it could more easily

---

[68] There are other examples of subgroupings within the list: "the sons of Pahath-moab of the sons of Jeshua and Joab" (v. 11), "the sons of Jedaiah of the house of Jeshua" (v. 39), and "the sons of Jeshu, namely of Kadmiel of the sons of Hodevah" (v. 43).

[69] "The Gaels of Scotland and the Jews of Poland were two ancient communities who long escaped surnames. Both had enjoyed communal autonomy, surviving for centuries with traditional name forms using either patronymics (such as the Jewish "Abraham Ben Isaac," i.e. Abraham, son of Isaac) or personal epithets. The famous Highland outlaw, whom English-speaking Lowlanders called Rob Roy MacGregor, c. 1660–1732, was known to his own as Rob Ruadh (Red Robert) of Inversnaid. Both Gaelic and Jewish nomenclatures fell victim to state bureaucracies in the late eighteenth century. After the Jacobite defeat, the Scottish Highlanders were registered according to clan names which they had previously rarely used, thereby giving rise to thousands upon thousands of MacGregors, MacDonalds, and MacLeods" [N. Davies, *History of Europe* (Oxford: Oxford University Press, 1996), p. 169].

absorb new members either via the amalgamation of two small kinship groups into a new מִשְׁפָּחָה (taking the name of a more distant
"common" ancestor as eponym) or, if the growth was internal occur-
ring at the level of say the בֵּית אָב, a large מִשְׁפָּחָה could split into
two (taking the name of a more recent "common" ancestor).[70]

The large size of the בֵּית אָבוֹת, on the one hand, and the absence
of any socially significant group at the extended family level, on the
other, suggests that the בֵּית אָבוֹת did not have the flexibility of the
מִשְׁפָּחָה. That is to say, the בֵּית אָבוֹת was not "designed" to accom-
modate that kind of growth and expansion. One could well imagine that in the immediate aftermath of deportation the exiled Jews
residing in various locations in Babylonia, formed new social groups
using a combination of real and fictive kinship ties in order to maintain their identity as a ethnic minority. Having re-grouped in this
way there was no need for a mechanism to incorporate new members or groups. Boundary maintenance was probably the order of
the day. The number of בתי אבות so formed and named would have
stayed the same and all those who belonged to a בית אבות would
have used the name of the founder in a manner analogous to the
use of the Scottish clan name, that is, as a surname. This is at any
rate one way of explaining the origin, size and inflexibility of the
eponymic בתי אבות.

But what about the other groupings, especially those named after
a locality? The members of the majority of these groups are described
as "the men of [locality]" which suggests both a post-exilic setting
and an expanding community.[71] But why not simply create new בתי
אבות named after an eponym? If it was done in the exile, why not
in the post-exilic setting? Why maintain this subtle distinction between
exilic and non-exilic groups (a distinction that would still obtain even
if they were both considered בתי אבות) and yet cover up this distinction at a higher level in claiming that all these groups came from
the exile?[72]

---

[70] Thus, the term מִשְׁפָּחָה as used in the OT can refer to a subdivision within a
tribe, a tribe or even all Israel. In the story of Achan, the tribe of Judah is called
a שֵׁבֶט and a מִשְׁפָּחָה (Josh. 7:14–17). Rogerson and Davies, *Old Testament World*,
p. 58. See also R. Fox, *Kinship and Marriage* (Harmondsworth: Penguin, 1967).

[71] The Nehemiah 7 version of this list is more consistent with the sons of [epo-
nym], men of [locality].

[72] If one were to take the view that the groups named after locality were also
exilic, one would still have to ask why they were not organised into eponymic בתי
אבות. Why the distinction?

The solution to these difficulties in understanding the social significance of the בית אבות might be found in considering another anom-
aly with regard to these lists; namely, why there are exilic groups
that are not בתי אבות. Why do these groups not have genealogical
records which link them to Israel via a בית אבות when the בית אבות
is itself somewhat of a fiction? Were they converts from Babylonia?
If not (and the fact that some of them were priests suggests that they
were not converts), why was it so important to have a particular
type of kinship connection when, according to the main criterion
(being a returnee), one was considered to be an acceptable member
of the assembly? The priestly families without the right connections
were not allowed to partake of the most holy food, but they were
free to partake of the lesser holy food. They were not excluded outright; they merely had to wait for the time when the high priest
would consult the Urim and Thummim.[73] All these groups did belong
to a kinship group of one description or another but, apparently,
not of a socially-significant kind. It appears, therefore, that the בית
אבות was also a mechanism of social discrimination within the community as well as a vehicle for identity maintenance. In other words,
more is involved in this list than "the determination of *true Israelites*."[74]

Whilst the overall concern is to distinguish between the community of returnees and the people of the land or remainees in terms
of descent from Israel (and even this was not a watertight distinction as testified to in the text in positive, negative and covert terms),[75]
the means by which this is done—the בית אבות—seems to have served
other and perhaps conflicting purposes. It was important to be a
returnee but it was not the only important issue. Whilst those unable
to prove their descent are clearly marked off in this list, the בתי אבות
named after a place are not distinguished in any way except by
being put at the end of the list of "the Israelites." Both groups had
kinship relations but, presumably, not of the right kind. Being able
to trace one's ancestry back to the right type of group—the eponymic
בית אבות—was clearly as important as the larger issue of being of
"exilic" and "Israelite" descent. My suspicion is that this "Golah list"

---

[73] Exod. 28:30, Lev. 8:8, Num. 27:21.

[74] Smith, *Religion*, p. 105. Japhet speaks of "true Jews" [S. Japhet, "People and
Land in the Restoration Period," in G. Stuecker (ed.), *Das Land Israel in biblischer
Zeit* (Göttingen: Vandenhoeck & Ruprecht, 1981), pp. 113–14].

[75] By positive terms I mean those texts which speak of those "who had joined them
and separated themselves from the pollutions of the peoples of the land" (Ezra 6:21).

and the kinship structures to which it refers were an essential element in the hierarchical structure of the post-exilic community.[76]

The "Heads of the Houses of the Fathers" (ראשי בתי אבות)
This suspicion is confirmed when we consider the only other context in Ezra-Nehemiah in which the בית אבות is mentioned, namely, in connection with the "heads of the houses of the fathers" [ראשי בתי אבות].

The following list of texts illustrates the degree to which these "heads" are involved in (or are portrayed as involved in) the central events and leading affairs of the community.

Ezra 1:5	the *heads* are the leaders of those who respond to Cyrus" edict.
Ezra 2:68–69	the *heads* donate large sums of money towards the construction of the temple (parallel in Neh. 7:70–2).
Ezra 3:12	the *heads* are among those who remember the First Temple.
Ezra 4:3	the *heads* respond to the charges of the "adversaries of Judah and Benjamin."
Ezra 8:1	Ezra gathers leaders "from Israel to go up with him. . . ." "These are the *heads* of the אבות and this is the genealogy of those who went up with me from Babylonia. . . ." The list generally follows the pattern: "from the sons of [eponym], x." Eleven of the seventeen eponyms found in the גולה list of Ezra 2//Neh. 7 are included here.
Ezra 10:16	Ezra selects *heads* to examine the matter of mixed marriage and those who agree to divorce their foreign wives are listed according to בתי אבות. Again, the pattern is "from the sons of [eponym]." Six of the seventeen eponyms from the גולה list are included here.
Neh. 8:13	the *heads*, the priests and the Levites come to Ezra to study the Law.
Neh. 11:3ff	the list of inhabitants who live in Jerusalem is a list of the *heads* only who are named as "x son of y son of z."
Neh. 12:12ff	lists the heads of the priestly and Levitical בתי אבות.

---

[76] Johnson puts it exactly the other way around when he says that "underneath the notion of legitimacy and racial purity is the desire to express the continuity of the people of God, that is to say, the identity of the new Israel of the restoration

These examples illustrate quite clearly the prominent role of the heads within the גולה community who work closely with representatives of the imperial administration, namely Ezra and Nehemiah.[77] The only exception to this pattern of leadership is the role played by the "elders of the Jews (שׁבי יהודיא)" in negotiating with Tattenai in the time of Darius (Ezra 5:5, 9; 6:7). Smith suggests that the elders were the leaders of the exilic community who retained some of their leadership functions in the post-exilic period. The heads are simply the most prominent members of the larger group of elders.[78] The list of functions could be expanded if the heads were among the סגנים and חרים.[79] The former filled local administrative positions relating to the province, including district governorships (Neh. 4:13).

The functions ascribed to the heads are community functions taken on by those who represent the community at a higher level. The heads act and speak on behalf of the community they represent; their actions are the community's actions and their interests are the interests of the community. At no time do we observe a clash of interests save the complaint of the destitute women against their fellow Jews in Nehemiah 5 (to be discussed below). But it is important to remember that this mode of representation is not representation on the parliamentary model; this mode of "representation" relates to a system of power and authority which is built right into the kinship structure. This hierarchical structure may indeed have been integral to the בתי אבות yet it was also capable of exploiting the community thus represented, as we will see below. Thus, what we seem to have here is a complex (and opaque) hierarchical structure which can only be got at, as it were, from the outside. The interests of the

---

with the old Israel of the monarchy" [M. D. Johnson, *The Purpose of Biblical Genealogies* (Cambridge: Cambridge University Press, 2nd edn., 1969), pp. 43–4].

[77] Their prominent position is also confirmed in Chronicles if Jehoshaphat's judicial reforms reflect post-exilic realities, for the heads are said to have given judicial duties (2 Chron. 19:8). Indeed, the genealogy of Levi is reduced to the genealogy of heads (1 Chron. 6) which indicated for Meyer the increasing prominence of certain families between Nehemiah and the Chronicler's time [Meyer, *Entstehung*, pp. 163–5].

[78] Smith, *Religion*, p. 97.

[79] Kippenberg, *Religion*, pp. 37–9. Cf. Ezra 9:2; Neh. 2:16; 12:40 for references to סגנים; and Neh. 2:16; 4:8[14], 13[19]; 5:7; 7:5; 13:11, 17 for סגנים and חרים. Blenkinsopp suggests that the former were hereditary nobility (Jer. 27:20; 39:6; Is. 34:12) whereas the latter were probably regional administrators (Jer. 51:23, 28, 57; Ezek. 23:6, 12, 23) [Blenkinsopp, *Ezra-Nehemiah*, pp. 223 and 252]. According to Williamson, the סגנים are indistinguishable from the חרים (cf. the last five references) and he concludes merely that they are leaders of the community [Williamson, *Ezra, Nehemiah*, p. 191].

heads and of the ruling classes as a whole are not (or could not be) articulated in the way in which, for example, the Chronicler articulates the temples claims to legitimacy and hegemony. The interests of the heads are intrinsically linked to, though not co-terminous with, the interests of the community.

To summarise: what this closer look at the "Golah list" of Ezra 2// Nehemiah 7 has disclosed is that social structures and ideologies which relate ostensibly to the interests of the community as a whole can also contain hierarchical structures which may distort the community and its discourses from the inside. The בית אבות especially, the basic social grouping of the post-exilic community, appears also to have been a fundamental aspect of the hierarchical structure of the community; that is, the heads of these בתי אבות were *individually* the ruling patriarchs of בתי אבות. To use Marx's terminology, the בתי אבות comprised the "community" while the heads as a group comprised the "higher community." This raises the possibility that what was at stake in the debate about community identity—the conflicting ideologies of identity discernible in the intermarriage crises narrated in Ezra-Nehemiah—was the status and position of the heads of the בתי אבות. In other words the ideology of identity as found in Ezra-Nehemiah which advocates a rigid separation of this community from the surrounding peoples was also potentially an ideology with functional consequences that worked in the interests of this "higher community." The purpose of the following discussion of Nehemiah 5 is to determine to what extent these consequences had an economic component.

Nehemiah 5 and the Potential for Economic Exploitation

Nehemiah 5 is one of the few texts in the Old Testament in which the poor speak for themselves and of their circumstances. It is, therefore, a rare window on the socio-economic situation in Judah in the post-exilic period. In verses 1–5, three groups complain about their plight:

> Now there was a great outcry of the people and of their wives against their Jewish kin. For there were those who said, "With our sons and our daughters, we are many; we must get grain, so that we may eat and stay alive." There were also those who said, "We are having to pledge our fields, our vineyards, and our houses in order to get grain during the famine." And there were those who said, "We are having to borrow money on our fields and vineyards to pay the king's tax. Now our flesh is the same as that of our kindred; our children are

the same as their children; and yet we are forcing our sons and our daughters to be slaves, and some of our daughters have been ravished; we are powerless, and our fields and vineyards now belong to others."

The three groups identify themselves with those they are accusing using the general term for kinship—"brother (אח)" appealing to the sense of solidarity that such a term implies. The exploitation (as they see it) has left them as "slaves (עבדים)," which runs counter to the ethos of kinship. The matter was brought to Nehemiah[80] and he ordered the nobles (חרים) and officials (סגנים) to restore the property and the interest that they took from the poor (vv. 6–11):

And I called a great assembly to deal with them, and said to them, "As far as we were able, we have bought back our Jewish kindred who had been sold to other nations; but now you are selling your own kin, who must then be bought back by us!" They were silent, and could not find a word to say. So I said, "The thing that you are doing is not good. Should you not walk in the fear of our God, to prevent the taunts of the nations our enemies? Moreover I and my brothers and my servants are lending them money and grain. Let us stop this taking of interest. Restore to them, this very day, their fields, their vineyards, their olive orchards, and their houses, and the interest on money, grain, wine, and oil that you have been exacting from them."

If one accepts the identification of the חרים and סגנים as proposed above—that is, that they are to be counted among the heads of the בית אבות—it then becomes clear as to what sort of crisis this may have been. Everywhere else in Ezra-Nehemiah one reads of the heads functioning in the interests of the community at large but in this text a whole different reality comes to light, namely, the reality of economic disparity on a scale high enough to register in the biblical text. The question is How does one reconstruct the context of this crisis? What were the larger social developments which gave rise to it?

In keeping with his overall argument about the erosion of the kinship mode of production in Judah in this period, Kippenberg interprets the three different groups as successive stages of impoverishment and exploitation which arise out of the expansion of the ancient mode of production. That is to say, he discerns a larger socio-economic

---

[80] In AramP 10 the debtor foregoes the possiblitity of appealing to the governor [A. Cowley (ed.) *Aramaic Papyri of the Fifth Century* (Osnabrück: Otto Zeller, reprint edn., 1967)].

trend which pitted the wealthy within the community against the poor. The first stage—the giving of one's children as security—involves the insolvent debtor being detained in the person of his children to pay off the debt. If the debtor had land and family, he would, argues Kippenberg, first have given his children as security before giving his land as security. In the second stage, the debtor gives his land as a pledge (because he has already pledged his children) though he continues to work the land and is required to pay some sort of interest on the loan from the surplus of the harvest. In the third stage the poor must borrow money to pay taxes but cannot give their land as security. The inability of the debtor to pay back the loan from his harvest (it is already out of his control) forces him to sell his children to satisfy the loan.[81]

In order to shed further light on this text, Kippenberg cites Solon of Athens who undertook similar measures with regard to a land dispute in the late 7th century BCE.[82] One of Solon's measures was to do away with security on the person.[83] On the face of it, this may appear to be a good thing in that the individuals involved would no longer live under the threat of debt-bondage, but paradoxically the security on the person was intended, in the context of kinship, to safeguard access to land within the kinship group. That is, one would not give the land for security because it was inalienable. Solon's reforms presuppose the emergence of economic hierarchies in the community and therefore represent an attempt to curtail its negative side-effects in the spirit of kinship solidarity. Similarly, the biblical laws concerning debt-bondage are clearly concerned with the more fundamental issue of maintaining access to land (on the basis of kinship affiliation) and are formulated with reference to Israel's deliverance from "slavery."[84] Thus, Solon's abolition of liability on

---

[81] Kippenberg, *Religion*, pp. 56–61. Kreissig, on the other hand, interprets the three groups as (1) those who have nothing but children to give as security, (2) those with land, and (3) those who have already given up their land as security. This is, therefore, a class conflict involving the landless, the small landowner and land possessors on one side and the large landowners on the other—that is, a clash between the ancient and Asiatic modes of production (as he defines them). Thus, both Kreissig and Kippenberg believe that the underlying problem is landownership; they simply disagree on how to model the complex web of social and economic relationships that landownership entails [Kreissig, *Sozialökonomische*, pp. 78–9].

[82] Kippenberg, *Religion*, pp. 54–5, 62.

[83] See Kippenberg, *Religion*, pp. 54–5 The primary texts relating to this episode are Aristotle, *Athenian Constitution*, chs 2 and 6; and Plutarch, *Solon*, ch. 13.

[84] Especially, Lev. 25:35–39; to be discussed below. Cf. Deut. 15:1–18.

the person can be interpreted as a departure from a kinship-based practice, even though it is done in the name of community solidarity.

Viewed in this light, the difference between these two reformers is very instructive. Solon's reforms paved the way for the expansion of the ancient mode of production (to use Marx's terminology) characterized by the free sale of private property, whereas Nehemiah's reforms did not sever the bond between community and land as reflected in the practice of liability on the person. In other words, his cancellation of debt did not amount to a radical restructuring of Judean society, either in the direction of the ancient mode of production (as in Solon's case) or along egalitarian kinship lines (as envisioned for example in the Jubilee laws).[85] The short term problem involved the apparent abuse of community norms[86] with regard to the taking of interest from ones "kin." The long term problem, according to Kippenberg, involved the expansion of the ancient mode of production characterized by an economy based on private property and trade which benefited the wealthier members of the community at the expense of poorer members and the basic kinship ethos of the community based on the בית אבות.

I would, however, have some reservations about the fundamental kinship-ethos of the post-exilic community in light of my comments on the בית אבות in general. I would argue that, if anything, the postexilic community was a cross between a miniature AMP—in that its hierarchical structure, and indeed economic structure, is built right into the community structures—and the ancient mode of production. The centripetal force of the former was in tension with the centrifugal force of the latter. Although an appeal is made here to kinship, kinship is a highly flexible concept and one must not confuse the *ideology* of kinship with the *reality* of kinship. Thus, when the term אחים is used—as it is throughout Ezra-Nehemiah—it is with reference to the citizen-temple community and as such is to be seen as denoting community membership,[87] but membership status in a בית אבות and in the larger theocratic community was by no means uniform.

Nor is the appeal to economic solidarity and the measures enacted by Nehemiah to be taken as an indication that the land was

---

[85] See the discussion below.

[86] Nehemiah does not appeal to biblical law so one can only speak of general norms which may or may not be related to the biblical laws cited above.

[87] Weinberg, *Citizen-Temple*, p. 102.

community-owned property. Both Kippenberg and Weinberg argue that the land ultimately belonged to the community and that the terms אחזה[88] and נחלה[89] designate "einen an Abstammung gebundenen Zugang zum Land."[90] Weinberg states that the "land was de facto inalienable property of the *'aḥuzzâ/naḥªlâ* of the *bêt 'abôt*, and was divided into parcels, which in turn were the possession of the families within the *bêt 'abôt*."[91] I would argue, however, that the principle of inalienability was already highly compromised within the בית אבות and that the concept of private property was already highly developed.

I base my argument, first of all, on the term אחזה which is used to designate the property of the members of the post-exilic community. The use of this term in the OT does not, in my view, correspond to the concept of community ownership of land. One is reminded of the way in which Marx defines the concept of community and private property in the *Grundrisse*. In the AMP, the land is the take-for-granted basis of community life: "Each individual regards himself as a *proprietor* or owner only qua MEMBER of such a community."[92] In the ancient community, on the other hand, the individual no longer takes (full) membership in the community for granted nor does the community take its relationship to the land for granted. The ancient community presupposes war and conquest. The use of אחזה in the OT (which occurs for the most part in late texts such as the Priestly source and Chronicles) reminds me of Marx's definition of the property relations of the ancient community, whether it refers to the land of Canaan as the future and perpetual אחזה of Israel (e.g. Gen. 17:8) or to the אחזה of individuals (e.g. Lev. 27:24).[93] The story of Israel's acquiring its אחזה is a story of conquest, and each individual's אחזה is clearly delineated from another's. The

---

[88] Neh. 11:3.

[89] Neh. 11:20.

[90] Kippenberg, *Religion*, p. 26.

[91] Weinberg, *Citizen-Temple*, p. 103.

[92] Marx, *Grundrisse*, p. 400.

[93] The relationship between אחזה and conquest is clearly stated in a passage such as Josh. 22:19. Joshua tells the eastern tribes that "if your possession [אחזה] is unclean, cross over into the LORD's possession [אחזה] where the LORD's tabernacle now stands and take for yourselves a possession [אחזה] among us." The combination of שוב and אחזה occurs five times in the Jubilee laws (Lev. 25:10, 13, 27, 28, 41) which suggests that the Jubilee was a symbolic reenactment of the conquest. To be discussed further below.

assumption is that the land rightly belongs to Israel and not to the Canaanites and membership in Israel is a pre-condition of (or pre-supposes?) individual ownership. This suggests to me a highly developed notion of property involving the question of legal entitlement in the face of the claims of others.

It is my view, therefore, that the hierarchies within the theocratic community were of economic consequence and that kinship and community structures and ideologies were also at the same time host to the interests of a dominant class of heads, nobles and officials. This ties in well with the view that the post-exilic community originated in the exile among the exiled elite of Judah. The initiative for the formation of the post-exilic citizen-temple community would, in this model, have come from the elders of the communities in exile and would have been based on the pattern of the citizen-temple communities in the region. As in the Babylonian assembly the citizen-temple community of Jerusalem eventually developed pronounced internal hierarchies with the heads of the lay and priestly בתי אבות in a dominant position.

Temple and Hierarchy

The relationship between the interests of the poor of Nehemiah 5 and the interests of the priests is raised by the text itself insofar as the situation envisaged is very similar to what is described in the Jubilee laws. The temple and its clergy clearly played a central role in the post-exilic community, in religious, social, political and economic terms. In the following I will argue that the temple at the centre of the theocratic community had a number of functions and that these various functions did not necessarily cohere. Furthermore, and related to this, I will argue that the interests of the clergy, which was as stratified a group as the community as a whole, where diverse.

The Temple as a Central Institution

The temple was, first of all, an institution of the empire. This is indicated in two ways in Ezra-Nehemiah. Firstly, the Cyrus decree and the various other "documents" in Ezra 4–6 claim that the Persians mandated that a temple should be built in Jerusalem and that those who take it upon themselves to do so have the legal right to do so. Secondly, these texts also indicate that the empire supported the temple financially, even to the point of giving it tax exempt status (Ezra 7:24). This was indeed an exceptional privilege, for the temples in Mesopotamia had to pay taxes.[94] In return for this generous support, the Persians had an institution, indeed a whole community, that not only fitted into their administrative agenda but also proclaimed its virtues. Is there any other mention in the Bible of the Jews praying for a foreign power or even suggesting that this might not be such a bad thing? And if these texts about Persian support are exaggerated, that in itself is evidence that someone is imaginatively participating in Persian imperial ideology.

I am not suggesting, however, that the role of the temple as a central institution of the state was uncontroversial or that those in charge of the temple were unwavering supporters of foreign domination. There is, in fact, a poignant witness to the contrary in Ezra's prayer.

> But now for a brief moment favor has been shown by the LORD our God, who has left us a remnant, and given us a stake in his holy place, in order that he may brighten our eyes and grant us a little sustenance in our slavery. For we are slaves; yet God has not forsaken us in our slavery, but has extended to us his steadfast love [חסד] before the kings of Persia, to give us new life to set up the house of our God, to repair its ruins, and to give us a wall in Judea and Jerusalem (Ezra 9:8–9).

Notice how the writer still gives the Persians a considerable advance in trust. The dominating power, the reason why they are enslaved, is the very agent God uses to deliver them from their slavery. He even goes so far as to call this Yahweh's חסד.[95] Thus, even though the imagery is of the Egyptian captivity and the exodus, the political perspective is entirely different. A sceptical reader might add that the best defence of a pro-Persian ideology is to bring up the strongest

---

[94] An important difference between the Persian and the Neo-Babylonians was that the Persians made the temples of Mesopotamia pay taxes. The Neo-Babylonians paid a tithe to the temples along with the rest of the population [M. Dandamaev, "Der Tempelzehnte in Babylonien während des 6.–4. Jh. v. u. Z.," in I. Steihl (ed.), *Beiträge zur Alten Geschichte und deren Nachleben. Festschrift für Franz Altheim I* (Berlin, 1969), pp. 82–9; and idem, "State and temple in Babylonia in the First Millennium BCE," in E. Lipinski (ed.), *State and temple Economy in the ANE, II* (OLA 6; Leuven: University Press, 1979), pp. 589–96]. The Persians continued to require that everyone else pay the tithe, but had the temples (because, presumably, they were major landowners) supply them with labour and produce. There were, however, some temples that were tax exempt, most notably the Jerusalem temple [Dandamaev, "Politische," pp. 52–3; and Tulpin, "Administration," pp. 149–53]. My guess is that if the Jerusalem temple had owned estates, it too would have paid taxes.

[95] On the significance of this term in Chronicles see chapter six.

anti-Persian argument and redirect it so that it misses the mark.
Either way, the role of the temple as a central institution was not
without its ambiguities.

The Temple as a Local Institution

These ambiguities were, however, part and parcel of the Persian
policy of integrating local institutions and giving them considerable
autonomy. The risk was of course that they would lose control over
these local powers from time to time.[96] But in between these rebel-
lions, the local authorities and elite could take advantage of the
opportunity to advance their own economic interests. I argued in
the previous section that there is a clearly defined hierarchical structure in the post-exilic community with the heads of the fathers'
houses, the סגנים, the חרים and officials in the administration at the
top. I would also include the higher clergy among the elite and it
would seem that their personal economic interests in terms of the
ancient mode of production were the same as the סגנים and חרים
who come in for a brow-beating in Nehemiah 5.

The presence of Tobiah is a case in point. He was in all likelihood taking advantage of the economic opportunities in Jerusalem
and he probably shared these same interests with the ruling classes
of Judah, including his relatives among the higher clergy.

> Moreover in those days the nobles of Judah sent many letters to Tobiah
> and Tobiah's letters came to them. For many in Judah were bound
> by oath to him, because he was the son-in-law of Shecaniah son of
> Arah: and his son Jehohanan had married the daughter of Meshullam
> son of Berechiah (Neh. 6:17–18).

> Now before this, the [high] priest Eliashib, who was appointed over
> the chambers of the house of our God, and who was related to Tobiah,
> prepared for Tobiah a large room [נשכה] where they had previously
> put the grain offering . . . (Neh. 13:4ff).

The presence of this "foreigner"[97] in the temple itself is no surprise
given the significance of trade in as large a cultic establishment as

---

[96] A. Kuhrt, "The Cyrus Cylinder and Achaemenid Imperial Policy," *JSOT* 25
(1983), pp. 83–97.

[97] As implied in the Nehemiah memoir (Neh. 2:10), but with a name like Tobiah
it is more likely that he was a Jew, maybe even a Jerusalemite of exilic descent
(Neh. 7:26) who as "the Ammonite servant" may have been Sanballat's and
Nehemiah's counterpart in Ammon [Blenkinsopp, *Ezra-Nehemiah*, pp. 217–19].

the one in Jerusalem. The importance of trade can be detected else-where as well. Neh. 3:30 speaks of Meshullam who made repairs opposite his living quarters (נשכה), the same word used in the text just quoted. We also read that "Malchijah, one of the goldsmiths, made repairs as far as the house of the temple servants and of the merchants . . . And between the upper room of the corner and the Sheep Gate the goldsmiths and merchants made repairs" (Neh. 3:31–32). All this indicates the close connection between the temple and trade with a "commercial quarter in the north-east corner of the temple mound."[98]

Nor should we, for that matter, exempt Nehemiah from the group of the elite who benefited from the opportunities for trade. If Nehemiah did not claim his food allowance as governor, how was it that he could still afford to feed one hundred and fifty at his table?[99] Was he also one of the wealthy landowners?[100]

These hierarchies needed to be legitimated just like imperial domination needed legitimation and the temple also served the purpose of legitimating this differential in power and wealth. The "higher community" of Judah had to appear to be looking out for the interests of the community at large and what better way to do this than to make a visual display of one's largesse in supporting the temple. "And some of the heads of the ancestral houses gave into the building fund twenty thousand darics of gold and two thousand minas of silver" (Neh. 7:71). These contributions equalled the amount given by all the rest of the people. Even though these numbers are probably exaggerated, the proportion of the heads's share of the wealth should indicate that the power differential had indeed translated into unequal access to the means of production. Another indication of support from the temple is found in the "constitution" of the community signed by "our officials, our Levites, and our priests" who pledge, on behalf of the whole community, "to charge ourselves yearly one-third of a shekel for the service of the house of our God: for the rows of bread, the regular grain offering, the regular burnt offering, the Sabbaths, the new moons, the appointed festivals, the sacred

---

[98] Blenkinsopp, *Ezra-Nehemiah*, p. 239.

[99] Neh. 5:14–18.

[100] D. J. A. Clines, "The Nehemiah Memoir: The Perils of Autobiography," in *What Does Eve Do to Help? and Other Readerly Questions to the Old Testament* (JSOTS 94; Sheffield: 1990), pp. 133–5.

donations, and the sin offerings to make atonement for Israel, and for all the work of the house of our God" (Neh. 10:32–33).

The Interests of the Clergy

As noted earlier, Nehemiah's reforms parallel the measures for debt-relief found in the Pentateuch and even though Nehemiah doesn't back up his actions by appealing to biblical law the parallel is suggestive of a common interest between the poor of Nehemiah 5 (or those who look out for the interests of the poor) and the biblical "jurists."[101] Of particular interest in this regard are the sabbath and Jubilee laws in Leviticus 25–27, the concluding chapters of the so-called Holiness Code.[102] The question to be asked is this: How does the idea of kinship solidarity, as expressed in the term "our brothers" (Neh. 5:1,5), relate to a solidarity based on the religious concept of the land as God's land (Lev. 25:23)?

Kippenberg believes that these laws are a "religiöse Neuinterpretation verwandschaftlicher Normen: die Solidarität ist nicht im Verwandschaftssystem begründet, sondern im sakralen Eigentumsverhältnis an Land und Menschen."[103] It presupposes the same process of class formation as found in Nehemiah and is an attempt to restrict its further development via an appeal to religious norms.[104]

According to this view, both the Jubilee and the נאלה institution presuppose the erosion of the concept of community solidarity in terms of access to the land and both try to redress the problem. The assertion that the land is Yahweh's (Lev. 25:23) is the very basis for the inalienability of the land as the inheritance of particular families. Land in Israel was *both* an inalienable right possessed by a family over generations and this because it was also the possession of Yahweh and he had given it to them. "Verschuldung räumt demgemäß dem Gläubiger kein Eigentumsrecht an Land und Menschen ein,

---

[101] Exod. 21:2–11 (release of the Hebrew slave after seven years); 22:25–27 ("no interest" law); 23:10 (sabbath year for benefit of poor); Lev. 25 (sabbath year and Jubilee); Deut. 15 (שמטה, seventh year remission of debts).

[102] Leviticus 25–26 appear to be an original unit to which chapter 27 was added. Chapter 27 does, however, fit into the context given that it deals with things devoted to Yahweh.

[103] Kippenberg, *Religion*, p. 66.

[104] Rogerson argues that the Holiness Code post-dates Nehemiah's reforms because he would not have failed to mention them if they were already available [Rogerson and Davies, *Old Testament World*, pp. 40–41].

sondern nur eine begrenzte Nutzung als Gegenwert für das Darlehen (Lev. 27,22–24)."[105] The basic principle of the Holiness Code in general, contends Kippenberg, is kinship solidarity and it is for this reason that the interests of the clergy and the poor overlap.

> Die Interessen der Priesterschaft waren durch zwei Merkmale geprägt. Das erste bestand darin, daß weder der Tempel noch die Leviten über nennenswertes Grundeigentum verfügten und möglicherweise nur bei Priesterfamilien Grundbesitz zu vermuten ist. Das begründet eine Abhängigkeit des Tempelkultus vom Staat sowie der priesterlichen Einkünfte von Abgaben der Produzenten bzw. Aristokraten. Zweitens war die landlose Priesterschaft an einer öffentlichen Kontrolle des Landbesitzes interessiert und nicht an einer Privatisierung des Grundeigentums. Nur auf diese Weise konnte sie der Ablieferung der Abgaben sicher sein. Die Sozialreform, die ihnen vorschwebte, sollte die traditionalen Institutionen den Erfordernissen von Rentabilität anpassen—zeitweilige Abhängigkeit, ja, Handelskapitalismus nein. Das Verbot der zinznahme (Lev. 25:35–38) war vielleicht der radikalste—aber wohl auch der wirkungsloseste—Ausdruck dieses Interesses, da es die Aneignung fremder Arbeit unmöglich machen sollte. Diese Konstellation von Interessen hatte zur Folge, daß Institutionen bäuerlicher Solidarität religiös begründet wurden. Dies war eine der Funktionen von Lev. 25.[106]

A number of factors indicate to me that Kippenberg's kinship solidarity versus ancient mode of production hypothesis is not correct. He is quite right in saying that the text presupposes the rise of something like the ancient mode of production and I would agree that a concept of inalienability is re-asserted, but the law of Jubilee transforms the kinship norm of inalienability to the point of making it quite unlike the kinship institution. Firstly, whereas the נאלה institution foresaw the immediate release of property and slaves, the Jubilee year seems to recognize the impracticalities of this and so sets a definite time frame for it to happen (i.e. far into the future).[107] Secondly, the principle of inalienability in the Jubilee is enforced via a central authority. Finally, the concept of inalienability presented here is based on the perpetual ownership of the land by individuals (notice the use of אחזה: Lev. 27:24) *not the community* as would be expected in a kinship society. The right to one's אחזה is still an inalienable right, but its enforcement every fifty years by a central authority makes it even less of a deterrent to latifundialization than the נאלה

---

[105] Kippenberg, *Religion*, p. 66.
[106] Kippenberg, *Religion*, p. 68.
[107] Kippenberg, *Religion*, p. 67.

institution. Given the lack of detail on implementation, does the writer really care about the actual everyday implications of the Jubilee law? Would they even have had a practical affect given the fact that one can do a great deal of exploiting in fifty years? Probably not.

Others argue that the Jubilee laws represent an exilic point of view. Fager argues that it is a priestly vision of a new social order which would secure the landholdings of the small landholder over against the large urban-dwelling landowners.[108] Kreissig also argues that the Holiness Code originated in the exile among the priests and was the legal tool by means of which they hoped to regain their land.[109] It could also reflect the aspirations of the extended families (משפחה; Lev. 25:10) in exile who looked forward to the day in which they could claim their land back. In other words, these laws do not reflect the self-interests of the priests but of the lay members of the exilic community.[110]

Another view is put forward by Habel who examines the ideological system of this text as a whole as it relates to the relationship between land, community and Yahweh. Yahweh is portrayed as the owner of the land on the model of the deity of a temple-community with the land as his extended sanctuary. This puts the people in the position of being Yahweh's tenants on the land much like the members of the citizen-temple communities we looked at in chapter three. That is to say, over against Yahweh they have no claim to ownership over the land but in relation to each other they have permanent access to their "possession" (אחזה): "The land shall not be sold in perpetuity, for the land is mine" (25:23).[111]

This ideology of land is not, of course, expressed directly but is rather presupposed in the laws of the land sabbaths and Jubilee which together compromise the basic conditions for the maintenance of the system of divine land tenure. Unlike Exodus 23:10–11 in which the sabbath year is prescribed for humanitarian purposes, the motivation in Lev. 25:1–7 is religious. Every seventh year Israel is to give the land back to the owner Yahweh who in return will ensure that the land will produce double in the sixth year (25:20–21). The

---

[108] J. Fager, *Land Tenure and Biblical Jubilee* (Sheffield: JSOT Press, 1993), pp. 38–9 and 88–89.

[109] Fager, *Land Tenure*, p. 85.

[110] N. C. Habel, *The Land is Mine: Six Biblical Land Ideologies* (Minneapolis: Fortress, 1995), p. 113.

[111] Habel, *Land is Mine*, pp. 98–101.

land itself is the object of these laws and forms part of a three-way bond together with deity/temple and people. The bond is secured if Israel keeps the sabbaths *and* reverences the sanctuary (26:2; cf. 19:29–30).[112]

The loss of land is envisioned in Leviticus 26. It is not with regard to moral impurity that Israel will be (read: was) expelled from the land but because Israel refuses to follow the principles of the land economy. The exile is understood as an imposition of sabbaths to make up for the lack of sabbath observance:

> Then the land shall enjoy its sabbath years as long as it lies desolate, while you are in the land of your enemies; then the land shall rest and enjoy its sabbath years. As long as it lies desolate, it shall have the rest it did not have on your sabbaths when you were living on it (26:34–35).

Exile can, of course, be reversed. If Israel confesses its iniquity . . .

> I will remember also my covenant with Isaac and also my covenant with Abraham, and I will remember the land. . . . I will remember in their favor the covenant with their ancestors whom I brought out of the land of Egypt in the sight of the nations to be their God: I am the LORD (26:42, 45).

The spectre of exile and the anticipation of restoration beyond exile raises the question of the overall intention and ideological function of this text. In the context of exile this text would have had a utopian ring to it in that it envisions a realignment of Israelite society on the model of a temple-community; a kind of getting back to the basics and re-thinking the fundamentals. In this view, the statement the "the land is mine" is not so much a question of establishing a particular economic practice (let alone the religious reinterpretation of kinship norms), but of establishing the fundamentals of a theocratic worldview with specific ideological implications for the community as a whole. In other words, this text has more to do with the relationship between land-people-deity as a whole than it does with the specifics of sabbath observance. At least this is how this text was understood in the post-exilic period. The post-exilic community looked back on the exile as just such a punishment (Ezra 9:6–9). God had indeed taken the land away from them on account of their sins leaving the land empty (2 Chron. 36:21); though not empty of people

---

[112] Habel, *Land is Mine*, pp. 101–104.

as such but empty in terms of its legitimate owners. According to
Carroll, the idea of the empty land (also found in 2 Kgs 24–25; Jer.
39–40, 52) is worked up into an ideological construct which, together
with the myth of the land being polluted by its Canaanite inhabitants (Leviticus 18), was used to legitimate the leading role of the
community centred about the Second Temple. Those who remain
"occupy space but that space is purely geophysical, it is not part of
the symbolic geography whose ideology underwrites so much of the
Hebrew Bible."[113] It is not surprising, therefore, that the return is
likened to a new exodus and a new conquest. Just as the first Israelites
were promised Canaan as an eternal possession (אחזה) so too were
the returnees. The land belonged to them as a community though
not in an AMP-like taken-for-granted way. It was the perpetual possession of this very community as opposed to the "peoples of the
lands." Each legitimate member of this community of Israelites had
his own private property (אחזה) within the larger אחזה.

What then are the interests of the temple and the clergy expressed
here? It seems to me that the Jubilee law, if anything, would have
allowed for the gradual expansion of the economic forces associated
with the ancient mode of production while at the same time insist-
ing on an essential commitment to the unique identity of the community as the only legitimate owners of the land of Israel. The latter
concern translates into an economic interest in that the temple, and
the priestly-classes that lived off of the income of the temple, needed
a "community" for which it could be the "higher community." It
would appear that the temple did not own land directly, unlike the
other citizen-temple communities described in chapter three, thereby
following the classic AMP pattern in which the higher community
has no direct access to the means of production and has to use
extra-economic—that is, ideological—means to extract the surplus.[114]

---

[113] R. P. Carroll, "The Myth of the Empty Land," in D. Jobling (ed.), *Ideological
Criticism of Biblical Text* (Semeia 59; Atlanta: Scholars), p. 84.

[114] The priests themselves probably owned land as indicated, for example, by the
reference to priests from the Jordan valley (Neh. 3:22). See Blenkisopp, *Ezra-Nehemiah*,
p. 238 and Kippenberg, *Religion*, p. 64. Kippenberg also cites Jer. 1:1; 32:6–15;
Amos 7:17; Neh. 11:20; 13:10; Lev. 27:21; and 1 Chron. 9:2. The wealthier priests
probably made a good living off of their estates, but the running of the temple
required more than the personal wealth of the higher clergy. That the concept of
community land was weak and that the needs of the temple and its staff was an
on-going issue is indicated by the fact that the Levites had difficulty in obtaining
their share of the produce (Neh. 13:10–14).

Thus, whilst the priests seem to have had legitimate interests in the general well-being of the members of the citizen-temple community, the way in which these general interests are secured, ideologically-speaking, would have also reinforced social patterns and trends that were detrimental to the long-term interests of the small landowner/holder. That is to say, the law of Jubilees does not seem to provide the sort of realistic checks and balances that would prevent the accumulation of wealth and power in the hands of the ruling classes in Jerusalem, priestly or otherwise. The wealthier priestly בתי אבות especially could have (and probably did) use this power differential to exploit the opportunities for trade and commerce just like the lay heads of the בתי אבות.

Conclusion

On the basis of the foregoing examination of the internal hierarchies of the theocratic community of the Second Temple, I conclude that the temple was the focal point of a system of hierarchies within the community and that it fulfilled a central, though ultimately equivocal, role in Judean society. It fulfilled contradictory functions as an institution of the empire, of the local elite, and of the community. The community was constructed on the basis of a system of kinship and pseudo-kinship groupings and differentiations which probably originated in the exile but which came to serve purposes quite unlike the straightforward concern for identity maintenance in a minority context. In fact, identity turns out to be a very complex notion indeed, playing host to ideologies and practices which distort at one level the very values which are affirmed at another. It is my view, therefore, that objectification—"the positive transformation of values into discourses, practices and institutions"—has given rise to alienation—"the distortion of these values, the reification of discourses, practices and institutions."[115] The question then is this: How does the Chronicler fit into this context?

---

[115] G. H. Taylor, "Editor's Introduction," in P. Ricoeur, *Lectures on Ideology and Utopia* (New York: Columbia University Press, 1986), p. xxvii.

CHAPTER SIX

THE CONSEQUENCES OF BELIEF

Introduction

In this third and final reading of Chronicles I will examine the wider social implications of the Chronicler's theocratic ideology against the backdrop of the hierarchical structure of Judean society as reconstructed in the last chapter. I will argue that from the point of view of the internal contextual functions of Chronicles, the work should be characterized as ideological in the sense of supporting the dominant position of the Second Temple within the post-exilic community. Furthermore, I will argue that the degree to which the Second Temple was an oppressive presence within the community is the degree to which the Chronicler's ideology—insofar as it supports the presence—is distorted.

I use the term "consequences" as shorthand for a range of social phenomena relating to the relationship between action, including the communicative action of the Chronicler, and social structures, including the hierarchical structures of Judean society and the economic inequalities that they engendered. By conceptualizing the Chronicler's ideology in terms of its consequences I am able to tap into the results of the first two readings of Chronicles and cast them in a new light. In the first two readings of Chronicles, attention was focused on the communicative intentions and motives of the Chronicler as it related to his ideology of identity and legitimacy. Beyond that I looked at the way in which these motives and intentions had certain implications in relation to the conventions or discourses concerning the identity of the community and the legitimacy of Judah, Jerusalem, and the Second Temple as the centre for "all Israel." In raising now the matter of "consequences of belief" I am explicitly expanding the frame of reference beyond conscious motives and intentions. There are, of course, intended consequences that can be linked to conscious motives and intentions, but the focus of attention will be less on these than on the unintended or less-than-fully-intended consequences of Chronicles.

As we noted in chapter two, these unintended consequences "feed back into" the social context at the level of system and lifeworld. That is to say, unintended consequences of actions are relevant with regard to the functional integration of the society as an economic system as well as the cultural conventions and discourses within which an action gains its currency. As Giddens puts it, "The complex conventions we observe in day-to-day life are not just a superficial gloss upon large-scale institutions, they are the very stuff of their continuity and fixity."[1] Consequences are in this view not simply linear and sequential having their origin in a discrete (unique) motive which, as it were, comes to life in a communicative act embodying certain intentions and finally bringing about certain effects in the "real world." Nor is it a matter of an economic force "expressing itself" in an interest as reflected in the ideology of a text which in turn has functional consequences for the economic base.

The word "belief" also emphasizes the point of transition from the conscious work of the ideologue, as understood within a motivational framework, to the consequences of the ideology produced. Ricoeur speaks of the gap between claims made by or on behalf of a dominant institution and the beliefs of those who are dominated by it. He sees ideology as bridging the gap between claim and belief. On the one hand, a text may put forward claims about the legitimacy of an institution such as the Second Temple (an ideology of legitimation), but, on the other hand, it may also encourage belief via ideological means—belief which goes beyond what the explicit terms of the claims themselves justify. In talking about the consequences of Chronicles I am talking about the way in which this text may have taken hold of the beliefs of its readers in the interests of power. The overall orientation of this final reading is that of critique as defined in the first two chapters of the study. That is to say that I am making a judgement about the Chronicler's ideology; specifically, that it represents a functionally-false consciousness (to use Geuss's terminology). This is, of course, more a judgement about the discourse of power associated with the Second Temple than it is about the Chronicler as an individual, but I suppose that I am holding him accountable for contributing to the ideological efforts of the Jerusalemite establishment. I am not saying that this is what Chronicles

---

[1] A. Giddens, *Social Theory and Modern Sociology* (Stanford: Stanford University Press, 1987), p. 14.

is *really* about but that this is a significant part of the meaning of this work. In making this judgement I am simply standing with the women of Nehemiah 5 who felt that "kinship" entailed social and economic solidarity, affirming with them the cultural value of egalitarianism in the face of alienation.

Ideological criticism of this sort is, therefore, not so much a matter of dispassionately proving a case but a matter of demonstrating that an attitude of suspicion is appropriate. In other words, this third reading is less objective and more speculative than the first two but, as I see it, that is all for the good. The aim of the entire project is understanding, but insofar as understanding may run into obstacles detours around these obstacles are required. This is such a detour.

The difficulty, of course, in exposing distortion within an ideological system is that one has to read against the grain of the text, taking up a position extrinsic to the text or situation in order to get at systemic distortion within. This extrinsic position is always in danger of losing touch with the symbolic nature of even ideologically-distorted social reality. Ideological criticism is thus always on the brink of counter-distortion in referring to models, forces, and causes and in its tendency to radically separate meaning and function, system and symbol, mind and body.

From Claim to Belief

As we saw in chapter four, the claims made on behalf of the theocratic community of the Chronicler's day are far grander than those made by the author of Ezra-Nehemiah. It is difficult to surpass the claim that Israel is the theocratic "kingdom of Yahweh in the hands of David" (2 Chron. 13:8). Even the scale of the narrative—from Creation to Restoration—speaks of an optimism quite out of step with historical realities. Israel in the Chronicler's day did not include "all Israel" nor was Jerusalem the centre of a kingdom stretching from Shihor of Egypt to Lebo Hammath (1 Chron. 13:5). But despite these realities the implication of the Chronicler's history of Yahweh's theocratic kingdom is that this kingdom as it exists *in nuce* in the Persian period is the legitimate social order for all Israel and for all time. The massive effort needed to write this history suggests that something was at stake for the Chronicler and his immediate social group in making this claim. What this something was is, of course, a matter of speculation but in light of chapter five I would argue that it was an internal matter having to do with the actual theocratic establishment.

If the Chronicler was an ideologue of the Second Temple and a member of the ruling classes in Jerusalem (or the least someone closely connected with the temple) then we can no longer interpret the Chronicler's theocratic ideology as some sort of benign necessity, whether as a response to local competition from Gerizim (Torrey, Noth), to sagging revenues (Braun) or to social divisions (Williamson). It was a necessity alright but of an altogether different kind. This is not to say that the claims he makes on behalf of the temple are distorting in and of themselves nor that he was necessarily consciously obscuring the darker side of power, but in light of chapter five one has to ask whether or not the beliefs of the people are not somehow being taken hold of in the interests of power. The Chronicler could make all the claims he wanted to based on all kinds of legitimate grounds, but without belief these claims would be so much wind. This applies to the primary audience of the ideology, the ruling class itself, as well as to the final audience, the majority of the people. The trick is to generate belief. It is one thing to intend to urge one's audience to support the Second Temple as the leading institution of the day (an illocutionary act), quite another to successfully persuade one's readers to actively support the temple (a perlocutionary act). It is the task of ideology to ensure the success of the perlocutionary act and to secure the belief in a legitimate order, hierarchies and all.

Like a ratchet that can only be turned one way, once beliefs are given they cannot be retracted. What sort of recourse did the ordinary members of the theocratic community have against this dominant institution?[2] And the fact that it was dominant is not a matter of chance; it was an ideological achievement that needed to be secured generation after generation. The ratchet had to turn, but in one direction only. It is in this sense that I would argue that the

---

[2] Even the prophetic critique of the cult was by this time an ancient tradition for the prophets of the post-exilic period are for the most part closely allied with the temple. And the idea that Trito-Isaiah and Zechariah 9–14 eminate from proto-apocalyptic circles disenfranchised from the cult and the priestly establishment has been challenged recently by S. L. Cook in *Prophecy and Apocalypticism: The Postexilic Social Setting* (Minneapolis: Fortress, 1995). There was no doubt serious disagreements within the community but none which question the fundamental validity of the theocratic institutions as such. That only happened in the late Second Temple period.

theocratic ideology of the Chronicler is distorting. The Chronicler provides the grease for the axle; the Second Temple, discourse and all, supplies the catch.

Only one question remains: How does the Chronicler's ideology persuade? How does he bridge the gap? My answer to this question begins with another look at the claims the Chronicler makes about the theocratic "kingdom of Yahweh" (2 Chron. 13:8).

There are two notions associated with the concept of the kingdom of Yahweh in Chronicles.[3] The first notion, that Israel under the Davidic dynasty is the kingdom of Yahweh, was discussed in chapter five. This view is clearly expressed in a number of important texts apart from 2 Chron. 13:8, including the so-called "dynastic promise" in 1 Chronicles 17. The Chronistic version of this promise has Yahweh speaking of "my house" and "my kingdom" (v. 14) as opposed to "your [that is, David's] house" and "your kingdom" (2 Sam. 7:16).[4] The effect of this change is to link the legitimacy of the temple in Jerusalem with the Davidic covenant and the promise of an everlasting kingdom. The link is not, however, fully forged until Solomon has completed the temple, the second of the two "houses" of the theocracy. This two-fold expression of the kingdom of Yahweh in the Davidic dynasty and the temple means that, on the one hand, the temple gains in significance on account of David and the promise.[5] On the other hand, the Davidic dynasty loses some of its independent significance on account of only being *a part of* the theocratic kingdom, the central institution of which is the temple, not the palace.

The simultaneous glorification and relativization of David and his dynasty is reinforced by the second notion associated with the kingdom of Yahweh; namely, the universal kingship of Yahweh.

1 Chronicles 16 tells of the celebration which followed the installation of the ark in Jerusalem. As argued in chapter 4, this text draws together a variety of concepts relating to Israel's identity as expressed in a number of Psalms.[6] Israel is constituted via the act

---

[3] I am following B. Kelly, *Retribution and Eschatology in Chronicles* (JSOTS 211; Sheffield: Sheffield Academic Press, 1996), pp. 211–13.

[4] See also 1 Chron. 28:5; 29:11. Cf 1 Chron. 10:14 and 29:23; as well as Pss. 45:6; 103:19; 145:11–13.

[5] It also suggests that the Davidic line also continued to be a focus of hope in the post-exilic period [Kelly, *Retribution*, p. 185].

[6] See the discussion in chapter four.

of worship before the central cult object. In this act of worship and through the singing of the hymn (vv. 8–36) Israel confesses Yahweh's kinship:

> Let the heavens be glad, and let the earth rejoice, and let them say among the nations, "The LORD is king" (v. 31).

Again and again reference is made to the peoples and the nations (vv. 8, 19, 24, 26, 28, 31) emphasizing Israel's vulnerability on the world stage. The psalm ends, therefore, with this appeal:

> Save us, O God of our salvation, and gather and rescue us from among the nations, that we may give thanks to your holy name, and glory in your praise. Blessed be the LORD, the God of Israel, from everlasting to everlasting (vv. 35–36).

This expression of Yahweh's universal kingship transcends the "incarnation" of Yahweh's rule in the house of David. This is not to say that it is simply a matter of Yahweh being king in heaven and David king on earth,[7] but the universal rule of Yahweh has its own this-worldly, institutional, focus in the cult of the Ark and in the temple. Thus, whilst the Davidic dynasty for the post-exilic community remains a question mark, Yahweh's universal kingship is forever recognizable and realizable in the temple and its cult. The implication of this text is that worship in the temple would remind the people that "the kingdom of Yahweh is a present, immanent fact."[8] And in as much as worship is the focal point, the "persuasive appeal of the Chronicler"[9] is aimed at the inner religious disposition of the individual in the community. The argument (or plea?) is not so much academic or legal but personal and emotive, having to do with attitude, motivation and disposition as much as with action vis-à-vis the cult.[10] In other words, the discourse of the Chronicler is individualistic and institutional at the same time.

---

[7] As suggested in Royal Psalms such as Psalm 2 and 72: see J. H. Eaton, *Kingship in the Psalms* (London: SCM, 1976); and K. Whitelam, "Israelite Kinship: The Royal Ideology and Its Opponents," in R. E. Clements (ed.) *The World of Ancient Israel: Sociological, Anthropological and Political Perspectives* (Cambridge: Cambridge University Press, 1989), pp. 119–39.

[8] Kelly, *Retribution*, p. 13.

[9] To use the title of R. K. Duke's, *The Persuasive Appeal of the Chronicler: A Rhetorical Analysis* (Bible and Literature Series 25; Sheffield: Almond, 1990).

[10] Duke analyses the rhetoric of the Chronicler under the following headings: "Logos: The Rational Mode of Persuasion"; "Ethos: The Ethical Mode of Persuasion"; and "Pathos: The Emotional Mode of Persuasion."

The Dynamics of Theocracy

We can explore further the dynamics of theocracy as it relates to the Chronicler's own action-consequence theory known as the "doctrine of retribution."[11] From an historians point of view the Chronicler's retributive theology is less than attractive, giving rise to a seemingly mechanistic historiography encumbered by a "divine pragmatism" or "strict theodicy."[12] More recently, Kelly has argued that the Chronicler's emphasis on reward and punishment should not be seen as a part of a general theory of divine action in history (which, I would add, runs counter to modern theories of history and is hence unwelcome) but rather as part of a covenant theology much in keeping with the blessings and cursings formula of Deuteronomy 28–29 (and to a lesser extent Leviticus 26). According to Kelly, the reward and punishment theme demonstrates "Yahweh's mercy and restorative will toward his sinful people."[13]

The central statement of the dynamics of the theocracy is found in 2 Chron. 7:12b–16a which contains most of the Chronicler's distinctive vocabulary relating to this theme. Kelly, following Williamson,

---

[11] See R. B. Dillard, "Reward and Punishment in Chronicles: The Theology of Immediate Retribution," *WTJ* 46 (1984), pp. 164–172.

[12] J. Wellhausen, *Prolegomena to the History of Ancient Israel* (trans. W. Robertson Smith; Gloucestor, MA: Peter Smith, reprint edn., 1973), p. 203; and S. Japhet, *The Ideology of the Book of Chronicles and its Place in Biblical Thought* (BEATAJ 9; trans. A. Barber; Frankfurt: Peter Lang, 1989), pp. 150–98, respectively. For a review of the discussion see Kelly, *Retribution*, pp. 29–45.

[13] Kelly, *Retribution*, p. 108. Rudolph also highlights the importance of the concepts of the grace and right response implicit in the doctrine of retribution. By grace God warns Judah of impending doom via the prophets (2 Chron. 12:5, 7ff; 15:2ff; 16:7ff; 19:2ff; 20:20, 37; 21:12ff; 24:19ff; 25:7ff, 15; 28:9ff; 33:10; 36:15). In the end, even though the kingdom of Judah was as sinful as the northern kingdom, by grace He allowed them to return. But God's action towards His people is not unilateral; the destiny of the people is also conditioned by their response to God (1 Chron. 28:9; 2 Chron. 12:5; 14:6; 15:2, 15). The right response is obedience that involves, first and foremost, proper worship, especially the giving of thanks and praise to God. Trust in God is another key component of right response to God's grace. Trust in God is shown through seeking Him and this is always effective (1 Chron. 21:9; 29:28; 2 Chron. 1:12; 13:18, 21; 14:4, 10; 15:15, 19; 16:7ff; 17:5, 10, 12; 18:31; 20:1ff, 25; 24:3, 15; 25:8; 26:5; 27:6; 32:1ff, 23, 27ff). The lack of trust brings ruin, which even extends to the quality of burial. The doctrine of retribution is, thus, not an independent mechanism, but is softened by the commitment of God to His people; a commitment that can wait for their obedience just as the people themselves sometimes have to wait for God. Trusting God and seeking Him in prayer are as important as law and ritual observance [Rudolph, *Chronikbücher* (HAT 21; Tübingen: Mohr, 1955), pp. xiv–xxi].

argues that this text expresses the ever-present possibility of repentance and restoration.[14] Again, the verbs used to express this theme emphasize the inner disposition of the individual. "*Seeking* Yahweh" בקש (v. 14) and its synonym דרש characterizes a personal commitment to Yahweh particularly as expressed in "prayer" התפלל (v. 14) and worship in the cult. "Seeking" and "praying" presuppose that one has "humbled oneself," כנע (v. 14) and "turned," שוב (v. 14), from one's wicked ways (מעל). Yahweh's response (v. 15) is to "hear" שמע, "forgive" סלח, and "heal" רפא the land. According to Kelly, this focus on individual internal motivation emphasizes the opportunity the people had "to pursue the path of full restoration, *assisted by the institution of the temple.*"[15]

Kelly has inadvertently put his finger on the very vital connection, ideologically-speaking, between the individual and the institution. I would agree, of course, with his view that it was the Chronicler's intention to portray the temple in terms of "assisting" the individual. But looking at the same thing *in terms of its functional properties* one would have to conclude that it had the reverse effect: It was the individual who was assisting the temple in restoring its fortunes in maintaining its dominant position in the community and perhaps even in extending its hegemony over the region as a whole. But in the ideology of the Chronicler this relationship is reversed and obscured. This is exactly the point where the beliefs of the individual are taken hold of in the interests of power. Thus, the individual addressed in the ideology of Chronicles is not the voluntary moral subject, freely offering support to the temple, so much as the *subject of* the temple and its discourses. What was at stake was not the fate of the individual so much as the fate of "the community" and the "higher community" within it.

An important illustration of the corporate and "institutional" dimension of the Chronicler's rhetoric is found in the reign of Jehoshaphat. 2 Chronicles 20 is unique to Chronicles and can be seen as a set piece example of the dynamics of theocracy. The chapter begins by telling how the Moabites, Ammonites and Meunites march against Judah. In response to this threat Judah assembles to seek help from the LORD (note the role of all the people in this, and

---

[14] Kelly, *Retribution*, p. 109.
[15] Kelly, *Retribution*, p. 109 [italics mine].

the calling of an assembly). Jehoshaphat then prays to the LORD, invoking the very things Solomon asked for in his prayer.

> O LORD, God of our ancestors, are you not God in heaven? Do you not rule over all the kingdoms of the nations? In your hand are power and might, so that no one is able to withstand you. Did you not, O our God, drive out the inhabitants of this land before your people Israel, and give it forever to the descendants of your friend Abraham? They lived in it, and in it have built you a sanctuary for your name, saying, "If disaster comes upon us, the sword, judgment, or pestilence, or famine, we will stand before this house, and before you, for your name is in this house, and cry to you in our distress, and you will hear and save." See now, the people of Ammon, Moab, and Mount Seir, whom you would not let Israel invade when they came from the land of Egypt, and whom they avoided and did not destroy—they reward us by coming to drive us out of your possession that you have given us to inherit. O our God, will you not execute judgment against them? For we are powerless against this great multitude that is coming against us. We do not know what to do, but our eyes are on you (2 Chron. 20:6–12).

The prayer begins by challenging Yahweh to reveal his universal kingship and to honour his special covenant with Israel (echoing 1 Chronicles 16). Jehoshaphat goes on to remind Yahweh of his promise to hear and to save the people who loyally seek him in prayer before his sancutary, the focal point of the theocracy. Except for Yahweh's rule (as exercised via the temple) the people are powerless. The story goes on to tell of a miraculous victory over these enemies, one in which the Judeans only had to sing praises to the LORD while Yahweh did the rest. There are allusions to the fall of Jericho as well as to Moses's charge to Israel "Do not fear them, for it is the LORD your God who fights for you" (Deut. 3:22). After Jehoshaphat's victory the land returns to normal "for his God gave him rest [נוח] all around" (2 Chron. 20:30). This story exemplifies in the starkest possible terms the ideological reversal described above. The people call upon Yahweh for assistance, believing that their worship and prayer—as manifested in their loyalty to the cult—is the only way of securing Yahweh's assistance and through that their place in the land and among the nations. Reading this same story from an ideological critical perspective one would have to say again that it is precisely the opposite: it is the belief of the people in the efficacy of the temple cult that is assisting Yahweh and (more accurately) his official representatives.

Exile and Restoration, Again (and Again)

This story also illustrates another dimension of the dynamics of theocracy. It is clear that the Chronicler intended this story, like the history as a whole, to say something about the present by saying something about the past. That is to say, the Chronicler's story of Israel has a paradigmatic, even atemporal, ahistorical quality which stands in tension with the narrative genre.

This tension is noticeable, first of all, in the genealogies. The time between Adam and David is not historical time, if time is the right word. The genealogies describe Israel as it always was, its inner structure and hierarchy, its geographical place. It treats of space not time. There is no contingency, no development, no promise to Abraham, no Moses, no exodus, no Sinai, no conquest,[16] no point at which Israel came into being. Israel emerged gradually, naturally, from Adam, Abraham and Israel. Israel emerged autochthonously in the land of Israel. This is God's order. Israel among the nations. Israel as always in the land. In the genealogies Israel's identity is taken-for-granted.

Yet, inserted into this picture are historical events, though no historical development as such. The tribes east of the Jordan are taken into exile (1 Chron. 5:25–26). Reuben lost his status as birthright to Joseph and Judah emerged as the most prominent tribe (1 Chron. 5:1–2). The Edomites had kings; that is, they had a history before David (1 Chron. 1:43). There were wars (1 Chron. 2:23; 4:41–43; 5:10, 19–22; 7:21; 8:13) but they form no sequence. They are mere fragments within a larger structure. The most important historical event mentioned in terms of identity is the Babylonian exile (1 Chron. 6:15; 8:6–7; 9:1) but it too has no consequences. In the Chronicler's picture of the past, the exile didn't really change anything. All Israel is centred around the Temple, before and after this event. Israel is back where it belongs, in its property (אחזה) and in its cities. A major disruption in terms of social identity is no disruption at all.

From Saul onward, the Chronicler no longer avoids history and development. The culmination of Israel's identity in the building of the temple is just that, a culmination; the result of a process of preparation. The temple had its origin in history, in the transition from one dynasty to another, in wars of conquest, in a promise given

---

[16] S. Japhet, "Conquest and Settlement in Chronicles," *JBL* 98 (1979), pp. 205–18.

at a particular time to a particular individual. In other words, it is not to be taken for granted, and that which has an origin might also have an end.[17] But to what extent is it conditional?

The reigns of David and Solomon have been described as the *Urzeit* of Israel; the realization of all that Israel was meant to be, the fulfillment of the promises and the culmination of the covenant relationship (Abrahamic, Mosaic and Davidic) between Yahweh and his people.[18] This *Urzeit* of the kingdom of Yahweh has structural effects backward and forward in time. Backward in the sense that Israel was always centred on Judah and Jerusalem. Forward in that this Urzeit sets in motion a spiralling pattern of punishment and forgiveness, exile and restoration. The oscillation between exile and restoration suggests that the kingdom of Yahweh is always under threat, yet never under threat. The spiral establishes an equilibrium which is vividly illustrated in the stories of Manasseh and Josiah. In Kings, Manasseh is thoroughly evil whereas Josiah is a righteous yet tragic figure (2 Kgs. 21–23:30). In Chronicles, on the other hand, Manasseh experiences his own personal exile and restoration (2 Chron. 33:10–13) whereas Josiah has only himself to blame for his death at the hand of Neco (2 Chron. 35:22). To look at a spiral from the side is to see linear development, but to look at it down the middle is to see a circle. Thus, although the rise of the Davidic dynasty and the building of the Temple are unique events, the consequences of these events are timeless. To judge by the way the book ends, the exile is overcome, the contingency of history is overcome, and Yahweh's theocracy endures.

But what about this spiral? What makes the line a spiral? What is the axis about which it turns? It is Yahweh's timeless commitment to Israel which transforms the linearity of the Chronicler's history into a spiral and Yahweh's abiding חסד about which the spiral turns. The word חסד "kindness/lovingkindness" occurs fifteen times in Chronicles. In the sphere of human relations the term denotes mutuality, that most essential of ingredients in preserving life in the family and in society.[19] When used of Yahweh (and most of the references

---

[17] D. Jobling, "Deconstruction and the Political Analysis of Texts: A Jamsonian Reading of Psalm 72," in D. Jobling (ed.), *Ideological Criticism of Biblical Texts* (Semeia 59; Atlanta: Scholars, 1992), p. 109.

[18] Riley, *King and Cultus*, pp. 57–8.

[19] In the following חסד is used to refer to human kindness: 1 Chron. 19:2; 2 Chron. 24:22; 32:32; 35:26.

in Chronicles have to do with Yahweh), the lovingkindness shown to David and/or Israel expresses the very heart of the relationship. This relationship is one-sided for it is impossible for humans to match Yahweh's kindness in terms of mutuality: thus, חסד is often translated "steadfast love" emphasizing the over-riding loyalty, permanence and constancy of the grace of Yahweh. Thus, the context in which one finds חסד used in Chronicles and elsewhere is that of petition and praise.

The occurrences in Chronicles can be divided into two groups. The first relates to the חסד shown to David and represents, if you will, Yahweh's commitment to Israel through time. The Davidic side of the theocracy is contingent for that which had an historical origin might also have an end. There is therefore a tension between the eternal promise to David of a dynasty and the fact that earthly dynasties are vulnerable.[20]

- 1 Chron. 17:13   "I will be a father to him, and he shall be a son to me. I will not take my steadfast love from him, as I took it from him who was before you."
- 2 Chron. 1:8   Solomon said to God, "You have shown great and steadfast love to my father David, and have made me succeed him as king."
- 2 Chron. 6:14   He said, "O LORD, God of Israel, there is no God like you, in heaven or on earth, keeping covenant in steadfast love with your servants who walk before you with all their heart."
- 2 Chron. 6:42   "O LORD God, do not reject your anointed one. Remember your steadfast love for your servant David."[21]

The second group of occurrences relates to Yahweh's "steadfast love" for Israel as expressed in the phrase "O give thanks to the LORD, for he is good; for his steadfast love endures forever." As argued in chapter three, this expression (which is found in Pss. 106:1; 107:1; 118:1–4, 29; 136:1–26; and Ezra 3:11) was the keynote of Second Temple worship—the central refrain in the theocratic anthem. In the Psalms the use of this phrase has an almost hypnotic effect, espe-

---

[20] Recent research has shown that the Chronicler was indeed hopeful of a restoration of the Davidic dynasty [see Kelly, *Retribution*, pp. 135–85]. But it is still a matter of *hope*!

[21] A further occurrence of this term with reference to David is found in the genealogy of Zerubbabel, a descendant of David. According to 1 Chron. 3:20 two of the five sons of Zerubbabel have חסד in their name: Hasadiah (חסדיה: "God is kind") and Jushab-hesed (יושב חסד: "kindness will be returned"). Williamson suggests that given the positive meaning of their names these two sons might well have been born after the return [Williamson, *1 and 2 Chronicles*, p. 57].

cially in Psalms 118 and 136. In the latter it is repeated in every single verse. The use of this phrase in Chronicles does, I suggest, have a similar effect beginning with the inaugural worship service before the Ark.

- 1 Chron. 16:34   O give thanks to the LORD, for he is good; for his steadfast love endures forever.
- 1 Chron. 16:41   With them were Heman and Jeduthun, and the rest of those chosen and expressly named to render thanks to the LORD, for his steadfast love endures forever.
- 2 Chron. 5:13   It was the duty of the trumpeters and singers to make themselves heard in unison in praise and thanksgiving to the LORD, and when the song was raised, with trumpets and cymbals and other musical instruments, in praise to the LORD, For he is good, for his steadfast love endures forever, and the house, the house of the LORD, was filled with a cloud.
- 2 Chron. 7:3   When all the people of Israel saw the fire come down and the glory of the LORD on the temple, they bowed down on the pavement with their faces to the ground, and worshiped and gave thanks to the LORD, saying, "For he is good, for his stead-fast love endures forever."
- 2 Chron. 7:6   The priests stood at their posts; the Levites also, with the instruments for music to the LORD that King David had made for giving thanks to the LORD—for his steadfast love endures for-ever—whenever David offered praises by their ministry. Opposite them the priests sounded trumpets; and all Israel stood.
- 2 Chron. 20:21   When he had taken counsel with the people, he appointed those who were to sing to the LORD and praise him in holy splendor, as they went before the army, saying, "Give thanks to the LORD, for his steadfast love endures forever."

Whereas there is a question mark over David, there is no question here. This isn't a matter of hope; it is a reality for Yahweh's "stead-fast love" is assured. It is assured because Yahweh is king of the universe and his kingship is forever centred on the temple. Even the exile and the end of the Davidic monarchy (though not the Davidic line) is no obstacle. The kingdom is Yahweh's kingdom before and after David and the exercise of his rule is not restricted to the Davidic line. Indeed, Yahweh's use of Cyrus as an agent of salvation for his people (2 Chron. 36:23) is also an expression חסד. At least this is the view expressed by Ezra in his prayer:

For we are slaves; yet our God has not forsaken us in our slavery, but has extended to us his steadfast love [חסד] before the kings of Persia, to give us new life to set up the house of our God, to repair its ruins, and to give us a wall in Judea and Jerusalem (Ezra 9:9).

Yahweh's commitment to Israel in time and space is his חסד and the temple is the focal point of Yahweh's חסד, the axis about which Israel's history revolves. Israel can take something for granted after all.

If Yahweh's חסד is the axis, it is Israel's response to God that provides the movement about the axis. How is Yahweh's חסד realized in time and space and from generation to generation? How does Israel escape the vicissitudes of history? How is Israel's identity as a people secured on the ground? The Chronicler's answer is very simple. Israel's identity as the people of God is secured by the right response of each generation, of each individual to God. The people of God are to live with a sense of the immediacy of God in his temple. They are to internalize their commitment to God and adopt the right attitude, humble themselves, pray, and seek Yahweh. Israel's identity is secured when it is loyal to God in his temple.[22] In ideological critical terms, what the Chronicler is asking his audience to do is to participate in this theocratic kingdom, imaginatively, actively, fully.

I conclude by returning to the middle of the story, to the *Urzeit* and David's final prayer on behalf of Israel and Solomon. In this prayer David affirms for the first and last time Yahweh's universal dominion:

> Blessed are you, O LORD, the God of our ancestor Israel, forever and ever. Yours, O LORD, are the greatness, the power, the glory, the victory, and the majesty; for all that is in the heavens and on the earth is yours; *yours is the kingdom, O LORD,* and you are exalted as head above all. Riches and honor come from you, and you rule over all. In your hand are power and might; and it is in your hand to make great and to give strength to all. And now, our God, we give thanks to you and praise your glorious name (1 Chron. 29:10b–13).

These are also the words of the Chronicler drawing the reader again and again to the temple and to worship.

Miles describes the literary effect of the ending of Chronicles (as read in the context of the current position of Chronicles in the Hebrew canon) as a "perpetual round."[23] I would suggest that the

---

[22] The king does, of course, play a major role in the narrative, but Yahweh's חסד does not only apply to the king. We noticed in chapter three how the promise to David is extended to include the people in 2 Chron. 6:36–42, 30:6–9 and elsewhere.

[23] J. Miles, *God: A Biography* (New York: Vintage), pp. 391–6. See chapter three.

internal oscillation of Chronicles has a similar effect: "The relationship between God and Israel, like that of the youth and his love [in Keats's Grecian Urn], is preserved by being frozen." To "hold the moment" in literary form "one must turn a continuing story into an endlessly recurring one."[24] In this vein one can all but audibly hear the people respond to David:

> O give thanks to the LORD, for he is good; for his steadfast love endures forever.
> O give thanks to the LORD, for he is good; for his steadfast love endures forever.
> O give thanks to the LORD, for he is good; for his steadfast love endures. . . .

Conclusion

These three readings of Chronicles have shown that the ideology of the Chronicler is a complex phenomena with many different aspects and interconnections. The above readings were not intended as a comprehensive interpretation of Chronicles nor was I working with the presupposition that what the Chronicler said can be reconstructed as one large coherent system of thought. My aim was rather to explore the ideological implications—in the fullest sense of that term—of what the Chronicler said and in the context in which he said it. The relationship between identity, legitimacy and distortion in Chronicles is at the level of discourse itself. If one thinks of Chronicles as a statue in a dark room, it is not so much a matter of shining a torch on Chronicles from three different angles, as noticing that the statue is at the centre of a room and that the room is part of a large and beautiful and awesome temple.

The Chronicler's ideology of identity and legitimacy was, in my view, a conscious reformulation of the ideology of the Second Temple; a reformulation which sought not only to reinforce its leading role in Judah but also to extend its claims over the whole land of Israel. The Chronicler adapted the history of the First Temple to this purpose by showing how the temple in Jerusalem was, from the beginning, the theocratic capital of all Israel. Identity and legitimacy

---

[24] Miles, *God*, p. 393.

are thereby secured in terms of the origins of theocratic "kingdom of Yahweh." But also at work within the Chronicler's ideology are the interests of Jerusalem's ruling classes, including the clergy. Chronicles can, therefore, be thought of as a cross-section of the discourse of the Jerusalem elite, perhaps in the period of its ascendancy.

ABBREVIATIONS

ADOG	Arbeiten des deutschen Orientalischen Gesellschaft
AGJU	Arbeiten zur Geschichte des antiken Judentums und des Urchristentums
AJSL	American Journal of Semitic Languages and Literature
AOS	American Oriental Studies
BEATAJ	Beiträge zur Erforschung des Alten Testaments und des antiken Judentums
BK	Biblischer Kommentar
BS	Bibliotheca Sacra
BTB	Biblical Theology Bulletin
BWANT	Beiträge zur Wissenschaft vom Alten und Neuen Testament
BZ	Biblische Zeitschrift
BZAW	Beihefte zur Zeitschrift für die alttestamentliche Wissenschaft
CBQ	Catholic Biblical Quarterly
CTM	Concordia Theological Monthly
EI	Eretz Israel
EvTh	Evangelische Theologie
FRLANT	Forschungen zur Religion und Literatur des Alten und Neuen Testaments
HAT	Handbuch zum Alten Testament
HUCA	Hebrew Union College Annual
ICC	International Critical Commentary
Int	Interpretation
JBL	Journal of Biblical Literature
JETS	Journal of the Evangelical Theological Society
JNES	Journal of Near Eastern Studies
JQR	Jewish Quarterly Review
JRel	Journal of Religion
JSNTS	Journal for the Study of the New Testament Supplement
JSOT	Journal for the Study of the Old Testament
JSOTS	Journal for the Study of the Old Testament Supplement
JSP	Journal for the Study of the Pseudepigrapha
JTS	Journal of Theological Studies
KAT	Kommentar zum Alten Testament
LS	Louvain Studies
NCB	New Century Bible
OBO	Orbis Biblicus et Orientalis
OLA	Orientalia Lovaniensis Analecta
OTL	Old Testament Library
RVV	Religionsgeschichtliche Versuche und Arbeiten
SBLDS	Society of Biblical Literature Dissertation Series
SBLMS	Society of Biblical Literature Monograph Series
SBM	Stuttgarter biblische Monographien
SUNT	Studien zum Umwelt des Neuen Testaments
TLZ	Theologische Literatur Zeitschrift
TrinJ	Trinity Journal
TynBul	Tyndale Bulletin
VT	Vetus Testamentum
VTS	Vetus Testamentum Supplement

WBC	Word Biblical Commentary
WMANT	Wissenschaftliche Monographien zum Alten und Neuen Testament
WTJ	Westminster Theological Journal
ZA	Zeitschrift für Assyriologie
ZAW	Zeitschrift für die alttestamentliche Wissenschaft

BIBLIOGRAPHY

Abercrombie, N., Hill, S. and Turner, B. S.
1980   *The Dominant Ideology Thesis*. London: Allen and Unwin.
Ackroyd, P. R.
1972   "The Temple Vessels—A Continuity Theme," *VTS* 23: 166–81.
1987   "The Written Evidence for Palestine," in H. Sancisi-Weerdenburg, A. Kuhrt, and J. W. Drijvers (eds.) *Achaemenid History*. Vol. 1, *Sources, Structures, and Synthesis* (Proceedings of the Gronigen 1983 Achaemenid History Workshop; Leiden: Nederlands Instituut voor het Nabije Oosten): 207–20.
1988   "Problems in the Handling of Biblical and Related Sources in the Achaemenid Period," in H. Sancisi-Weerdenburg, A. Kuhrt, and J. W. Drijvers (eds.), *Achaemenid History*. Vol. 3, *Method and Theory* (Proceedings of the London 1985 Achaemenid History Workshop; Leiden: Nederlands Instituut voor het Nabije Oosten): 33–54.
1990   "The Biblical Portrayal of Achaemenid Rulers," in H. Sancisi-Weerdenburg, A. Kuhrt, and J. W. Drijvers (eds.), *Achaemenid History*. Vol. 5, *The Roots of the European Tradition* (Proceedings of the Groningen 1986 Achaemenid History Workshop. Leiden: Nederlands Instituut voor het Nabije Oosten): 1–16.
1991   *The Chronicler in His Age*. JSOTS 101. Sheffield: JSOT Press.
Albertz, R.
1994   *A History of Israelite Religion in the Old Testament Period*. Translated by J. Bowden. London: SCM.
Albright, W. F.
1921   "The Date and Personality of the Chronicler." *JBL* 40: 104–124.
Alt, A.
1953   "Die Role Samarias in der Entstehung des Judentums," in *Kleine Schriften zur Geschichte des Volkes Israel*, II (München: C. H. Beck).
1953   "Zur Geschichte der Grenze zwischen Judäa und Samaria," in *Kleine Schriften zur Geschichte des Volkes Israel*, II (München: C. H. Beck).
Anderson, R. T.
1992   "Samaritans," in D. N. Freedman (ed.), *The Anchor Bible Dictionary* (New York: Doubleday).
Auld, A. G.
1994   *Kings without Privilege: David and Moses in the Story of the Bible's Kings*. Edinburgh: T & T Clark.
Austin, J. L.
1975   *How to Do Things with Words*. Second edition. Oxford: Clarendon.
Austin, M. M.
1981   *The Hellenistic World from Alexander to the Roman Conquest: A Selection of Ancient Sources in Translation*. Cambridge: Cambridge University Press.
Avigad, N.
1976   *Bullae and Seals from a Post-exilic Judean Archive*. Jerusalem: Israel Exploration Society.
Bailey, A. M. and Llobera, J. R.
1981   *The Asiatic Mode of Production: Science and Politics*. London: Routledge and Kegan Paul.
Barnes, W. E.
1896/7   "The Religious Standpoint of the Chronicler." *AJSL* 8: 14–20.

Barth, F.
1969   *Ethnic Groups and Boundaries: The Social Organization of Culture Difference.* Bergen: Scandinavian University Press.

Batten, L. W.
1913   *Ezra and Nehemiah.* ICC. Edinburgh: T & T Clark.

Becker, J.
1980   *Messianic Expectation in the Old Testament.* Translated by D. E. Green. Edinburgh: T & T Clark.

Bedford, P. R.
1991   "On Models and Texts: A Response to Blenkinsopp and Petersen," in P. R. Davies (ed.), *Second Temple Studies.* Vol. 1, *The Persian Period* (JSOTS 117; Sheffield: JSOT Press): 154–62.

Begg, C. T.
1982   "'Seeking Yahweh' and the purpose of Chronicles." *LS* 9: 128–141.

Ben Zvi, E.
1988   "The Authority of 1–2 Chronicles in the Late Second Temple Period," *JSP* 3: 59–88.

Berger, P.-R.
1975   "Der Kyros-Zylinder mit dem Zusatzfragment BIN II Nr. 32 und die akkadischen Personennamen im Danielbuch." *ZA* 64: 192–234.

Bickerman, E. J.
1976   "The Edict of Cyrus in Ezra 1," in *Studies in Jewish and Christian History*, vol. 1 (AGJU IX; Leiden: Brill): 72–108.

Blenkinsopp, J.
1981   "Interpretation and the Tendency to Sectarianism," in E. P. Sanders, et al. (eds.), *Jewish and Christian Self-Definition.* Vol. 2, *Aspects of Judaism in the Graeco-Roman Period* (Philadelphia: Fortress): 1–26.
1987   "The Mission of Udjahorresnet and those of Ezra and Nehemiah." *JBL* 106: 409–21.
1988   *Ezra-Nehemiah.* OTL. Philadelphia: Westminster.
1990   "A Jewish Sect of the Persian Period." *CBQ* 52: 5–20.
1991   "Temple and Society in Achaemenid Judah," in P. R. Davies (ed.), *Second Temple Studies.* Vol. 1, *The Persian Period* (JSOTS 117; Sheffield: JSOT Press): 22–53.

Boyce, M.
1992   "Zoroaster, Zoroastrianism." D. N. Freedman (ed.), *The Anchor Bible Dictionary* (New York: Doubleday).

Braun, R.
1971   "The Message of Chronicles: Rally 'Round the Temple." *CTM* 42: 502–514.
1976   "Solomon, the Chosen Temple Builder: The Significance of 1 Chronicles 22, 28 and 29 for the Theology of Chronicles." *JBL* 95: 581–590.
1977   "A Reconsideration of the Chronicler's Attitude toward the North." *JBL* 96: 59–62.
1979   "Chronicles, Ezra and Nehemiah: Theology and literary History," in J. A. Emerton (ed.), *Studies in the Historical Books of the Old Testament* (VTS 30; Leiden: Brill): 52–64.
1986   *1 Chronicles.* WBC. Waco, TX: Word.

Brett, M. G.
1990   "Four or Five Things to do with Texts," in D. Clines, S. Fowl, and S. Porter (eds.), *The Bible in Three Dimensions: Essays in Celebration of Forty Years of Biblical Studies in the University of Sheffield* (JSOTS 87; Sheffield: JSOT Press): 357–77.
1991   *Biblical Criticism in Crisis? The Impact of the Canonical Approach on Old Testament Studies.* Cambridge: Cambridge University Press.
1991   "Motive and Intention in Genesis 1." *JTS* 42: 1–16.

Brinkman, J. A.
1984   *Prelude to Empire*. Occasional Papers of the Babylonian Fund. Philadelphia: University of Pennsylvania Museum Press.

Caquot, A.
1965   "Les 'grâces de David'. A propos de'Isaie 55/3b." *Semitica* 15: 45–59.

Carroll, R. P.
1986   *Jeremiah*. OTL. London: SCM.
1990   "Silence, Exile, and Cunning: Reflections on the 'Buerger-Tempel-Gemeinde' Thesis Approach to the Early Second Temple Period." Paper read at the SBL International Meeting, Vienna.
1990   "Torrey, C. C," in R. J. Collins and J. H. Houlden (eds.), *A Dictionary of Biblical Interpretation*. London: SCM.
1991   "Textual Strategies and Ideology in the Second Temple Period," in P. R. Davies (ed.), *Second Temple Studies*. Vol. 1, *The Persian Period* (JSOTS 117; Sheffield: JSOT Press): 108–124.
1992   "Co-opting the Prophets: Nehemiah and Noadiah," in E. Ulrich, J. Wright, R. P. Carroll, and P. R. Davies (eds.), *Priests, Prophets and Scribes: Essays on the Formation and Heritage of Second Temple Judaism in Honor of Joseph Blenkinsopp* (JSOTS 149; Sheffield: JSOT Press): 87–101.
1992   "The Myth of the Empty Land," in D. Jobling (ed.), *Ideological Criticism of Biblical Texts* (Semeia 59; Atlanta: Scholars): 79–93.
1994   "Israel, History of (Post-Monarchic Period)," in D. N. Freedman (ed.), *The Anchor Bible Dictionary* (New York: Doubleday).

Carter, C.
1994   "The Province of Yehud in the Post-Exilic Period: Soundings in Site Distribution and Demography," in T. Eskenazi and K. Richards (eds.), *Second Temple Studies*. Vol. 2, *Temple and Community in the Persian Period* (JSOTS 175; Sheffield: JSOT Press): 106–45.

Charlesworth, J. H. (ed.)
1985   *The Old Testament Pseudepigrapha*. Vol. 2, *Expansions of the "Old Testament" and Legends, Wisdom and Philosophical Literature, Prayers, Psalms and Odes, Fragments of Lost Judeo-Hellenistic Works*. New York: Doubleday.

Clines, D. J. A.
1990   "The Nehemiah Memoir: The Perils of Autobiography," in *What Does Eve Do to Help? and other Readerly Questions to the Old Testament* (JSOTS 94; Sheffield: JSOT Press): 124–64.
1995   *Interested Parties: The Ideology of Writers and Readers of the Hebrew Bible*. JSOTS 205. Sheffield: Sheffield Academic Press.

Cogan, M.
1988   "For we, like you, Worship your God: Three Biblical Portrayals of Samaritan Origins." *VT* 38: 286–292.

Coggins, R. J.
1975   *Samaritans and Jews. The Origins of Samaritanism Reconsidered*. Growing Points in Theology. Oxford: Blackwell.

Cook S. L.
1995   *Prophecy and Apocalypticism: The Postexilic Social Setting*. Minneapolis: Fortress.

Cowley, A., (ed.)
1967   *Aramaic Papyri of the Fifth Century*. Reprint edition. Osnabrück: Otto Zeller.

Cross, F. M.
1975   "A Reconstruction of the Judean Restoration." *JBL* 94: 4–18.

Crown, A. D.
1993   *A Bibliography of the Samaritans*. Second edition. Metuchin, NY/London: American Theological Library Association.

Crown, A. D., Pummer, R. and Tal, A. (eds.)
1993 *A Companion to Samaritan Studies*. Tübingen: J. C. B. Mohr (Paul Siebeck).
Curtis, E. L. and Madsen, A. A.
1910 *The Books of Chronicles*. ICC. Edinburgh: T & T Clark.
Dandamaev, M. A.
1969 "Achaemenid Babyonia," in I. M. Diakonoff (ed.), *Ancient Mesopotamia: Socio-Economic History. A Collection of Studies by Societ Scholars* (Moscow: Nauka): 296–311.
1969 "Der Tempelzehnte in Babylonien während des 6.–4. Jh. v. u. Z." in I. R. Steihl (ed.), *Beiträge zur Alten Geschichte und deren Nachleben. Festschrift für Franz Altheim I* (Berlin): 82–9.
1972 "Politische und Wirtschaftliche Geschichte," in G. Walser (ed.), *Beiträge zur Achämenidengeschichte* (Historia Einzelschriften 18; Wiesbaden: Harrassowitz): 19–24.
1979 "State and Temple in Babylonia in the First Millenium BCE," in E. Lipinski (ed.), *State and Temple Economy in the Ancient Near East, II* (OLA 6; Leuven: University Press): 589–96.
1982 "The Neo-Babylonian Elders," in M. Dandamaev, et al. (eds.), *Societies and Languages of the Ancient Near East. Festschrift I. M. Diakonoff* (Warminster: Aris and Phillips): 38–41.
1984 "Babylonia in the Persian Age," in W. D. Davies and L. Finkelstein (eds.), *The Cambridge History of Judaism*. Vol. 1, *Introduction; The Persian Period* (Cambridge: Cambridge University Press): 326–42.
1986 *Slavery in Babylonia from Nabopolassar to Alexander the Great (626–331 BC)*. Revised edition. Edited by V. A. Powell. Translated by V. A. Powell, M. A. Powell and D. B. Weisberg. DeKalb, IL: Northern Illinois University Press.
Dandamaev, M. and Lukonin, V. G.
1989 *The Culture and Social Institutions of Ancient Iran*. Cambridge: Cambridge University Press.
Davies, N.
1996 *History of Europe*. Oxford: Oxford University Press.
Davies, P. R.
1992 "Defending the Boundaries of Israel in the Second Temple Period: 2 Chronicles 20 and the 'Salvation Army'," in E. Ulrich, J. Wright, R. P. Carroll, and P. R. Davies (eds.), *Priests, Prophets and Scribes: Essays on the Formation and Heritage of Second Temple Judaism in Honour of Joseph Blenkinsopp* (JSOTS 149; Sheffield: JSOT Press): 43–54.
Davies, P. R., (ed.)
1991 *Second Temple Studies*. Vol. 1, *The Persian Period*. JSOTS 117. Sheffield: JSOT Press.
Delcor, M.
1962 "Hinweise auf das Samaritanische Schisma im Alten Testament." *ZAW* 74: 281–291.
De Vries, S. J.
1988 "Moses and David as Cult Founders in Chronicles." *JBL* 107: 619–639.
De Wette, W. M. L.
1843 *A Critical and Historical Introduction to the Canonical Scripture of the Old Testament*. Translated by T. Parker. Boston: Little and Brown.
1971 *Beiträge zur Einleitung in das Alte Testament*. Vol. 1, *Kritischer Versuch über die Glaubwürdigkeit der Bücher der Chronik mit Hinsicht auf die Geschichte der Mosaischen Bücher und Gesetzgebung*. Reprint of 1806 edition. Darmstadt: Ohms Verlag.
Diakonoff, I. M.
1969 "The Rise of the Despotic State in Ancient Mesopotamia," in I. M. Diakonoff (ed.), *Ancient Mesopotamia: Socio-Economic History. A Collection of Studies by Soviet Scholars* (Moscow: Nauka): 173–203.
Dillard, R. B.
1984 "Reward and Punishment in Chronicles: The Theology of Immediate Retribution," *WTJ* 46: 164–72.

Dion, P. E.
1990   *The Jews during the Persian Period: A Bibliography*. Supplement to the Newsletter for Targumic and Cognate Studies 5. Toronto: University of Toronto Press.
1991   "The Civic and Temple Community of Persian Period Judea: Neglected Insights from Eastern Europe." *JNES* 50: 281–7.
Douglas, M.
1993   *In the Wilderness: The Doctrine of Defilement in the Book of Numbers*. JSOTS 158. Sheffield: JSOT Press.
Duke, R.
1990   *The Persuasive Appeal of the Chronicler: A Rhetorical Analysis*. Bible and Literature Series 25. Sheffield: Almond.
Dumbrell, W. J.
1984   "The Purpose of the Books of Chronicles." *JETS* 27: 257–266.
Durkheim, E.
1947   *The Division of Labour in Society*. Translated by G. Simpson. Glencoe, IL: Free Press.
1964   *The Rules of Sociological Method*. New York: Free Press.
Eagleton, T.
1976   *Marxism and Literary Criticism*. London: Methuen.
1991   *Ideology: An Introduction*. London: Verso.
Eagleton, T. (ed.)
1994   *Ideology*. London: Verso.
Eaton, J. H.
1976   *Kingship in the Psalms*. London: SCM.
Eph'al, I.
1978   "The Western Minorities in Babylonia in the 6th–5th Centuries BC: Maintenance and Cohesion." *Orientalia* 47: 74–90.
Eskenazi, T.C.
1988   *In an Age of Prose: A Literary Approach to Ezra-Nehemiah*. SBLMS 36. Atlanta, GA: Scholars Press.
Eskenazi, T. C. and E. P. Judd.
1994   "Marriage to a Stranger in Ezra 1–9," in T. Eskenazi and K. Richards (eds.), *Second Temple Studies*. Vol. 2, *Temple and Community in the Persian Period* (JSOTS 175; Sheffield: JSOT Press): 266–85.
Ewald, H.
1867   *History of Israel*. Translated by R. Martineau. London: Longmans and Green.
Fager, J.
1993   *Land Tenure and Biblical Jubilee*. Sheffield: JSOT Press.
Finley, M.
1980   *Ancient Slavery and Modern Ideology*. London: Chatto and Windus.
Fisch, H.
1988   *Poetry with a Purpose: Biblical Poetics and Interpretation*. Bloomington: Indiana University Press.
Fishbane, M.
1985   *Biblical Interpretation in Ancient Israel*. Oxford: Clarendon.
Fortes, M.
1969   *Kinship and Social Order*. Chicago: University of Chicago Press.
Fowl, S.
1995   "Texts don't have ideologies." *Biblical Interpretation* 3: 15–34.
Fowler, R.
1981   *Literature as Social Discourse: The Practice of Linguistic Criticism*. London: Batsford.
Fox, R.
1967   *Kinship and Marriage*. Harmondsworth: Penguin.
Freedman, D. N.
1961   "The Chronicler's Purpose." *CBQ* 23: 436–42.

Frei, H.
1984   "Zentralgewalt und Lokalautonomie im Achämenidenreich," in H. Frei
       and K. Koch, *Reichsidee und Reichsorganization im Perserreich.* OBO 55. Göttingen:
       Vandenhoeck & Ruprecht.
Fretheim, T. E.
1968   "The Priestly Document: Anti-Temple?" *VT* 18: 313–329.
Garlan, Y.
1988   *Slavery in Ancient Greece.* Translated by J. Lloyd. Ithaca, NY: Cornell University
       Press.
Geertz, C.
1975   *Interpretation of Cultures: Selected Essays.* London: Hutchinson.
Geuss, R.
1981   *The Idea of a Critical Theory: Habermas and the Frankfurt School.* Cambridge:
       Cambridge University Press.
Giddens, A.
1976   *New Rules of Sociological Method: A Positive Critique of Interpretative Sociologies.*
       London: Hutchinson.
1987   *Social Theory and Modern Sociology.* Stanford: Stanford University Press.
Godelier, M.
1977   *Perspectives in Marxist Anthropology.* Translated by R. Brain. Cambridge: Cambridge
       University Press.
1978   "Infrastructure, Societies, and History." *Current Anthropology* 19: 763–8.
1981   "The Asiatic Mode of Production," in A. M. Bailey and J. R. Llobera
       (eds.), *The Asiatic Mode of Production: Science and Politics.* London: Routledge and
       Kegan Paul.
Goldingay, J.
1975   "The Chronicler as a Theologian." *BTB* 5: 99–126.
Grabbe, L. L.
1991   "Reconstructing History from the Book of Ezra," in P. R. Davies (ed.), *Second
       Temple Studies.* Vol. 1, *The Persian Period* (JSOTS 117; Sheffield: JSOT Press):
       98–106.
1992   *Judaism from Cyrus to Hadrian.* Minneapolis: Fortress.
Graham, M. P.
1990   *The Utilization of Chronicles in the Reconstruction of Israelite History in the Nineteenth
       Century.* SBLDS 116. Atlanta: Scholars Press.
Graham, M. P., Hoglund, K. G. and McKenzie, S. L. (eds.)
1997   *The Chronicler as Historian.* JSOTS 238. Sheffield: Sheffield Academic Press.
Grayson, A. K.
1972   *Assyrian Royal Inscriptions.* Vol. 1, *From the Beginning to Ashur-resha-ishi I.* Wiesbaden:
       Harrassowitz.
Groder, M. and Kreiswirth, M., (eds.)
1994   *Johns Hopkins Guide to Literary Theory and Criticism.* Baltimore: Johns Hopkins
       University Press.
Gunneweg, A. H.
1982   "Die aramäische und die hebräische Erzählung über die nachexilische Restau-
       ration—ein Vergleich." *ZAW* 94: 299–302.
Habel, N. C.
1995   *The Land is Mine: Six Biblical Land Ideologies.* Minneapolis: Fortress.
Habermas, J.
1984   *The Theory of Communicative Action.* Vol. 1, *Reason and the Rationalization of Society.*
       Translated by T. McCarthy. Cambridge: Polity.
1987   *The Theory of Communicative Action.* Vol. 2, *Lifeworld and System.* Translated by
       T. McCarthy. Cambridge: Polity.
Hanson, P.
1975   *The Dawn of Apocalyptic.* Philadelphia: Fortress.

Harris, M.
1980   *Cultural Materialism: The Struggle for a Science of Culture*. New York: Harper and Row.
Heltzer, M.
1992   "The Provincial Taxation in the Achaemenian Empire and 'Forty Shekels of Silver' (Neh. 5, 15)." *Michmanim* 6: 15–25.
1992   "A Recently Published Babylonian Tablet and the Province of Judah after 516 BCE." *Transeuphratene* 5: 57–62.
Hirsch, E. D., Jr.
1967   *Validity in Interpretation*. New Haven, CO: Yale University Press.
Hoglund, K.
1991   "The Achaemenid Context," in P. R. Davies (ed.), *Second Temple Studies*. Vol. 1, *The Persian Period* (JSOTS 117; Sheffield: JSOT Press): 54–72.
1992   *Achaemenid Imperial Administration in Syria-Palestine and the Missions of Ezra and Nehemiah*. SBLDS 125. Atlanta, GA: Scholars Press.
Holloday, W.
1989   *Jeremiah 2 : A Commentary on the Book of the Prophet Jeremiah Chapters 26–52*. Hermeneia. Minneapolis: Fortress.
Horsley, R. A.
1991   "Empire, Temple and Community—but no Bourgeoisie! A Response to Blenkinsopp and Petersen," in P. R. Davies (ed.), *Second Temple Studies*. Vol. 1, *The Persian Period* (JSOTS 117; Sheffield: JSOT Press): 163–75.
Iser, W.
1978   *The Act of Reading: A Theory of Aesthetic Response*. Baltimore: Johns Hopkins University Press.
Jameson, F.
1981   *The Political Unconscious: Narrative as a Socially Symbolic Act*. Ithaca, NY: Cornell University Press.
Janssen, J. J.
1979   "The Role of the Temple in the Egyptian Economy during the New Kingdom," in E. Lipinski (ed.), *State and Temple Economy in the Ancient Near East, II* (OLA 6; Leuven: University Press): 505–15.
Japhet, S.
1968   "The Supposed Common Authorship of Chronicles and Ezra-Nehemiah, Investigated Anew." *VT* 18: 330–371.
1979   "Conquest and Settlement in Chronicles." *JBL* 98: 205–18.
1981   "People and Land in the Restoration Period," in G. Strecker (ed.), *Das Land Israel in biblischer Zeit* (Göttingen: Vandenhoeck & Ruprecht): 103–25.   .
1982   "Sheshbazzar and Zerubbabel." *ZAW* 94: 66–98.
1989   *The Ideology of the Book of Chronicles and its Place in Biblical Thought*. BEATAJ 9. Translated by A. Barber. Frankfurt: Peter Lang.
1993   *I & II Chronicles*. OTL. Louisville, KY: Westminster/John Knox.
Jobling, D.
1987   "Sociology and Literary Approaches to the Bible." *JSOT* 38:85–93.
1991   "Texts and the World—An Unbridgeable Gap? A Response to Carroll, Hoglund and Smith," in P. R. Davies (ed.), *Second Temple Studies*. Vol. 1, *The Persian Period* (JSOTS 117; Sheffield: JSOT Press): 175–82.
1992   "Deconstruction and the Political Analysis of Texts: A Jamsonian Reading of Psalm 72," in D. Jobling (ed.), *Ideological Criticism of Biblical Text* (Semeia 59; Atlanta: Scholars): 95–127.
Johnson, M. D.
1969   *The Purpose of Biblical Genealogies*. Second edition. Cambridge: Cambridge University Press.
Johnstone, W.
1986   "Guilt and Atonement: The Theme of 1 and 2 Chronicles," in J. D. Martin

and P. R. Davies (eds.) *A Word in Season: Essays in Honour of William McKane* (JSOTS 42; Sheffield: JSOT Press): 113–38.

Kartveit, M.
1989   *Motive und Schichten der Landtheologie in I Chronik 1–9.* ConBOT 28. Stockholm: Almqvist & Wiksell.

Kelly, B.
1996   *Retribution and Eschatology in Chronicles.* JSOTS 211. Sheffield: Sheffield Academic Press.

Kent, J. H.
1948   "The Temple Estates of Delos, Rheneia and Mykonos." *Hesperia* 17: 243–338.

Kent, R. G.
1953   *Old Persian: Grammar, Texts, Lexicon.* AOS 33. Second edition. New Haven, CO.: Yale University Press.

Kippenberg, H.
1971   *Garizim und Synagoge: Traditionsgeschichtliche Untersuchungen zur samaritanischen Religion der aramische Periode.* RVV 30. Berlin: Walter de Gruyter.
1982   *Religion und Klassenbildung im antiken Judäa: Eine religionssoziologische Studie zum Verhältnis von Tradition und gesellschaftlichen Entwicklung.* SUNT 14. Second edition. Göttingen: Vandenhoeck & Ruprecht.

Kippenberg, H. (ed.)
1977   *Seminar: Die Enstehung der antiken Klassen-gesellschaften.* Frankfurt: Suhrkamp.

Koch, K.
1984   "Weltordnung und Reichsidee im alten Iran," in K. Koch and H. Frei, *Reichsidee und Reichsorganization im Perserreich.* OBO 55. Göttingen: Vandenhoeck & Ruprecht.

Krader, L.
1975   *The Asiatic Mode of Production: Sources, Development and Critique in the Writings of Karl Marx.* Assen: Van Gorcum.

Kreissig, H.
1971   "'Antike' Produktionsformen im hellenistischen Asien, 'Orientalische' Produktionsformen in der klassischen Ägäis." *Acta Conventus XI* (Warsaw).
1973   *Die sozialökonomische Situation in Juda zur Achämenidenzeit.* Schriften zur Geschichte und Kultur des alten Orients 7. Berlin: Akademie.

Kuhrt, A.
1983   "The Cyrus Cylinder and Achaemenid Imperial Policy." *JSOT* 25: 83–97.

Kuhrt, A. and Sherwin-White, S.
1991   "Aspects of Seleucid Royal Ideology: The Cylinder of Antiochus I from Borsippa." *Journal of Hellenic Studies* 111: 71–86.

Kümmel, H. M.
1979   *Familie, Beruf und Amt in spätbabylonischen Uruk: Prosopographische Untersuchungen zu Berufsgruppen des 6. Jahrhunderts v. Chr. in Uruk.* ADOG 20. Berlin: Mann.

Lang, B.
1982   "The Social Organization of Peasant Poverty in Biblical Israel." *JSOT* 24: 47–63.

Lebram, L.
1987   "Die Traditionsgeschichte der Esragestalt und die Frage nach dem historischen Esra," in H. Sancisi-Weerdenburg, A. Kuhrt, and J. W. Drijvers (eds.) *Achaemenid History.* Vol. 1, *Sources, Structures, and Synthesis* (Proceedings of the Grönigen 1983 Achaemenid History Workshop; Leiden: Nederlands Instituut voor het Nabije Oosten): 103–38.

Levenson, J. D.
1984   "The Temple and the World." *JRel* 64: 275–98.

Liverani, M.
1973   "Memorandum on the Approach to Historiographic Texts." *Orientalia* 42: 178–94.

1979   "The Ideology of the Assyrian Empire," in M. Trolle Larsen (ed.), *Power and Propaganda: A Symposium on Ancient Empires* (Mesopotamia 7; Copenhagen: Akademisk Forlag): 297–318.

Luckenbill, D. D.
1927   *Ancient Records of Assyrian and Babylon*. Vol. 2, *Historical Records of Assyria: From Sargon to the End*. Chicago: University of Chicago Press.

Magen, Y.
1986   "A Fortified Town of the Hellenistic Period on Mt. Gerizim." *Qadmoniot* 19.3–4: 91–101.
1986   "The Temple of Zeus on Mt. Gerizim [Hebrew]," in *Proceedings of the Twelfth Archeological Congress* (Jerusalem: Israel Exploration Society): 14–15.
1990   "Mt. Gerizim, A Temple City [Hebrew]." *Qadmoniot* 23.3–4: 69–96.
1993   "Gerizim, Mt.," in E. Stern (ed.), *The New Encyclopedia of Archaeological Excavations in the Holy Land* (Jerusalem: Israel Exploration Society/New York: Simon & Schuster).

Mantel, H. D.
1973   "The Dichotomy of Judaism during the Second Temple." *HUCA* 44: 55–87.

Marsden, E. W.
1969   *Greek and Roman Artillery*. Oxford: Clarendon.

Marx, K.
1964   *The Economic and Philosophic Manuscripts of 1844*. Edited by D. J. Struik. New York: International Publishers.
1965   *Karl Marx: Selected Correspondence*. Moscow: Progress.
1967   *Capital: A Critique of Political Economy*. Vol. 1, *The Process of Capitalist Production*. New York: International Publishers.
1967   *Grundrisse der Kritik der politischen Ökonomie*. Frankfurt: Europäische Verlagsanstalt.
1970   "A Contribution to the Critique of Hegel's 'Philosophy of Right'," in *Critique of Hegel's "Philosophy of Right."* Edited by J. O'Malley. Translated by A. Jolin and J. O'Malley. Cambridge: Cambridge University Press.

Marx, K. and Engels, F.
1969   *Basic Writings on Politics and Philosophy*. Edited by L. S. Feuer. London: Fontana.
1987   *Karl Marx-Frederick Engels: Collected Works*. Vol. 29, *Karl Marx: 1857–61*. London: Lawrence and Wishart.

Mayes, A. D. H.
1993   "On Describing the Purpose of Deuteronomy." *JSOT* 58: 13–33.

McCarthy, T.
1984   "Translator's introduction" in J. Habermas, *The Theory of Communicative Action*. Vol. 1, *Reason and the Rationalization of Society*. Cambridge: Polity.

McKenzie, S. L.
1985   *The Chronicler's Use of the Deuteronomistic History*. Harvard Semitic Monographs 33. Atlanta, GA: Scholars.

Meyer, E.
1896   *Die Enstehung des Judenthums: Eine historische Untersuchung*. Halle: Niemeyer.

Meyers, C.
1983   "The Israelite Empire: In Defense of King Solomon." *Michigan Quarterly Review* 22: 412–28.
1987   "David as Temple Builder," in P. D. Miller, Jr., P. D. Hanson, and S. D. McBride (eds.), *Ancient Israelite Religion. Essays in Honor of Frank Moore Cross* (Philadelphia: Fortress): 357–76.

Meyers, E. M.
1985   "Shelomith Seal." *EI* 18: 33–38.

Miles, J.
1996   *God: A Biography*. New York: Vintage.

Milgrom, J.
1985   "Hezekiah's Sacrifices at the Dedication Services of the Purified Temple

(2 Chr 29:21–24)," in A. Kort and S. Morschauser (ed.), *Biblical and Related Studies Presented to Samuel Iwry* (Winona Lake, IN: Eisenbraun): 159–61.

Montrose, L.
1989   "Professing the Renaissance: The Poetics and Politics of Culture," in H. Aram Veeser (ed.), *The New Historicism* (London: Routledge).

Mosis, R.
1973   *Untersuchungen zur Theologie des chronistischen Geschichtswerkes.* Freiburger theologische Studien 92. Freiburg: Herder.

Mowinckel, S.
1960   "Erwägungen zum chronistischen Geschichtswerk." *TLZ* 85: 1–8.
1964/5   *Studien zu dem Buche Ezra-Nehemiah.* Oslo: Universitetsforlaget.

Murray, D. F.
1993   "Dynasty, People, and the Future: The Message of Chronicles." *JSOT* 58: 71–92.

Muscarella, I.
1969   "Review of G. Walser, *Die Völkerschaften.*" *JNES* 28.

Myers, J. M.
1966   "The Kerygma of the Chronicler: History and Theology in the Service of Religion." *Int* 20: 259–273.

Newsome, J.
1975   "Towards a New Understanding of the Chronicler and His Purpose." *JBL* 95: 201–17.

North, R.
1963   "Theology of the Chronicler." *JBL* 82: 369–381.

Noth, M.
1987   *The Chronicler's History.* JSOTS 50. Translated by H. G. M. Williamson. Sheffield: JSOT Press.

Nylander, C.
1979   "Achaemenid Imperial Art," in M. Trolle Larsen (ed.), *Power and Propaganda: A Symposium on Ancient Empires* (Mesopotamia 7; Copenhagen: Akademisk Forlag): 345–59.

Oeming, M.
1990   *Das wahre Israel: Die "genealogische Vorhalle" 1 Chronik 1–9.* BWANT. Stuttgart: Kohlhammer.

O'Leary, B.
1989   *The Asiatic Mode of Production: Oriental Despotism, Historical Materialism and Indian History.* Oxford: Blackwell.

Petersen, D. L.
1991   "The Temple in Persian Period Prophetic Texts," in P. R. Davies (ed.), *Second Temple Studies.* Vol. 1, *The Persian Period* (JSOTS 117; Sheffield: JSOT Press): 125–44.

Pfeiffer, R. H.
1952   *Introduction to the Old Testament.* New York: Harper.

Plöger, O.
1968   *Theocracy and Eschatology.* Translated by S. Rudman. Oxford: Blackwell.

Postgate, J. N.
1972   "*The Role of the Temple in the Mesopotamian Secular Community,*" in P. J. Ucko, R. Tringham, and G. W. Dimbleby (eds.), *Man, Settlement and Urbanism* (London: Duckworth): 811–25.

Polzin, R.
1976   *Late Biblical Hebrew.* Missoula, MT: Scholars Press.

Poulssen, N.
1967   *König und Tempel im Glaubenszeugnis des Alten Testaments.* SBM 3. Stuttgart: Kohlhammer.

Premnath, D. N.
1988   "Latifundialization and Isaiah 5:8–10." *JSOT* 40: 49–60.
Pummer, R.
1982   "Antisamaritanische Polemik in jüdischen Schriften aus der intertestamen-
       tarischen Zeit." *BZ* NF 26.2: 224–42.
Rad, G. von.
1930   *Das Geschichtsbild des Chronistischen Werkes.* BWANT. Stuttgart: Kohlhammer.
1966   "The Levitical Sermon in I and II Chronicles," in *The Problem of the Hexateuch
       and other Essays.* Translated by E. W. Trueman Dicken. Edinburgh: Oliver and
       Boyd.
Ricoeur, P.
1977   *The Rule of Metaphor.* Translated by R. Czerny, et al. Toronto: University of
       Toronto Press.
1986   *Lectures on Ideology and Utopia.* Edited by G. H. Taylor. New York: Columbia
       University Press.
Riley, W.
1993   *King and Cultus in Chronicles: Worship and the Reinterpretation of History.* JSOTS
       160. Sheffield: JSOT Press.
Rogerson, J. W.
1984   *Old Testament Criticism in the Nineteenth Century: England and Germany.* London:
       SPCK.
1985   "The Use of Sociology in Old Testament Studies," in J. A. Emerton (ed.),
       Congress Volume Salamanca (1983) (VTS 36; Leiden: Brill): 245–56.
1989   "Anthropology and the Old Testament," in R. E. Clements (ed.), *The World
       of Ancient Israel: Sociological, Anthropological and Political Perspectives* (Cambridge:
       Cambridge University Press): 17–37.
Rogerson, J. W. and Davies, P. R.
1989   *The Old Testament World.* Cambridge: Cambridge University Press.
Rothstein, J. W. and Hänel, J.
1927   *Das erste Buch der Chronik.* KAT. Leipzig: Reichart.
Rowland, C. C.
1991   "The Second Temple: Focus of Ideological Struggle?" in W. Horbury (ed.),
       Templum Amicitae: Essays on the Second Temple Presented to Ernst Bammel (JSNTS
       48; Sheffield: JSOT Press): 175–98.
Rowley, H. H.
1962   "The Samaritan Schism in Legend and History," in B. W. Anderson and
       W. Harrelson (eds.), *Israel's Prophetic Heritage: Festschrift J. Muilenburg* (London:
       SCM): 208–222.
Rudolph, W.
1947   *Ezra und Nehemia.* HAT. Tübingen: J. C. B. Mohr
1955   *Chronikbücher.* HAT. Tübingen: J. C. B. Mohr.
Ruffing, A.
1992   *Jahwekrieg als Weltmetapher: Studien zu Jahwekriegtexten des chronistischen Sondergutes.*
       Stuttgart: Katholisches Bibelwerk.
Runciman, W. G.
1983   *A Treatise on Social Theory.* Vol. 1, *The Methodology of Social Theory.* Cambridge:
       Cambridge University Press.
Sailhamer, J.
1989   "1 Chronicles 21: A Study in Inter-biblical Interpretation." *TrinJ* 10:
       33–48.
Sarkisian, G. Kh.
1969   "City Land in Seleucid Babylonia," in I. M. Diakonoff (ed.), *Ancient Mesopotamia.
       Socio-Economic History: A Collection of Studies by Societ Scholars* (Moscow: Nauka):
       312–31.

Schaefer, G. E.
1972   "The Significance of Seeking God in the Purpose of the Chronicler." Th.D. diss., Southern Baptist Theological Seminary.
Schwartz, J.
1988   "On Priests and Jericho in the Second Temple Period." *JQR* 79: 23–48.
Shaver, J. R.
1990   *Torah and the Chronicler's History Work.* Atlanta, GA: Scholars Press.
1992   "Ezra and Nehemiah: On the Theological Significance of Making them Contemporaries," in E. Ulrich, J. Wright, R. P. Carroll, and P. R. Davies (eds.), *Priests, Prophets and Scribes: Essays on the Formation and Heritage of Second Temple Judaism in Honor of Joseph Blenkinsopp* (JSOTS 149; Sheffield: JSOT Press): 76–86.
Skinner, Q.
1972   "Motives, Intentions and the Interpretation of Texts," *New Literary History* 3: 393–408.
Smith, A. D.
1994   "The Politics of Culture: Ethnicity and Nationalism," in *Companion Encyclopedia of Anthropology* (London: Routledge).
Smith, D. L.
1989   *The Religion of the Landless: The Social Context of the Babylonian Exile.* Bloomington, IN: Meyer Stone.
Smith-Christopher, D. L. (= Smith, D. L.)
1991   "The Politics of Ezra: Sociological Indicators of Postexilic Judaean Society," in P. R. Davies (ed.), *Second Temple Studies.* Vol. 1, *The Persian Period* (JSOTS 117; Sheffield: JSOT Press): 73–97.
1994   "The Mixed Marriage Crisis in Ezra 9–10 and Nehemiah 13: A Study of the Sociology of the Post-Exilic Judean Community," in T. Eskenazi and K. Richards (eds.), *Second Temple Studies.* Vol. 2, *Temple and Community in the Persian Period* (JSOTS 175; Sheffield: JSOT Press).
Smith, M.
1971   *Palestinian Parties and Politics that Shaped the Old Testament.* New York: Columbia University Press.
Steck, O. H.
1968   "Das Problem theologischer Strömungen in nachexilischer Zeit." *EvTh* 28: 445–458.
Stein, G.
1997   "Zur Datierung der Chronik: Ein neuer methodischer Ansatz." *ZAW* 109: 84–92.
Stern, E.
1982   *The Material Culture of the Land of the Bible in the Persian Period (538–322 BCE).* Warminster: Aris & Phillips.
Stillwell, R., (ed.)
1976   *The Princeton Encyclopedia of Classical Sites.* Princeton: Princeton University Press.
Stinespring, W. F.
1961   "Eschatology in Chronicles." *JBL* 80: 209–219.
Stolper, M. W.
1989   "The Governor of Babylon and Across-the-River in 486 B.C." *JNES* 48: 283–305.
1985   *Entrepreneurs and Empire: The Murashu Firm and Persian Rule in Babylonia.* Istanbul: Nederlands Historisch-Archaeologisch Instituut Istanbul.
Strübind, K.
1991   *Tradition als Interpretation in der Chronik: König Josaphat als Paradigma chronistischer Hermeneutik und Theologie.* BZAW 201. Berlin: Walter de Gruyter.
Struve, V. V.
1969   "The Problem of the Genesis, Development, and Disintegration of the Slave

Societies in the Ancient Orient," in I. M. Diakonoff (ed.), *Ancient Mesopotamia. Socio-Economic History: A Collection of Studies by Soviet Scholars* (Moscow: Nauka): 17–69.

Taylor, G. H.
1986   "Editor's introduction," in P. Ricoeur, *Lectures on Ideology and Utopia* (New York: Columbia University Press).

Thompson, J. B.
1981   *Critical Hermeneutics: A Study in the Thought of Jürgen Habermas and Paul Ricoeur.* Cambridge: Cambridge University Press.

Throntveit, M. A.
1987   *When Kings Speak: Royal Speech and Royal Prayer in Chronicles.* SBLDS 93. Atlanta: Scholars.

Torrey, C. C.
1986   *The Composition and Historical Value of Ezra-Nehemiah.* BZAW 2. Giessen.
1970   "The Chronicler as Editor and Independent Narrator," in *Ezra Studies* (New York: reprint edn., Ktav): 208–51.

Townsend, J. L.
1987   "The Purpose of 1 and 2 Chronicles." *BS* 144: 277–292.

Tulpin, C.
1987   "The Administration of the Achaemenid Empire," in I. Carradice (ed.), *Coinage and Administration in the Athenian and Persian Empires: The Ninth Oxford Symposium on Coinage and Monetary History* (BAR Int'l Series 343; Oxford: B.A.R.): 109–66.

Walser, G.
1966   *Die Völkerschaften auf den Reliefs von Persepolis.* Berlin: Gebrüder Mann.

Waltke, B.
1992   "Samaritan Pentateuch." D. N. Freedman (ed.), *The Anchor Bible Dictionary* (New York: Doubleday).

Washington, H. C.
1994   "The Strange Woman of Proverbs 1–9 and Post-Exilic Judean Society," in T. Eskenazi and K. Richards (eds.), *Second Temple Studies.* Vol. 2, *Temple and Community in the Persian Period* (JSOTS 175; Sheffield: JSOT Press): 217–42.

Weber, M.
1978   *Economy and Society: An Outline of Interpretive Sociology.* Translated by G. Roth and C. Wittich. Berkeley: University of California Press.

Weinberg, J. P.
1987   "Königtum und Königreich im Weltbild des Chronisten." *Klio* 69: 28–45.
1992   "Die Mentalitat der Jerusalemischen Burger-Tempel-Gemeinde des 6.–4. Jh. v. u. Z.," *Transeuphratene* 5: 133–42.
1988   "Gott im Weltbild des Chronisten: Die vom Chronisten verschwiegenen Gottesnamen." *ZAW* 100 (Supplement): 170–189.
1992   *The Citizen-Temple Community.* JSOTS 151. Translated by D. L. Smith-Christopher. Sheffield: JSOT Press.

Welch, A. C.
1939   *The Work of the Chronicler: Its Purpose and Date.* Schweich Lectures 1938. London: British Academy.

Wellhausen, J.
1973   *Prolegomena to the History of Ancient Israel.* Translated by W. Robertson Smith. Reprint edition. Gloucestor, MA: Peter Smith.

Welten, P.
1973   *Geschichte und Geschichtsdarstellung in den Chronikbüchern.* WMANT 42. Neukirchen-Vluyn: Neukirchener.
1979   "Lade-Temple-Jerusalem: Zur Theologie der Chronikbucher," in A. Gunneweg and O. Kaiser (eds.), *Textgemäss: Aufsätze und Beiträge zur Hermeneutik des Alten Testaments* (FS Würthwein; Göttingen: Vandenhoeck & Ruprecht): 169–83.

White, S. K.
1988   *The Recent Work of Jürgen Habermas: Reason, Justice and Modernity.* Cambridge:
       Cambridge University Press.
Whitelam, K. W.
1989   "Israel's Traditions of Origin: Reclaiming the Land," *JSOT* 44: 19–42.
1989   "Israelite Kinship: The Royal Ideology and Its Opponents," in R. E. Clements
       (ed.), *The World of Ancient Israel: Sociological, Anthropological and Political Perspectives*
       (Cambridge: Cambridge University Press): 119–39.
Widengren, G.
1977   "The Persian Period," in J. Hayes and J. M. Miller (eds.), *Israelite and Judean
       History* (Philadelphia: Fortress): 489–538.
Willi T.
1972   *Die Chronik als Auslegung: Untersuchungen zur literarischen Gestaltung der historischen
       überlieferung Israels.* FRLANT 106. Göttingen: Vandenhoeck & Ruprecht.
1991   *Chronik.* BK. Neukirchen-Vluyn: Neukirchener.
1995   *Juda, Jehud, Israel: Studien zum Selbstverstandnis des Judentums in persischer Zeit.*
       Tübingen: J. C. B. Mohr (Paul Siebeck).
Williamson, H. G. M.
1977   "Eschatology in Chronicles." *TynBul* 28: 115–54.
1977   *Israel in the Books of Chronicles.* Cambridge: Cambridge University Press.
1982   *1 and 2 Chronicles.* NCB. London: Marshall, Morgan & Scott.
1983   "The Composition of Ezra i–vi." *JTS* 34: 1–30.
1985   *Ezra, Nehemiah.* WBC. Waco, TX: Word.
1988   "The Governors of Judah under the Persians." *TynBul* 39: 59–82.
1991   "The Temple in the Books of Chronicles," in W. Horbury (ed.), *Templum
       Amicitae: Essays on the Second Temple Presented to Ernst Bammel* (JSNTS 48; Sheffield:
       JSOT Press): 15–31.
Wimsatt W. K. and Beardsley, M. C.
1972   "The Intentionality Fallacy," in D. Lodge (ed.), *20th Century Literary Criticism*
       (London: Longman): 334–45.
Winton Thomas, D. (ed.)
1958   *Documents from Old Testament Times.* New York: T. Nelson.
Wittfogel, K. A.
1957   *Oriental Despotism: A Comparative Study of Total Power.* New Haven: Yale University
       Press.
Wright, J. W.
1991   "The Legacy of David in Chronicles: the Narrative Function of 1 Chronicles
       23–27." *JBL* 110: 229–242.
1992   "From Center to Periphery: 1 Chronicles 23–27 and the Interpretation of
       Chronicles in the Nineteenth Century," in E. Ulrich, J. Wright, R. P. Carroll,
       and P. R. Davies (eds.), *Priests, Prophets and Scribes: Essays on the Formation and
       Heritage of Second Temple Judaism in Honor of Joseph Blenkinsopp* (JSOTS 149;
       Sheffield: JSOT Press): 20–42.
Yadin, Y.
1963   *The Art of Warfare in Biblical Lands in the Light of Archaeological Discovery.* London:
       Weidenfeld and Nicolson.
Yamauchi, E.
1990   *Persia and the Bible.* Grand Rapids, MI: Baker.
Zizek, M. (ed.)
1994   *Mapping Ideology.* London: Verso.
Zunz, L.
1832   *Die gottesdienstlichen Vorträge der Juden, historisch entwickelt.* Berlin: Asher.

INDEX OF BIBLICAL REFERENCES

36:15	219n	4	36
36:17–19	79	4:1–3	89, 89n, 91, 108, 120
36:20–21	79		
36:20	31, 80, 82	4:1	87
36:21	80, 82, 146, 210	4:1–2	40
36:22–23	81–83, 124	4:3	89, 196
36:23	151, 225	4:4–5	89n
		5:1–6:18	89
Ezra		5:3ff	102
1–6	42, 84, 85n, 88, 88n, 90	5:3	89n
		5:5	102, 197
1	81, 84, 86	5:6–23	89n
1:1–4	81, 82, 88n	5:9	197
1:1	84	5:24	89n
1:3	83, 118n	6:3–5	88n, 89
1:4	80n	6:6–11	89
1:5–11	85	6:7	197
1:5	85, 131, 196	6:10	94
1:6	85	6:17	37n
1:7	85	6:19–21	87
1:11	86	6:21	195n
2	86, 103, 189–191, 198	7–10	90
		7:13	118n
2:1	87, 87n, 190	7:24	204
2:2	132n	7:28	37n
2:2–35	191	8:1	196
2:6	189	8:17	108n
2:11	193n	8:25	37n, 118n
2:16	192	8:33	190n
2:22	190n	8:35	37n, 118n
2:36–39	191	8:36	102n
2:39	193n	9–10	109, 111, 113, 115
2:40	49n, 191		
2:41	191	9	107, 112, 114, 192
2:42	191	9:1–2	43n, 111
2:43–54	191	9:1	37n, 192
2:43	193n	9:2	192, 197n
2:55–58	191	9:4	115
2:59–63	191	9:6–9	210
2:59	37n, 87, 119, 132n, 192	9:7	112
		9:8–9	204
2:61	190n	9:8	80n
2:62	191	9:9	225
2:63	191	9:15	80n
2:64	87, 107n, 190, 192	10	114
		10:1ff	37n
2:65	192	10:1	107n, 112
2:68–69	196	10:3	113, 115
2:69	151	10:5	37n, 118n
2:70	118n	10:8	107n, 113, 177n
3:8	80n	10:10	37n
3:11	140n, 154, 224	10:12	107n
3:12	196	10:14	107n
4–6	89, 203	10:16	196

INDEX OF APOCRYPHAL/
DEUTERO-CANONICAL REFERENCES

INDEX OF EXTRA-BIBLICAL REFERENCES

INDEX OF MODERN AUTHORS

BIBLICAL INTERPRETATION SERIES

ISSN 0928-0731

1. VAN DIJK-HEMMES, F. & A. BRENNER. *On Gendering Texts*. Female and Male Voices in the Hebrew Bible. 1993. ISBN 90 04 09642 6
2. VAN TILBORG, S. *Imaginative Love in John*. 1993. ISBN 90 04 09716 3
3. DANOVE, P.L. *The End of Mark's Story*. A Methodological Study. 1993. ISBN 90 04 09717 1
4. WATSON, D.F. & A.J. HAUSER. *Rhetorical Criticism of the Bible*. A Comprehensive Bibliography with Notes on History and Method. 1994. ISBN 90 04 09903 4
5. SEELEY, D. *Deconstructing the New Testament*. 1994. ISBN 90 04 09880 1
6. VAN WOLDE, E. *Words become Worlds*. Semantic Studies of Genesis 1-11. 1994. ISBN 90 04 098879
7. NEUFELD, D. *Reconceiving Texts as Speech Acts*. An Analysis of 1 John. 1994. ISBN 90 04 09853 4
8. PORTER, S.E., P. JOYCE & D.E. ORTON (eds.). *Crossing the Boundaries*. Essays in Biblical Interpretation in Honour of Michael D. Goulder. 1994. ISBN 90 04 10131 4
9. YEO, K.-K. *Rhetorical Interaction in 1 Corinthians 8 and 10*. A Formal Analysis with Preliminary Suggestions for a Chinese, Cross-Cultural Hermeneutic. 1995. ISBN 90 04 10115 2
10. LETELLIER, R.I. *Day in Mamre, Night in Sodom*. Abraham and Lot in Genesis 18 and 19. 1995. ISBN 90 04 10250 7
11. J.C.O'Neill. *Who Did Jesus Think He Was?* 1995. ISBN 90 04 10429 1
12. TOLMIE, D.F. *Jesus' Farewell to the Disciples*. John 13:1-17:26 in Narratological Perspective. 1995. ISBN 90 04 10270 1
13. RYOU, D.H. *Zephaniah's Oracles against the Nations*. A Synchronic and Diachronic Study of Zephaniah 2:1-3:8. 1995. ISBN 90 04 10311 2
14. SONNET, J.-P. *The Book within the Book*. Writing in Deuteronomy. 1997. ISBN 90 04 10866 1
15. SELAND, T. *Establishment Violence in Philo and Luke*. A Study of Non-Conformity to the Torah and Jewish Vigilante Reactions. 1995. ISBN 90 04 10252 3
16. NOBLE, P.R *The Canonical Approach*. A Critical Reconstruction of the Hermeneutics of Brevard S. Childs. 1995. ISBN 90 04 10151 9
17. SCHOTTROFF, L.R & M.-T. WACKER (Hrsg.). *Von der Wurzel getragen*. Christlich-feministische Exegese in Auseinandersetzung mit Antijudaismus. 1996. ISBN 90 04 10336 8
18. BECKING, B. & M. DIJKSTRA (eds.). *On Reading Prophetic Texts*. Gender-Specific and Related Studies in Memory of Fokkelien van Dijk-

Hemmes. 1996. ISBN 90 04 10274 4
19. BRETT, M.G. (ed.). *Ethnicity and the Bible*. 1996. ISBN 90 04 10317 1
20. HENDERSON, I.H. *Jesus, Rhetoric and Law*. 1996. ISBN 90 04 10377 5
21. RUTLEDGE, D. *Reading Marginally*. Feminism, Deconstruction and the Bible. 1996. ISBN 90 04 10564 6
22. CULPEPPER, R.A. (ed.). *Critical Readings of John 6.*
23. PYPER, H.S. *David as Reader*. 2 Samuel 12:1-15 and the Poetics of Fatherhood. 1996. ISBN 90 04 10581 6
26. BRENNER, A. *The Intercourse of Knowledge*. On Gendering Desire and 'Sexuality' in the Hebrew Bible. 1997. ISBN 90 04 10155 1
27. BECK, D.R. *The Discipleship Paradigm*. Readers and Anonymous Characters in the Fourth Gospel. 1997. ISBN 90 04 10700 2
28. EVANS, C.A. & S. TALMON (eds.) *The Quest for Context and Meaning*. Studies in Biblical Intertextuality in Honor of James A. Sanders. 1997. ISBN 90 04 10835 1
29. VAN WOLDE, E. (ed.) *Narrative Syntax and the Hebrew Bible*. Papers of the Tilburg Conference 1996. 1997. ISBN 90 04 10787 8
30. DAWES, G.W. *The Body in Question*. Metaphor and Meaning in the Interpretation of Ephesians 5:21-33. 1998. ISBN 90 04 10959 5
31. NEUENSCHWANDER, B. *Mystik im Johannesevangelium*. Eine hermeneutische Untersuchung aufgrund der Auseinandersetzung mit Zen-Meister Hisamatsu Shin'ichi. 1998. ISBN 90 04 11035 6
32. RESSEGUIE, J.L. *Revelation Unsealed*. A Narrative Critical Approach to John's Apocalypse. 1998. ISBN 90 04 11129 8
33. DYCK, J.E. *The Theocratic Ideology of the Chronicler*. 1998. ISBN 90 04 11146 8
34. VAN WIERINGEN, A.L.H.M. *The Implied Reader in Isaiah 6–12*. 1998. ISBN 90 04 11222 7
35. WARNING, W. *Literary Artistry in Leviticus*. 1998. ISBN 90 04 11235 9 (In preparation)
36. MARAIS J. *Representation in Old Testament Narrative Texts*. 1998. ISBN 90 04 11234 0